HEKATE SOTEIRA
A Study of Hekate's Roles in the
Chaldean Oracles and Related Literature

American Philological Association
American Classical Studies

The Harmonics of Nicomachus and the Pythagorean Tradition	Flora R. Levin
The Etymology and the Usage of ΠΕΙΡΑΡ *in Early Greek Poetry*	Ann L. T. Bergren
Two Studies in Roman Nomenclature	D.R. Shackleton Bailey
The Latin Particle Quidem	J. Solodow
On the Hymn to Zeus in Aeschylus' Agamemnon	Peter M. Smith
The Andromache of Euripides	Paul David Kovacs
A Commentary on the Vita Hadriani in the Historia Augusta	Herbert W. Benario
Creation and Salvation in Ancient Orphism	Larry J. Alderink
Eros Sophistes: Ancient Novelists at Play	Graham Anderson
Ancient Philosophy and Grammar: The Syntax of Apollonius Dyscolus	David Blank
Autonomia: Its Genesis and Early History	Martin Ostwald
Language and Metre: Resolution, Porson's Bridge, and Their Prosodic Basis	A. M. Devine
Descent from Heaven: Images of Dew in Greek Poetry and Religion	Deborah Boedeker
Iamblichus and the Theory of the Vehicle of the Soul	John F. Finamore
Epicurus on the Swerve and Voluntary Action	Walter G. Englert
Seneca's Anapaests	John G. Fitch
Xoana and the Origins of Greek Sculpture	A. A. Donohue
ANAΓKH in Thucydides	Martin Ostwald
Old Comedy and the Iambographic Tadition	Ralph M. Rosen
EKΩN and AKΩN in Early Greek Thought	GailAnn Rickert
Hekate Soteira	Sarah Iles Johnston

Sarah Iles Johnston

HEKATE SOTEIRA
A Study of Hekate's Roles in the Chaldean Oracles and Related Literature

Scholars Press
Atlanta, Georgia

HEKATE SOTEIRA

Sarah Iles Johnston

© 1990
The American Philological Association

Library of Congress Cataloging in Publication Data

Johnston, Sarah.
    Hekate soteira : a study of Hekate's role in the Chaldean oracles
and related literature / Sarah Johnston.
    p. cm. -- (American classical studies ; no. 21)
    Includes bibliographical references.
    ISBN 1-55540-426-X (alk. paper). -- ISBN 1-55540-427-8 (pbk. :
alk. paper)
    1. Julianus, the Theurgist. Chaldean oracles. 2. Hecate (Greek
deity) I. Title. II. Series.
BF1762.J843J64 1990
292.2'1114--dc20   89-24269
                                                                                          CIP

Printed in the United States of America
on acid-free paper

The cover illustration, by LeRoy Johnston III, is based on photographs of a third-century B.C. relief from Aegina. The relief was formerly in the Metternich collection of Schloss Königswart, Marienbad; its current whereabouts are unknown.

DIS MANIBUS

JOHN B. BREMNER

Haec studia adulescentiam acuunt, senectutem oblectant, secundas res ornant, adversis perfugium ac solacium praebent, delectant domi, non impediunt foris, pernoctant nobiscum, peregrinantur, rusticantur.

Cicero, Pro Archia *VII.16*

HEKATE SOTEIRA

Acknowledgments	viii
Introduction	1
Part I: Hekate's Cosmological Duties	
Chapter I: The Middle Platonic Cosmic Soul	13
Chapter II: Hekate's Earlier Nature	21
Chapter III: Hekate's Later Roles as a Guide or Intermediary	29
The Mistress of the Moon	29
Hekate Κλειδοῦχος	39
Chapter IV: Hekate and the Chaldean Cosmic Soul	49
The Transmission of the Ideas	49
Hekate as a Dividing Bond	59
Hekate as an Ensouler and Enlivener	62
Chapter V: Hekate Μεταξύ: How She Became What She Did	71
Part II: Hekate and Theurgy	
Chapter VI: Theurgy and Magic	77
Chapter VII: Hekate's Top and the Iynx-Wheel	90
Chapter VIII: The Epiphany of Hekate	111
Chapter IX: The Chaldean Daemon-Dogs	134
Chapter X: Hekate and Magic: Conclusions	143
Summary	149
Appendix : Evidence for the Equation of Hekate and the Cosmic Soul	153
Bibliography	164
Indices of Topics Discussed	175
Index of Passages Discussed	182
Index of Oracle Fragments Discussed	190

Acknowledgments

My thanks go first to Kevin Clinton, Cornell University, and Fritz Graf, Universität Basel, who served as the directors of the dissertation from which this book grew. It is impossible to summarize, in a single paragraph, the many reasons that I have to thank Professors Graf and Clinton--here it must suffice to say that they were generous with their help, that they were encouraging in their comments and that their knowledge of Graeco-Roman religion and magic was invaluable to me both during the completion of the dissertation and while I worked on later, revised versions of this work.

I also am grateful to Phillip T. Mitsis and Judith Ginsburg, both of Cornell, for their many insightful comments, and to Robert Lamberton, Princeton University, whose knowledge of the transmission of ideas and literature in later antiquity helped me to unravel the puzzling remarks of the Neoplatonic exegetes. Among the people who read and commented on the work at later stages, Peter Brown (Princeton) Christopher Faraone (Virginia Polytechnical) and Jan Bremner (University of Utrecht) gave particularly valuable advice, as did the two anonymous readers to whom the APA Editorial Board for Monographs sent the manuscript. The manuscript for this book was completed in 1987-88, while I taught in the Princeton Department of Classics. I thank the faculty there for a pleasant and stimulating year; many members of the Department offered criticisms of selected portions of this book while it was being revised.

Preparation of the camera-ready text for this book would not have been possible without the help of Professors Margaret Cook, Diane Juffras and James O'Hara--expert κυβερνῆται of the Macintosh. I also thank my student assistant, Eric Burke, who proofread the Greek and Latin of the final version.

Finally, I thank my husband, LeRoy--talented executor of the cover illustration and patient proofreader of the English portions of the manuscript.

Columbus, Ohio
September 16, 1989

Introduction

Hekate is best known to classicists and historians of religion as the horrific patroness of witches. But from the Hellenistic age onwards, some Greek and Roman philosophers and magicians portrayed her quite differently, allotting to her such duties as ensouling the cosmos and the individual men within it, forming the connective boundary between the divine and human worlds, and facilitating such communication between man and god as could lead eventually to the individual soul's release. She was celestial and potentially beneficent, rather than chthonic and threatening.

The literary corpus that most consistently portrays Hekate in this way is the fragmentary collection of verses commonly called the "Chaldean Oracles."[1] In these Oracles, and in the theurgical system for which they served as sacred literature, Hekate was identified with the Platonic Cosmic Soul. Her prominence in the Oracles is notable: her name occurs in five of the 226 extant Oracle fragments (far more often than the name of any other traditional deity);[2] we can deduce, by analysis of the fragments and the comments of their ancient exegetes, that Hekate/Soul is discussed in at least 66 other fragments. Indeed, the goddess herself speaks in up to eleven fragments.[3]

---

[1] Citations of Oracle fragments throughout this book refer to the edition of E. Des Places, *Oracles Chaldaïques, Avec un Choix de Commentaires Anciens* (Paris 1971); See also Des Places' addenda to this edition, "Notes sur quelques "Oracles Chaldaïques," in *Melanges Edouard Delebecque* (Aix-en-Provence Cedex 1983) pp. 321-9. Fragments 211-226 are considered *fragmenta dubia* by Des Places; see also M. Tardieu, "Les Oracles Chaldaïques," in *The Rediscovery of Gnosticism*, vol. I *The School of Valentinus*, ed. Bentley Layton (Leiden 1980) pp. 194-237, which criticizes Des Places' inclusion of frs. 26, 98, 155. 165-66, 171-74 and 177-78. Citations for W. Kroll's earlier edition of the Oracle fragments (*De Oraculis Chaldaicis*, Breslauer Philologische Abhandlung, VII, 1 [Breslau 1894; rpt. Hildesheim 1962]) and references for the ancient works from which the Oracle fragments are derived are given within parentheses following the citations for Des Places' edition. All translations, except where noted, are my own. Kroll and Des Places both provide comments on the history of the texts. A concordance of the fragment numbers and references to discussion of individual fragments in other secondary works can be found on pp. 679-80 of Hans Lewy, *Chaldean Oracles and Theurgy* (1956; 2nd ed. Paris 1978). A concordance of Kroll's and Des Place's fragments can be found in Des Places, pp. 251-52. Complete information for editions of the other works to which I refer, e.g., Damascius, Porphyry, can be found in the bibliography. The works of Kroll and Lewy, and the edition of Des Places, will be referred to hereafter by the author's last name only.

Recently, H.-D. Saffrey, "Les Néoplatoniciens et les Oracles Chaldaïques," *REAug*. 28 (1981) 209-225, has proposed adding four citations from Proclus' *In Parmenides* to the corpus of Oracles fragments; these fragments do not enter into the topics discussed in this book, however.

[2] Frs. 32, 35, 50, 52; 221 (*fragmentum dubium*). Few other traditional Greek deities are mentioned in the extant fragments: Eros, frs. 44, 45; Rhea, fr. 56; Zeus, frs. 215, 218 (*fragmenta dubia*); the nymphs, fr. 216 (*fragmentum dubium*); Helios, fr. 216 (*fragmentum dubium*).

[3] Frs. 38, 53, 72, 146, 147, 148, 219, 221, 222, 223, 224 (the five last being *fragmenta dubia*). That Hekate is the speaker of these fragments is not stated in the fragments themselves; it must be deduced from the statements of the ancient commentators of the Oracles or by analysis of the

INTRODUCTION

Most previous studies of philosophy and magic in the Imperial Age only have nodded to Hekate's cosmogonic and soteriological importance in the Oracles, doing little to elucidate the reasons for it. Many of those that do offer brief explanations rely too heavily on the most familiar of Hekate's traditional roles--mistress of witches--and overlook the fact that throughout antiquity, she was a goddess of great diversity. Such explanations often overlook, too, the opportunity of illuminating Hekate's roles in the Chaldean system by closely examining her appearances in theurgical, magical and philosophical sources approximately contemporaneous with the Oracles. The goal of this book is to give a more complete and integrated picture of Hekate's roles in the Chaldean Oracles and then, based on that picture, to suggest reasons for her prominence in both the Oracles and related literature. An enhanced understanding of Hekate's importance in these sources not only will clarify our picture of the goddess herself, but also will provide insight into the ways in which the spheres of theurgy, magic and philosophy intersected during the Imperial Age.

The Chaldean Oracles consist of theological, cosmological and theurgically practical information presented in dactylic-hexameter verse. Tradition said that they were written down by Julian "The Theurgist," son of Julian "The Chaldean,"[4] in the second century A.D.[5] The younger Julian was supposed by later Platonists to have

---

fragments themselves. I have listed here only those fragments that modern scholars generally agree to have been spoken by Hekate. Because all of the Chaldean Oracles were presumed to have been spoken by gods, it is likely that other fragments could be assigned to Hekate if more of the complete texts were extant.

[4]Suid. s.v. "Ἰουλιανός" (433 and 434 Adler); cf. C.A. Lobeck, *Aglaophamus* (Königsberg 1829) p. 102, where the suggestion first is made, on the basis of the statements in Suidas, that the younger Julian was the "author" of the Oracles. For a review of subsequent argument concerning the question of authorship, and of the legends surrounding the two Julians, see Lewy, pp. 3-6 and Des Places, pp. 7-8. Most recently, H-D. Saffrey, above, n. 1, has argued that the "theurgical" or "magical" Oracle fragments were composed by Julian *pater* and the more philosophical ones by Julian *filius*. Full discussion of the Oracles' authorship is outside the bounds of this book; for brevity of expression I will acquiesce with the opinion of late antiquity and most modern scholars (including Saffrey) by referring to the composer(s) of the Oracles as "Julian(s)," but this use of the name indicates my agreement only with the premise that the Oracles emerged during the mid to late second century and not necessarily with the premise that they were composed by one or both of the Julians. See also the following note on the related issue of the date of the Oracles' composition.

[5]The most recent discussion of the date of the Oracles' composition is found in E. Des Places, "Les Oracles Chaldaïques," *ANRW* II 17.4 (Berlin, 1984) 2299-2335. Des Places newly discusses the problem of the Oracles' relationship to Albinus (*fl.* 151-2) and Numenius (first half of the second century); he places the composition of the Oracles after both but before Porphyry, i.e., in the late second century. Recently, H.-D. Saffrey, above, n. 1, has argued that the ancient evidence describing the Juliani as performing various miracles reflects a Neoplatonic eagerness to connect them with any remarkable occurrence, and, therefore, can be used only to show how the Neoplatonists themselves viewed the Juliani--not to date the Juliani. This, as Saffrey notes, complicates the dating of the Oracles. It should also be noted that the traditional date of the Oracles' composition (whether their authors were the Juliani or not) can never be accepted fully until the question of why the erudite Plotinus makes no mention of the Oracles is answered (see pp. 5-6 below). However, even those scholars who doubt Julian's authorship place the composition of the Oracles in the mid to late second century, A.D.; certainly by the time of Porphyry's *floruit* (mid-third century) they were well enough

INTRODUCTION 3

flourished during the reign of Marcus Aurelius and to have taken part in the emperor's campaigns. In fact, as early as the fourth century a story began to circulate that Julian had caused by magic the rain that was a decisive factor in the battle against the Quadi (172 A.D.);[6] Psellus added that he also created a human mask of clay that shot thunderbolts at the enemy during a battle with the Dacians.[7] Modern scholarship rightly has called into question not only the authorship of the Oracles but also the most basic details of the Julians' lives. Fowden, in an article that closely examines variant legends surrounding the rain miracle,[8] shows insight when he calls the younger (and more famous) Julian "an almost proverbial figure, perhaps the most famous of all the pagan thaumaturges." Proverbial, yes--like another famous thaumaturge, Apollonius of Tyana, Julian seems to have been a man for whom there is some historical basis but around whom such an accretion of fables is deposited that the shape of the historical facts can be discerned only vaguely.[9] Despite the murkiness that surrounds the Juliani, however, there remains general scholarly agreement that whatever their actual source, the Oracles emerged during the mid to late second century.[10]

According to the ancient exegetes of the Oracles, Julian alleged that the doctrines contained within the Oracles were handed down directly by "the god" or "the gods;"[11] Hekate and Apollo were the two divinities usually credited with the

---

established to be treated as documents deserving reverence (see below, pp.4-5, on Porphyry and the Oracles).

[6]Suid. s.v. "Ἰουλιανός" (434 Adler). For the dating of the story to the fourth century, see the article by Fowden cited in n. 8 below. For further citations for the story and discussion of the event's implications see Fowden; H.-D. Saffey, above, n. 1, 213-14; Lewy, p. 4; E.R. Dodds, "Theurgy and its Relationship to Neoplatonism," *JRS* 37 (1947; rpt. with minor revisions as Appendix II: "Theurgy" in *The Greeks and the Irrational* [Berkeley 1951]; citations in this book refer to page numbers in *The Greeks and the Irrational* and are hereafter cited as "Dodds, *G&I* p. **") p. 285 and nn. 22 and 23.

[7]Psellus *Script. Min.* I.446.28 K-D (pp. 221-22 in Des Places' edition of the Oracles). This seems to be an example of Chaldean *telestika*. For discussion, see C. A. Faraone, "The Protection of Place: Talismans and Theurgy in Ancient Greece," in *Magika Hiera: Greek Magic and Religion*, ed. C. A. Faraone and Dirk Obbink (Oxford forthcoming 1990).

[8]Garth Fowden, "Pagan Versions of the Rain Miracle of A.D. 172," *Historia* 36/1 (1987) 83-95. On the question of the Oracles' authorship, see also P. Hadot, "Bilans et perspectives sur les *Oracles Chaldaïques*, " in Lewy pp. 703-6.

[9]Indeed, Anastasius the Sinaite (*PG* 89 525 a) tells us that Julian and Apollonius--whom most traditions and modern scholarship separate by several decades--met in a sort of "battle of the thaumaturges" during the reign of Domitian. Apuleius, another historical figure who received his share of accreted legends, was a third competitor. Charged with delivering Rome from the plague, Apuleius guaranteed to do so in fifteen days and Apollonius in ten; Julian, however, merely spoke and the plague ended (on this story, see Fowden, above, n. 8).

[10]See n. 5, above.

[11]For summary and discussion of the ancient opinions that the Oracles were divinely inspired see W. Theiler, "Die chaldäischen Orakel und die Hymnen des Synesios" *Schriften der Königsberger Gelehrten Gesellschaft* XVIII, 1 (Halle 1942; rpt. in W. Theiler, *Forschungen zum Neuplatonismus*,

divine messages. The fact that many of the Oracles were spoken in the first person by a god or goddess (who sometimes even identifies him or herself by name)[12] supported the illusion of divine authorship. Later, the Neoplatonists implicitly assumed that the Oracles could be used as direct proof concerning the nature or wishes of the gods, although they sometimes found it necessary to "interpret" these divine utterances in ways that conveniently suited their own ideas. Indeed, the Chaldean Oracles and the writings attributed to Orpheus became "sacred books" in certain Neoplatonic circles and were esteemed beyond even those of Aristotle and Plato; before a student was allowed to approach the former two, he had to study the latter.[13]

This introduction would be of considerable length if it were to list all the authors of late antiquity who used the Oracles or their doctrines in support of their own premises or as the targets of their Christian polemic; most authors with an interest in Platonism or magic who wrote after the advent of the Oracles had something, however brief, to say on the subject of the Chaldean Oracles. But it would be useful to describe at this point the five authors from whose works most of the Oracle fragments and ancient exegeses of them are gleaned, as their names will be met with constantly throughout this study.[14]

Although there is still disagreement about which of the specific oracles cited in the extant works of Porphyry (232-305 A.D.) are Chaldean,[15] recent scholarship has solidified the general picture of Porphyry as a devoted student of the Chaldean Oracles and an essential link between Chaldean doctrine and later Neoplatonic ideas.[16] Porphyry's comments, when carefully evaluated, can help in the recon-

---

Berlin 1966, all citations in this book, hereafter cited by "Theiler," refer to the 1966 printing) pp. 252-4. See also, more briefly, Lewy pp. 6-7.

[12]E.g., frs. 53, 72, 147; *fragmenta dubia* 211, 219, 220, 222, 224.

[13]Marinus *Procl.* 13 and 26. See R.T. Wallis, *Neoplatonism* (London 1972) p. 105, for discussion. Proclus further suggested, according to Marinus, that of all ancient literature only the Chaldean Oracles and Plato's *Timaeus* were worthy of study (*Procl.* 38).

[14]This review will be brief. More thorough explorations of the subject can be found in Des Places, "Les Oracles Chaldaïques," above, n. 5; in the *notice* preceding Des Places' edition of the fragments; and in Lewy, Chapter I. Also useful for an overview of the period following the composition of the Oracles is Wallis' work. Further discussion of the ancient authors' attitudes towards theurgy and citations of modern works on that subject will be found in Chapter VI.

[15]Bidez's opinion that Porphyry did not know of the Oracles at the time that he wrote *Philosophy from Oracles* now generally is rejected (J. Bidez, "Note sur les mystères néoplatoniciens" *Rev. Belg. de Phil. et. d'Hist.* 7 (1928) 1477 ff. Terzaghi, Lewy, Hadot and O'Meara (cited in the note that follows) all have argued for the Chaldean origin of some oracles found in *The Philosophy from Oracles* and the *On the Return [of the Soul]*; Augustine specifically says that Porphyry quotes Chaldean Oracles in the latter (*De Civ. Dei* X.32). The question now is which Porphyrian oracles are Chaldean. See also Chapter VI, p. 79.

[16]Scholarship that elucidates Porphyry's reliance on the Chaldean system includes Lewy's excursus, "Porphyry and the Chaldeans" (pp. 449-56), which does a thorough job of citing previous scholarship; P. Hadot, *Porphyry et Victorinus*, 2 vols. (Paris 1968); John J. O'Meara, *Porphyry's Philosophy from Oracles in Augustine* (Paris 1956) and *Porphyry's Philosophy from Oracles in*

struction of the Chaldean system. His works also provide information about theurgy in general and its relationship to philosophy and more traditional magic. Particularly important in this respect are *On the Return [of the Soul]*, fragments of which are found in Augustine,[17] *Philosophy from Oracles*,[18] fragments of which are collected mainly from Eusebius' *Praeparatio Evangelica*, and the *Letter to Anebo*, an address to an Egyptian priest that requests information on Egyptian theurgical practices.[19] Iamblichus responded to the latter in his *De Mysteriis*.

Given the influence that the Oracles had on Porphyry, it is notable that no certain reference to them can be found in the works of Porphyry's teacher, Plotinus (205-269/70 A.D.).[20] Because it seemed impossible that a thorough scholar of such

---

Eusebius' Praeparatio Evangelica and Augustine's Dialogues of Cassiciacum (Paris 1969); and Andrew Smith, *Porphyry's Place in the Neoplatonic Tradition* (The Hague 1974). The ancient evidence includes the citation from Augustine, mentioned above; Suid. s.v. "Πορφύριος," which lists among his works *On the Doctrines of Julian the Chaldean;* and Aeneas of Gaza who mentions a work of Porphyry's called *On the Descent [of the Soul]* (*Theophrastus*, p. 51 Boissonade; quoted by Kroll, p. 6, with the emendation by suggested by Boissonade and Wolff). Aeneas specifically says that the doctrines Porphyry discussed in the work were identical with those of the Chaldeans. On Aeneas, see further Lewy, p. 450 and n. 7.

[17]See Aug. *De Civ. Dei* X.32 and Lewy, p. 7. J. Bidez assembled the fragments of *On The Return [of the Soul]* in *Vie de Porphyry* (Gand 1913). More recently, O'Meara (above, n. 16, esp. the earlier of his two works) has argued for the possibility that *On Return* and the *Philosophy from Oracles* are actually parts of a single Porphyrian work (but see Des Places, above, n. 5, pp. 2308-2311, who argues against this). Lewy (p. 449) also suggested that *On the Return* was not a separate work, but did not suggest a relationship to the *Philosophy from Oracles* in particular.

[18]The fragments of this work first were collected and edited by G. Wolff, *Porphyrii de philosophia ex oraculis hauriendia librorum reliquiae* (Berlin 1856). Bidez, "Note sur les mystères néoplatoniciens" *Rev. Belg. de Phil. et. d'Hist.* 7 (1928) 1477 ff. argued that Porphyry did not know the Chaldean Oracles when he composed the *Philosophy from Oracles*. N. Terzaghi, "Sul Commento di Niceforo Gregorio al ΠΕΡΙ ΕΝΥΠΝΙΩΝ di Synesio," *Studi italiani filologia classica* XII (1904) 191 ff., however, identified several of the oracles found in Eusebius as Chaldean; Des Places includes several of these in his edition of the Oracles as *fragmenta dubia*. Lewy also suggests that some of the Porphyrean oracles are Chaldean. Not all of Lewy's identifications are convincing; for critical evaluation of Lewy's proposals, see E.R. Dodds' review of Lewy's book "New Light on the Chaldean Oracles," *Harvard Theological Review* 54 (1961) 263-273 (rpt. in the second edition of Lewy's book, pp. 693-701; hereafter cited as "Dodds, "New Light" with the pagination of the reprint). Dodds does admit in his review, however, that it is strange "that an oracle hunter so learned and diligent as Porphyry should have missed at this time a collection which had been in circulation for seventy years" (p. 697). This marks a departure from the staunch stand against Chaldean influence in Porphyry's work that Dodds expressed in *G&I*, p. 287. Hadot and O'Meara (above, n. 16) more recently have argued against Dodds' hesitancy and in favor of Lewy's suggestions, discerning considerable Chaldean influence and citations in *Philosophy From Oracles* and also in *On the Return*. See also discussion of some of the Porphyrian oracles in Chapter VI and in the Appendix.

[19]Ed. and trans. (Italian) by A. Sodano (Naples 1958).

[20]Psellus does claim that a statement made at the beginning of *Enn.* I.9 is inspired by Chaldean fr. 166 (*PG* 122, 1125 d; not in Kroll): ...μὴ 'ξάξῃς, ἵνα μή τι ἔχουσα ἐξίῃ.... Modern opinion, however, tends towards rejecting the validity of Psellus' remark. See Des Places' edition of the Oracles, p. 165 n. 1; A.H. Armstrong's Loeb Cl. Lib. edition of Plotinus, (Cambridge and London 1966) I, 322 n. 1; and Dodds, *G&I* p. 285 and n. 26. Armstrong suggests that the growing corpus of Chaldean Oracles may have borrowed the "oracle" from Plotinus, rather than the reverse. Dodds

broad theological and philosophical interests as Plotinus[21] would have been unaware of the Oracles and their teachings, some modern scholars assumed that he ignored the Oracles because their soteriological doctrines contradicted his own approach to salvation; however, as Dodds notes,[22] Plotinus did criticize the teachings of men such as Zoroaster and Zostrianus, with whom he disagreed. Dodds argues from this observation that the Oracles were not yet composed by the time of Plotinus or that they had not come to Plotinus' attention. But Plotinus' silence could be explained in other ways: perhaps, for example, Plotinus perceived the study of the Oracles as a "philological" rather than "philosophical" pursuit, appropriate to those, such as Porphyry, who were interested in religious and oracular lore, but not to himself. In short, given our current lack of knowledge on the subject, the absence of reference to the Oracles in Plotinus' works tells us little about either the Oracles or Plotinus' personal attitudes to theurgy with any certainty.[23]

Iamblichus (250-325 A.D.), who studied with Porphyry either in his homeland of Syria or in Rome, was more enthusiastic about theurgy than was his teacher, advocating its use towards the salvation of the soul. Iamblichus' lost exposition on Chaldean theurgy would have been of great help to us; his previously mentioned reply to Porphyry's *Letter to Anebo, De Mysteriis*,[24] provides information on the Oracles in the course of discussing supposedly Egyptian mysteries.[25] *De*

---

also rejects a Chaldean origin for Plotinus' statement, suggesting instead a "pythagorean" source (but "pythagorean" is such a general term as to be useless). Des Places apparently accepts the fragment as found in Psellus as Chaldean, as he includes it in his edition of the Oracles. He gives no opinion on the question of whether Plotinus borrowed from or knew of the Oracles, although he does assume that they existed by the time Plotinus wrote.

[21] Certainly, as the affair in the Iseum implies, Plotinus generally was acquainted with the activities of theurgists (Porph. *Plot*. 10 [16.12 ff. Volk]). The affair is discussed by G. Luck, "Theurgy and Forms of Worship in Neoplatonism" in *Religion, Science and Magic In Concert and in Conflict*, ed. Jacob Neusner, Ernest S. Frerichs and Paul V.M. Flesher (New York and Oxford 1989), pp. 185-225; Dodds, *G&I* p. 289 ff.; A.H. Armstrong, "Was Plotinus a Magician?" *Phronesis* I (1955) 73 ff. and Philip Merlan, "Plotinus and Magic," *Isis* 44 (1953) 341-8.

[22] *G&I* p. 285.

[23] On the general question of Plotinus, the Oracles and theurgy, see Des Places, p. 165 n. 1; A. H. Armstrong's edition of Plotinus, p. 322 n. 1; Dodds, *G&I* pp. 285-89 and 301 n. 26, and Merlan and Armstrong, above, n. 21. More generally, on Plotinus and the challenge of deriving information about him from ancient sources, see M.O. Goulet-Cazé, "L'Arrière-Plan Scholaire de la *Vie de Plotin*" and Richard Goulet, "L'Oracle D'Apollon dans la *Vie De Plotin*," both in *Porphyre: La Vie de Plotin*, ed. L. Brisson et al. (Paris, 1982), I 231-281 and 371-412.

[24] The most recent edition and translation (French) of *De Mysteriis* is by E. Des Places (Paris 1966). See also Des Places' comments on Iamblichus in the *notice* of his edition of the Oracles, pp. 24-29.

[25] For the relationship between Iamblichus and the Oracles, see John F. Finamore, *Iamblichus and the Theory of the Vehicle of the Soul*, Amer. Philol. Assoc. American Classical Studies, no. 14 (Chico, CA 1985); F.W. Cremer, *Die Chaldäischen Orakel und Jamblich de Mysteriis*, Beitr. z. Klass. Philol., 35 (Meisenheim 1969); Des Places, above, n. 5, pp. 2311-2313 and Des Places' *notice*, pp. 24-29. Chapter VIII will deal with the relationship between the Oracles and Iamblichus' remarks in more depth.

INTRODUCTION   7

Mysteriis was harshly--and wrongly--judged by Dodds to be "ill-written and philosophically worthless," and "a manifesto of irrationalism;"[26] this has led later scholars to overlook both the importance of Iamblichus as a source of information concerning theurgy and the importance of theurgy's influence on Neoplatonic soteriology. As Gregory Shaw demonstrated in a 1985 article,[27] Iamblichus accepted theurgy, and its rituals, as a method of reaching salvation that was different from but equal to--indeed, in some ways superior to--strict, philosophical reasoning or contemplation; it was by no means the lesser method of accomplishing soteriological goals.

The most lucrative source of Oracle fragments is Proclus (412-485 A.D.), a man who claimed to have seen luminous visions of Hekate,[28] and who, like Porphyry and Iamblichus, wrote a now lost commentary on the Chaldean Oracles as well as the lost *Concerning Ascension [of the Soul]*. Originally from Lycia, he studied in Athens with Syrianus and later became head of the Academy. His commentaries on Plato's works, particularly those on the *Timaeus* and the *Republic*,[29] supply many of the Oracle fragments, and his other works provide useful *comparanda* for evaluation of the Chaldean system. Especially interesting for students of Hekate's nature is his *Hymn to Hekate and Janus* (no. VI), which will be discussed briefly in Chapter X (pp. 147 n.19).

Damascius was head of the Academy in Athens at the time that Justinian closed it in 529. A pupil of Proclus and Isidorus, he transmitted many of the extant fragments in his *Dubitationes et Solutiones de Primis Principiis* and in his *In Platonis Parmenidem*,[30] and a few in his *Vita Isidori*.[31] He primarily used the Oracles--often rather creatively--to support his own sometimes convoluted interpretations of Platonic cosmology and philosophy.

The doctrines of the Chaldean Oracles continued to fascinate philosophers and theologians, both pagan and Christian, into the early Renaissance. The eleventh-

---

[26] Dodds, "Iamblichus," *OCD* 2nd ed.; *G&I* p. 287.

[27] Gregory Shaw, "Theurgy: Rituals of Unification in the Neoplatonism of Iamblichus," *Traditio* XLI (1985) 1-28. Compare the remarks made by Luck in an article published a few weeks before the completion of this book (above n. 21), pp. 210-11, and the conclusions of Garth Fowden, *The Egyptian Hermes: A Historical Approach to the Late Pagan Mind* (Cambridge, 1986), chps. 3-6, esp. chp. 5.

[28] Marinus, *Procl.* 26.

[29] The standard editions of these works remain those of W. Kroll, *In Rem Publicam*, 2 vols. (Leipzig 1899-1901) and E. Diehl *In Timaeum*, 3 vols. (Leipzig 1903-06). Citations in this book refer to volume, page and line numbers within these editions. More recently, A.-J. Festugière has translated these works into French, *In Rem Publicam*, 3 vols. (Paris 1970); *In Timaeum*, 5 vols. (Paris 1966-68).

[30] These two works were last edited, in a single, two-volume edition, by C-A. Ruelle (Paris 1889). All citations in this book refer to Ruelle's edition. A translation into French was done by A.-Ed. Chaignet (Paris 1898).

[31] Edited by C. Zintzen (Hildesheim 1967). French translation and commentary by A.-Ed. Chaignet in *Proclus, Commentaire sur le Parménide* (Paris 1903), pp. 241-371.

century scholar Michael Psellus, from whose works many Oracle fragments are derived, provides exegesis of and commentary on the Oracles. His main sources for Oracle fragments and information about the Chaldean system were Proclus and Porphyry.

Psellus worked from the standpoint of a Christian determined whenever possible to prove the concordance of pagan sacred literature with the precepts of the Christian God, and when not, to prove the superiority of the latter.[32] However, as N.G. Wilson has noted,[33] "Psellus displays far more knowledge of [theurgy] than was discreet," and Psellus himself expressed great admiration for the author of the Oracles at *Chronographia* 6.38. Whether it was Neoplatonism that took him into these "more dangerous areas of thought" as Wilson suggests,[34] or simply intellectual curiosity, he is one of our richest sources of information about theurgy and the Chaldean Oracles. Wilson discusses the magnetic pull Psellus had for students, and Psellus himself said that his students included Arabs, Celts, Persians, Ethiopians and Egyptians;[35] we only can guess at the degree to which his didactic skills promoted the dispersal of Chaldean doctrine throughout the respective nations. Later students of theurgy, such as Marsilio Ficino and Michael Italicus, drew most of their information and many of their opinions about the Oracles from Psellus.

Porphyry, Iamblichus, Proclus, Damascius and Psellus: among the ancient commentators, these men are the most important to study of the Oracles, and we will meet them often in the pages to follow. It would also be helpful at this point to synopsize the views of the modern scholars whose opinions on the Oracles and Hekate will be cited frequently.

The earliest modern editor and interpreter of the Oracles in any detail was Wilhelm Kroll.[36] Kroll's exposition of the Oracles heavily influenced the opinion of Martin P. Nilsson, whose brief discussion of them in his *Geschichte der Griechischen Religion* (II.2 479-81) is the basis of most classicists' acquaintance with the Oracles. Kroll understood Hekate's prominence in the Oracles, as well as their emphasis on fire and fiery light, to signify that they were documents associated with a mystery cult (p. 68). He suggested that this mystery cult was an oriental,

---

[32]The works of Psellus that are most relevant to the study of the Chaldean Oracles have been edited and translated into French by E. Des Places in his edition of the Oracles. Lewy includes an excursus (pp. 473-79) on Psellus' interest in the Chaldean Oracles.

[33]N.G. Wilson, *Scholars of Byzantium* (Baltimore 1983), p. 160. Wilson's entire chapter on Psellus is useful for a general understanding of this scholar and his motivations, although Wilson's evaluation of Psellus seems to be colored by his hesitancy to allow that Psellus genuinely may have been interested in theurgy, e.g., "recently his scholarship [of *De Operatione Daemonum*] has been denied, and one must hope the skeptical view is correct" (p. 160).

[34]Wilson, p. 160.

[35]C. Sathas, *Bibliotheca graeca medii aevi* V (Paris 1874), 508.

[36]Above, n. 1.

perhaps Persian, solar cult, adducing the fact that the Oracles "neglect other Greeks gods in favor of Hekate" in support of this suggestion. He further explained Hekate's prominence in the Oracles by noting that by the second century she had become syncretized with other goddesses, particularly oriental goddesses. She was an omnipotent goddess, worthy of the extraordinary attention that this alleged mystery cult paid her.

Kroll offered little description or interpretation of the roles that Hekate played in the Chaldean system; he did note briefly, however, that she probably was equated with the Platonic Cosmic Soul. In general, Kroll denied Hekate as great and diverse a role as later scholars have, although he candidly summed up his opinion of her with the words *"Confiteor tamen me nihil nosse, quod ad mirabilem huius Hecates formam prope accedat"* (p. 69).

W. Theiler[37] compared the Chaldean Oracles to the hymns of the Christian Neoplatonist Synesius of Cyrene (370-413), from whose writings a few of the extant Oracle fragments are derived. Theiler argued that the theological and philosophical systems of Synesius were based largely on those of the Oracles as presented in later Neoplatonists.

Theiler's work is generally instructive and provocative, but offers little analysis of Hekate's role in the Chaldean system. It does, however, discuss two problems that are important to study of the Oracles in general and, in particular, to the study of Hekate in later antiquity. First, there is the question of how far Neoplatonic interpretation of the Oracles can be trusted; the Neoplatonists, in attempting to show agreement between the Oracles and Plato's own writings, sometimes misinterpreted the tenets of the Oracles or equated the deities of the Chaldean system with other deities or concepts. Specifically, Theiler argued that, in their quest to trinitize everything, Neoplatonists forced third components into what were originally dyads, or broke single deities into three separate deities or entities. Second, Theiler noted, Rhea and Hekate sometimes were equated by the exegetes of the Oracles, in an attempt to make the Chaldean theological system agree with the "Orphic" or "Hellenic" theological system in which Rhea was important, when the Oracles did not genuinely do so themselves. When using Neoplatonic remarks about Hekate to elucidate the Oracle fragments, therefore, it is essential to discriminate between "Hekate," "Rhea" and "Hekate/Rhea."

The most complete discussion of the Oracles is still Hans Lewy's *Chaldean Oracles and Theurgy*,[38] which includes discussions of Hekate's roles and nature;

---

[37] Above, n. 11

[38] Above, n. 1. Lewy's work was reviewed by Dodds, "New Light." Although he finds fault with many of Lewy's individual arguments, Dodds generally praises the work for its comprehensiveness. Lewy died before the work was completed; although its substantive misinterpretations are probably Lewy's, many of its careless errors and inconsistencies must be laid at the doors of its posthumous

Lewy's opinions concerning Hekate and the Chaldean system as a whole will be evaluated frequently in the pages that follow. Lewy identified Hekate with the Cosmic Soul, as did Kroll, but he also identified her with the Chaldean personifications of Physis, Zoë, Heimarmene and Ananke.

Lewy made only incidental suggestions concerning the reasons for Hekate's connection with the Cosmic Soul or for her general prominence in the Oracles. Overall, he presumed both to have arisen from her role as a witches' and magicians' goddess and from her syncretization with other goddesses. Following Kroll's lead, he suggested that by the time the Oracles were composed, Hekate had become a sort of "All-goddess," and that this, at least in part, justified her exaltation.

R.T. Wallis referred to the Chaldean Oracles throughout his *Neoplatonism*.[39] Like Lewy, he suggested that Hekate's prominence in the Chaldean system reflected her previous role as a witches' goddess, and, like Lewy, he understood her to have been equated with the Cosmic Soul (p. 106). Although Wallis' remarks on Hekate are brief, his comments on the relationship of the Chaldean system to more traditional Platonism form a useful basis for more detailed analyses.

In his commentary on individual fragments, E. Des Places[40] largely followed Lewy's opinions concerning Hekate. In the *notice* preceding his edition of the fragments, he offered a brief description and analysis of the primary entities found in the Chaldean system, including Hekate, whom he identified with the Cosmic Soul (p. 13). Des Places described Hekate as:

> ...un intermédiare à la fois dissociant et unifiant entre les deux Transcendants ("Ἅπαξ et Δὶς ἐπέκεινα). Son rôle est celui de l'amour, "lien lourd de feu," "lien admirable," "lien auguste qui unifie toutes choses et surmonte toutes."

Des Places certainly was correct in all he said about Hekate; it is necessary, however, to go further than he did, to define more precisely the nature and implications of her role as "mediator" in the Chaldean system, and to identify the reasons for which this role was developed.

John Dillon[41] discussed the Chaldean Oracles in the final chapter of *The Middle Platonists,* in a section entitled "The Platonic Underworld;" the title itself concisely expresses the attitude of most modern scholars toward the Oracles and their connection with "mainstream" philosophy. Dillon, like Wallis, studied the Oracles in

---

editors. The second edition, undertaken by Michael Tardieu, has corrected many of these errors and provided extensive indices. Also included, in addition to the reprint of Dodds' review, are *compléments* by Tardieu and P. Hadot. The second edition was reviewed favorably by Gedaliahu G. Stroumsa, "Chaldean Oracles," *Numen* XXVII fasc. 1 (1981) 167-171.

[39] Above, n. 13.
[40] Above, n. 1.
[41] John Dillon, *The Middle Platonists: 80 B.C. to A.D. 220* (Ithaca 1977), pp. 392-6.

the context of the Platonic and Pythagorean movements from which they developed; his work provides a excellent basis for their closer evaluation.

Dillon described Hekate's role in the Chaldean system in terms similar to those of Des Places (p. 394):

> Standing on the border between the intelligible and the sensible worlds, acting both as a barrier and as a link between them, we find an entity personified as Hecate, the goddess of the Underworld in traditional Greek religion.

It will be shown below that Hekate's importance in the Chaldean system is not based exclusively on her role as a goddess of the Underworld; the other part of Dillon's comment, however, expresses two of Chaldean Hekate's most important functions-- mediating between and dividing the two portions of the universe, called here the "Sensible" and "Intelligible" worlds. Dillon also made the important observation that in the Chaldean Oracles, as well as in many other philosophical and mystic systems, the basic female principle of the universe can manifest itself at several different levels, even under different names. This observation will be useful in understanding some of Hekate's roles.

Finally, M. Tardieu's most recent discussion of the Oracles[42] briefly addresses Hekate's roles. Like most other scholars, he identifies her with the Cosmic Soul, places her between the Sensible and Intelligible spheres as a *frontière,* and emphasizes her dual role as a boundary and a transmitter between them. Although he notes (p. 216) that some of the traits Hekate displays in the Oracles are similar to those she displays in the Greek magical papyri (he cites *PGM* IV.1443, 2551-2, 2559), he offers no analysis of *why* this goddess became the Platonic Soul. More generally, however, his analyses of how the tenets of the Oracles are similar to those of Valentinian Gnosticism are very helpful in understanding the cosmogonic and soteriological doctrines of the Chaldean system.

No other scholars have offered significant analyses of Hekate's roles in the Chaldean Oracles. Only a few others (whose works will be discussed in subsequent chapters) have studied the Oracles in any depth at all;[43] occasionally, brief mention of them has been made in studies of other Middle or Neoplatonic philosophical systems. Such relative neglect of the Oracles is puzzling in view of the importance that con-

---

[42] Above, n. 1.

[43] Notably Saffrey, above, n. 1; Cremer, above, n. 25; O. Geudtner, *Die Seelenlehre der Chaldäischen Orakel* Beitr. z. Klass. Philol. 35 (Meisenhiem, 1971) and Dodds, *G&I* and "New Light." Cremer and Geudtner briefly mention Hekate during discussion of other matters; both equate her with the Cosmic Soul (p. 100; p. 35). Ruth Thompson Majercik, "Chaldean Oracles: Text, Translation and Commentary," Diss. University of California at Santa Barbara 1982, mentions Hekate only in connection with specific fragments and briefly in her introductory remarks, giving no detailed analysis of the goddess' nature and duties. She follows the lead of previous scholars in equating Hekate with the Cosmic Soul (p. 10).

temporaneous and later authors placed on these "divine" documents. The neglect of Chaldean *Hekate* is particularly surprising, considering the frequency with which Hekate appears in the literature of the Imperial Age and in the magical papyri; the examination of Chaldean Hekate provides new *comparanda* for the elucidation of her appearances in contemporary literature.

The study that follows is divided into two parts. Part I analyzes the philosophical and cosmological roles that Hekate played in the Chaldean and similar systems and suggests that she was elected to play them because of her earlier importance in traditional Graeco-Roman religion as a goddess associated with liminal points (e.g., crossroads, doorways). Part II examines the ways in which Hekate was imagined to help the individual man--the theurgist--and how these differ from the ways she was imagined to interact with the magicians (γόητες) who invoked her. Like the first part, it suggests that many of her more practical, theurgical roles find their basis in her earlier nature as a goddess associated with liminal points, although her established patronage of witches and magicians doubtlessly played a part as well. The final portions of each part--Chapters V and X--show how this study's arguments about Hekate in the Oracles and other mystic literature can elucidate the overall picture of a goddess who long has puzzled scholars of ancient religion and magic.

PART I
HEKATE'S COSMOLOGICAL DUTIES

Chapter I
The Middle Platonic Cosmic Soul

Scholars of the Oracles, ancient and modern alike, agree that Hekate represents the Cosmic Soul in the Chaldean system.[1] Modern adherents of this opinion, including Kroll, Lewy, Wallis, Des Places and Tardieu, were mentioned in the Introduction. An appendix to this book, "Evidence for the Equation of Hekate and Soul," summarizes the ancient evidence on which the modern opinions are based.

Chapters I through V will examine the significance of Hekate's equation with the Cosmic Soul and her assumption of similar roles, primarily studying her appearances in philosophical and mystic literature of the Hellenistic and Imperial ages. In particular, Hekate's duties as Cosmic Soul in the Chaldean System will be examined in detail. Additionally, based on what is known about Hekate's functions in earlier literature and cult, a reason for her assumption of cosmological roles in later antiquity will be offered. The unravelling of all these problems requires, first and foremost, a brief survey of the development of the concept of the Platonic Cosmic Soul itself.

The Cosmic (or World) Soul is mentioned by Plato in the *Philebus* (30 a ff.), in the *Laws* (896 e-898 d) and the *Timaeus* (30 b ff.). Discussions in the *Philebus* and the *Laws* are brief. In the *Philebus,* Socrates says that the souls of individual bodies are derived from that one which ensouls the body of the Cosmos; this soul is similar to, but fairer than, the souls of men. In the *Laws,* the idea of two Cosmic Souls--a "good" one and a "bad" one--is discussed.

The idea of a Cosmic Soul is developed to a much greater extent in the *Timaeus*. It is logical to assume, says Timaeus (30 b ff.), that the Cosmos was created by the providence of God as a living creature endowed with soul and intelligence (κόσμον ζῷον ἔμψυχον ἔννουν τε...γενέσθαι). Another, extended passage in the *Timaeus* (34 b-37 c) gives further information about the Soul. It lies at the

---

[1] There is no single ancient term for what modern scholars refer to as the "Cosmic" or "World" Soul. Often (e.g., in the *Timaeus*) the word ψυχή, without further modification, is used, although the cosmic implication can be deduced from the passage. Sometimes a genitive, such as "τοῦ παντός," is added. In late writings, various adjectives signify the cosmic status, such as "πηγαία."

very center of the body of the Cosmos, yet it is diffused throughout it in such a way as to enclose the body of the Cosmos as well; in other words, the omnipresent Soul marks at once the axial point around which the Cosmos is formed and its outer boundary (34 b ff.).

The Soul is a mixture of compounds intermediate between opposing substances: indivisible (unchanging) existence and divisible (physical) existence; indivisible (unchanging) sameness and divisible (physical) sameness; indivisible (unchanging) difference and divisible (physical) sameness. The most significant act of this process is the forced unification of sameness and difference in the final mixture (35 a ff.). The Soul is compounded of, and thus unifies, opposing principles.

Within the Soul's structure is the basis of mathematical proportions and harmony. When the Creator has compounded the basic material of the Soul from the opposites listed above, he subdivides it (35 b ff.). Plato's description of the measurements according to which the subdivisions are made is too lengthy to repeat here; the important point is that the resultant proportions of the division are those basic to ancient mathematical and musical theories. From the laws governing the structure of the soul can be derived the limits, divisions and other relationships that give physical and artistic cohesion to the Cosmos. The same concept is reflected in the description of the division of the Soul into interlocking circular strips turning at different, but proportionally related, speeds (36 b ff.). The Soul provides a standard for the correct, harmonious delineation and demarcation of the physical world.

The final part of this portion of Plato's description of the Soul (36 d-37 c) briefly reiterates the ideas already discussed, but also builds upon them to reach the concluding (and for Plato's purposes perhaps the most significant) statements about the Soul. The Soul, infiltrating and enclosing the entire body of the Cosmos, provides a divine and eternal source of rational life; it is the crowning creation of all intelligible and eternal entities and is endowed with reason and harmony. Because it is compounded of sameness, difference and existence, is divided in a proportionately logical manner, and "revolves upon itself" (seemingly a reference to the strips of the soul that revolve in appropriately contrasting ways), whenever it meets with an entity whose being is either dispersed or indispersible, the Soul is able to calculate and declare the degree to which that entity participates in sameness or difference. Finally, because the Soul is able to discern and evaluate the qualities of sameness and difference--qualities that are related closely to the realm of the eternally true (the Intelligible World) and the realm of the ever-changing (the Sensible World)--Soul plays a crucial role in the formation of correct opinion or belief and of knowledge.

A little more is learned about the Cosmic Soul later in the dialogue. At 41 d ff., Plato says that the Father and Demiurge gathered together the remains of the Cosmic Soul and, adding to them other, less pure (41 d), mortal (cf. 69 c ff.) ingredients, created a mixture not quite as pure as that of the Soul, but similar to it. From this mixture were created individual souls--part immortal, part human.

The functions and qualities of Plato's Cosmic Soul can be summarized as follows: the Soul sits at the center of, yet encloses, the Cosmos, thereby representing the threshold between the Sensible World (to which the term "Cosmos" regularly refers in philosophical literature) and the Intelligible World. It is composed of and unifies opposing principles that are essential to the functioning of the Cosmos. It contains within itself the divisions and proportions (mathematical, musical, etc.) that enable man to structure his world usefully and harmoniously . It plays an essential role in the development and recognition of correct opinion and knowledge. Finally, it is a constituent and thus a partial source of the human soul, which also includes mortal elements.

It was from the picture presented in the *Philebus*, the *Laws* and the *Timaeus* that later Platonists as well as other philosophers or mystics developed their own theories about the Cosmic Soul.[2] They took Plato's words not as a literary exercise hinting at or representing the way things *might* be or *ought* to be (a *fable vraisemblable* as P. Hadot calls it[3]), but as gospel truth--an accurate description of the way in which the universe was created and operated. The *Timaeus*, indeed, was one of the works most frequently studied and explicated in late antiquity; still extant, for example, are Proclus' lengthy commentary and Plutarch's *De Animae Procreatione in Timaeo*. Proclus, in fact, advocated the elimination of all ancient works except the *Timaeus* and the Chaldean Oracles (Marinus, *Procl.* 38).

The role of the Cosmic Soul that most markedly increased in importance was the multi-faceted one of an intermediary between two worlds. This emphasis on Soul as an intermediary agreed with the growing tendency of philosophers and mystics to insist upon the presence of intermediary principles in general, particularly ones that mediated between God and man. The idea was reflected in what has been called by modern scholars the "Principle of Continuity." The term refers to the ancient belief

---

[2] This discussion of the later concepts of the Cosmic Soul relies in great part on the indispensible works of John Dillon, *The Middle Platonists* (Ithaca 1977) and R.T. Wallis, *Neoplatonism* (New York 1972) (hereafter cited as "Dillon" and "Wallis"), who throughout their books, with reference to specific philosophers, discuss the topic in greater depth than it is possible to do here. The conclusions based on this summary discussion are my own, however, unless specifically credited to Dillon or Wallis. Other scholars whose work was taken into consideration are cited in the pertinent footnotes. Some of the material used to compose this portrait of the Platonic Cosmic Soul is derived from authors later than the supposed date of the Chaldean Oracles. Unfortunately, knowledge about views of the Cosmic Soul at or before the mid-second century is slight; the sources are largely Aristotle, Xenocrates, Apuleius and Plutarch. However, because much of what we know about the theology of the Oracles themselves is derived from later authors, an awareness of later authors' views will be of help.

[3] P. Hadot, "Physique et Poésie dans le Timée de Platon," *Rev. Theol. Philos.* 115 (1983) 133-33. Cf. also: S. Breton, "Téléologie et ontogénie. Variations sur les Oracles Chaldaïques," *RecSR* LXVI (1978) 5-26.

that there could be no gaps or discordances in the universe, physically or theologically; therefore, dissimilar entities must be unified or at least buffered by a third entity that possessed characteristics of each.[4] The third and middle entity served as an interface. This doctrine had many applications. Plutarch and Apuleius used it to prove and justify the existence of daemons, who mediated between gods and men. It was the impetus behind the uncontrolled "triadization" (multiplication of hypostases) that was found in almost all later philosophical, theological and mystical systems, beginning with Iamblichus' insertion of mean terms into all sets of opposites.[5] One important aspect of the general principle is its double implication: the intermediate entity not only helped to delineate the differences between the two entities it separated but also provided a means of connecting them.

The Cosmic Soul became a favorite intermediary. In the *Timaeus*, the opposing principles of sameness and difference were unified within Soul (35 a). Later interpreters understood these principles to represent what came to be called the Intelligible and Sensible Worlds, or the worlds of unchanging divinity and changing humanity;[6] they described Soul as establishing a boundary between yet connecting the ephemeral world of bodily perceptions, from which the intelligent man sought to free his soul, and the world of incorporeal perfection. A corollary to this was the fact that Soul's physical position between the two realms made it the encloser, or limit, of the Sensible World; in fact, this idea was expressed already in the *Timaeus* by the description of Soul as enwrapping (περικαλύψασα) the outer edges of the Sensible World (36 e).

Later philosophers, beginning with Plotinus, understood the *Timaeus* to place the Soul between Time (under whose divisions and laws the mortal world operated) and Unlimited Eternity (under which the divine, hypercosmic portion of the

---

[4]The "Principle of Continuity," or "Law of Mean Terms," is discussed by Wallis, pp. 130-132, who points out that it is in evidence as early as the *Timaeus* itself. See also R. MacMullen, *Paganism in the Roman Empire* (New Haven and London 1981), pp. 79 ff. Ancient examples and explications of the idea--of which there are many--include Iamb. *De Myst.* I.5-7; 14,10-23,7; Plot. *Enn.* V.2.2, 26-9; Procl. *ET.* 28, 106-7, 132, 190-1; Procl. *In T.* II.119.25. See also Wallis, p. 11, where the body-soul dualism introduced in Plato's later works is mentioned as a motivation for the development of mediating principles.

[5]Wallis, p. 132, points out one of the most interesting applications of the theory: Sallustius (*DM* XVI.2) justifies animal sacrifice by making the animal's life the bridge between human and divine life.

[6]For example, Numenius, p. 97.8 (Leemans), "the mediator between the φυσικῶν and the ὑπερφυῶν;" Plotinus *Enn.* V.1.7 (a light streaming forth from the Intellect but occupied with the phenomenal world) and IV.4.3 (the boundary line between Sensible and Intelligible Worlds, pulled in both directions); Plutarch *De proc. an.* 1024 b (in the middle of the Sensible and Intelligible Worlds); Proclus *In T.* II.1.14 "the mediator (μέση) between divisible and indivisible...the boundary (ὅρος) of the ungenerated and the generated...the limit (πέρας) of Eternity and Being."

universe operated) as well as between sameness and difference.[7] By virtue of this intermediary position, the Cosmic Soul also became the producer of the Sensible World. Into the Cosmic Soul were cast the eternal Ideas of the divine mind; the Cosmic Soul in turn cast images of these Ideas onto the shapeless Prime Matter, producing the Sensible World, which was ruled by Time. The intermediary function of the Soul thus took on a creative, transmissive aspect, reminiscent of the traditional feminine one of receiving fertilization and subsequently bearing life.

The intermediary character of the Cosmic Soul was expressed in other ways, as well.[8] For the sake of brevity, only those expressions that were drawn most directly from the description in the *Timaeus* were reviewed above; in general, however, Soul became for Platonism and related systems the entity that mediated not only between the Sensible and Intelligible Worlds but also between any opposing terms that somehow characterized them. Further examples of this development will be given in subsequent chapters as particular forms of mediation associated with theurgy and Hekate are discussed.

Although the role of intermediary was the one most emphasized in later Platonic discussions of the Cosmic Soul, Soul's other functions and attributes were not forgotten. The fact that the *Timaeus* situated in the Soul the basic mathematical and musical proportions, by means of which the Cosmos was ordered and organized, led to the theory that the Soul itself was composed of Number, or of all numbers. This theory was encouraged by (and in turn gave credence to) the Platonic equation of the Ideas or Forms with mathematical entities.[9] It was related, too, to the belief that Soul received the Ideas and then cast them unto chaotic matter in order to construct the Cosmos; Number, in Pythagorean and Platonic theory, was responsible for the organization of physical space and thereby for the construction of the physical Cosmos.

Such theories seem to have begun with Aristotles' exposition of Plato's doctrines concerning the Ideas: Dillon's analysis of Aristotle's evidence, pp. 6-7, con-

---

[7] For example: Proc. *ET.* 191 (and commentary in Dodds' edition) and Plot. *Enn.* IV.4.15, 16-20, where the same is said of the human soul. Discussion in Wallis, pp. 118-20.

[8] For example: Iamblichus (*De anima, ap.* Stobaeus I.365.5 Wachs ff.) argues that the soul is an intermediary by her very nature or essence, which is inferior to that of the intelligence but superior to that of the body (discussion in Wallis, pp. 118-20). Cf. Procl. *In T.* II.105.15 ff.; II.215.29 ff. (the Soul as a μεταξύ between the divided and undivided); Nicomachus of Gerasa (in *Theolog. Ar.* p. 45, 6, De Falco; see Dillon p. 358: the Soul, by bringing harmony to opposites, imposes form on matter); and Porph. *Sent.* 5. Dillon, p. 29, finds the Soul portrayed as the primal intermediary entity as early as Xenocrates. Dillon, pp. 45-7, discusses the importance and development of the Soul as intermediary entity in early Middle Platonism; however the other two entities are described, Dillon shows, the third and middle entity was almost always equated with Soul. Cf. also Tardieu, pp. 209 ff. and the passage from Calcidius, quoted below, p. 20.

[9] General discussion is found at Dillon, pp. 6-8, and Wallis, pp. 16, 50-1; more extensive discussion of the Soul and mathematicals, especially in Posidonius, can be found in Philip Merlan, *From Platonism to Neoplatonism,* 2nd ed. (The Hague 1960), chs. I and II.

cludes that Plato conceived of the Soul as receiving the Ideas, converting them into "Mathematicals," and then projecting those Mathematicals unto Matter in order to construct the physical World. Such a process was in its own way, of course, a form of mediation, as it involved the transmission of material from one realm to another. Our evidence for the beliefs of Plato's pupil Xenocrates is fragmentary and derived largely from other authors; it is likely, however, that he considered Ideas and Numbers to be identical, that he situated them at the level of Soul, which was itself described as "self-moving Number," and that he thereby made the Soul responsible for the physical delineation of the Cosmos.[10]

Later Platonists developed these ideas in a variety of ways. Posidonius (*ap.* Plut. *De Proc. An.* 1023 b-d = fr. 391 a Theiler) based many of his beliefs about the Soul on the fact that it was constructed according to Number and Harmony.[11] Eudorus (*ap.* Plut. *De Proc. An.* 1013 b) echoed an opinion of Xenocrates when he said that the creation of Soul in the *Timaeus* actually described the generation of Number from One and the Unlimited Dyad. According to Iamblichus' *De Anima* (*ap.* Stob. *Anth.* I.364 ff. Wachs.), Moderatus defined Soul as Number, which contained all the significant ratios and made things that differed from one another symmetrical and agreeable. Nicomachus of Gerasa constructed a numerical scheme under which the Soul was the Hexad (in contradiction to the many systems in which it was identified with the Decad and Tetractys). It also was called "Form of Forms" as its duty was to give form to the formless by imposing harmony on opposites (or, as Dillon, p. 358, suggests, by imposing the basic triangles on Matter). Interestingly, an epithet of the Hexad and six, "ἑκατηβελέτις," was etymologized by Nicomachus as "projection of Hekate," whom he equated with the Triad (*Theol. Ar.* p. 49,11 de Falco) Dillon (pp. 358-59) suggests that, as the Hexad was the projection of the Triad, the Cosmic Soul was understood as the projection or emanantion of Hekate.

Such are some of the ways in which the relationship between the Cosmic Soul and Number was expressed by Platonists. To summarize "Middle Platonic" views, the Soul contained--or was--Number and all qualities associated with Number, such as Ratio and Harmony. Number, in turn, was in various manners related to or identified with the Ideas. The Ideas, perhaps incarnated as the Mathematicals, were cast by Soul upon Primal Matter, which then became the physical Cosmos. This act of casting brought about the structuring of the Cosmos into its proper physical proportions, the delineation of chaotic matter. The process in its entirety reflected at least two of the functions or attributes attached to the Cosmic Soul in the *Timaeus:* the Soul's intermediary, transmissive position between the Intelligible

---

[10]The best summation of Xenocrates' views of this matter, with citations, is Dillon, pp. 24 ff.

[11]Discussion of Posidonius' theories of the Soul at Dillon, pp. 110-112.

and Sensible Worlds and its possession of all significant ratios --arithmetic, harmonic or otherwise.

It has been shown that the Cosmic Soul played a role in generating the physical Cosmos. Soul also generated, or was the source of, individual souls; Middle-Platonic evidence for this role is discussed in the appendix. The idea that the individual soul was sent to earth by the Cosmic Soul may have been encouraged by the belief, quite popular in later mystic thought, that the soul descended (and after death reascended) through a series of planetary spheres.[12] This relationship between Soul and souls found its basis in *Phileb.* 30 a ff., where Socrates argued that if our bodies are to be understood as derived from the greater body of the Cosmos, then logically our souls must be derived from the Cosmic Soul. The description at *Tim.* 41 d ff. of the material of individual souls being created in part from the remains of the Cosmic Soul undoubtedly also contributed this belief.

Finally, some Middle-Platonic authors hypothesized the existence of an evil or irrational Cosmic Soul or of two opposing Cosmic Souls. Plutarch[13] is one of the more notable proponents of this idea; it was perhaps his interest in Egyptian theology--which has much stronger dualistic tendencies than does Greek theology[14]--that led to his adoption of it. Dillon's suggestion that Plutarch may have borrowed the idea from Persian theology also would make sense.[15] Platonic justification for the theory of a dual Cosmic Soul could be found by those who sought it in *Laws* 896 d ff., where Plato hypothesized a Cosmic Soul that was opposed to the "good" Cosmic Soul and was the cause of all irrational motion in the sublunar portion of the universe. Although many Neoplatonists rejected the idea of an irrational or outright evil Soul, it did resurface occasionally, especially after the introduction of Christian dogma. The concept played a part in the development of Chaldean doctrine (see Chapter IX, "The Chaldean Daemon-dogs").

In the preceding pages the most prominent traits and functions associated with the Cosmic Soul from the time of its description by Plato through early Neoplatonism have been reviewed. Those traits and functions revolve around Soul's role as an intermediary principle between the Sensible and Intelligible Worlds; by virtue of this cosmological position, Soul was also the entity that enclosed the Sensible World. As the receiver and subsequent transmitter of the Ideas--which were understood to travel from the Intelligible World to the Sensible World through Soul--Soul was involved with Number and with the standards for proportion and harmony; as a result Soul

---

[12] See I.P. Culianu, *Psychoanodia I: A Survey of the Evidence Concerning the Ascension of the Soul and its Relevance* (*EPRO* 99) (Leyden 1983), especially chs. III-VII. See also discussion in Wallis, p. 35.

[13] E.g., *De Is.* 370 f; *De proc. an.* 1026 e-1027 a.

[14] *De Is.*

[15] Dillon, pp. 202-6. For Plutarch's interest in Persian theology, see, e.g., *De Is.* 369 e).

was involved intimately with providing physical delineation and structure to the Cosmos. Finally, Soul was responsible for the ensouling of individual men, perhaps because their souls were all but part of her.

This discussion of the Platonic Cosmic Soul can be closed with a quotation from Calcidius, a third- or fourth-century[16] Platonist who translated the *Timaeus* into Latin and wrote a commentary on it. Calcidius' work is considered by modern scholars to provide particularly good *comparanda* for the Chaldean system.[17] He says about Soul (*In Plat. Tim.* 53):[18]

> Haec est illa rationabilis anima mundi, quae gemina iuxta meliorem naturam veneratione tutelam praebat inferioribus, divinis dispositionibus obsequens, providentiam nativis impertiens, aeternorum similitudine propter cognationem beata, dissolubilium rerum auxiliatrix et patrona, cuius in consulendo ratiocinandoque virtutis in moribus hominis apparent insignia, qui cultor eximius dei diligentiam mansuetis impertit animalibus.

Calcidius emphasizes the position of Soul between the human and divine worlds and the varied roles it allows Soul to play. These roles include those of *"patrona"* and *"auxiliatrix;"* the chapters that follow will discuss how the concept of Soul as the beneficient aider of man developed from the role of intermediary that has been discussed above.

First, however, Chapter II will examine the early development of Hekate's role as a goddess concerned with the crossing of boundaries.

---

[16] Calcidius' date is problematic. See Dillon, pp. 401 ff., for an evaluation of the scholarly arguments, in particular a refutation of Waszink's late fourth century dating of Calcidius. Dillon himself finds it "almost incredible" that such a work as Calcidius' commentary on the *Timaeus* could have been written later than 350 B.C., and prefers to place him in the "Middle Platonic spectrum," after Numenius and Origen, whom Calcidius mentions by name. Dillon's careful examination of the pertinent facts is convincing; Calcidius probably belongs in the late third or early fourth century.

[17] Wallis, p. 166, notes that Calcidius' work most clearly shows the influence of Numenius, a second-century Middle Platonist whose works reflect knowledge either of Chaldean system itself or of the same doctrines that determined its development. On Numenius and the Chaldean Oracles, see Tardieu, p. 234; Lewy, ch. VI, esp. pp. 313-21, and E.R. Dodds' brief article "Numenius" in *OCD*. On Numenius' possible influence on Calcidius and Calcidius in general, see also Dillon, pp. 401-8. Calcidius certainly shows an interest in many of the same questions Chaldean doctrine sought to elucidiate--the cosmic position and purpose of daemones, for example.

[18] This passage is also cited by Lewy, p. 366 n. 207, who rightfully finds it a useful *comparandum* for Proclus' exuberant *Hymn to Hekate and Janus* (quoted below, pp. 147 n. 19).

Chapter II
Hekate's Earlier Nature

Modern scholarship has suggested that Hekate's identification with the Chaldean Cosmic Soul and the attribution to her of similar cosmically significant roles springs from her connection with magic or from her extensive syncretism with other goddesses by late antiquity.[1] Although both of these factors contributed to such an equation, a third, more important factor has been overlooked. Chapters III, IV and V will show that most of the duties late philosophical and mystic literature assigned to Hekate portrayed her as the intermediary between the Sensible and Intelligible Realms, at whose discretion passage from one to the other was facilitated. This chapter will show that these roles represent an extension of her well known role as a goddess associated with the passage through crossroads, doors, and other liminal places, a role alluded to as early as Aeschylus (fr. 388 Nauck), where she is described as standing before the entrances to palaces. A summary of evidence will show how pervasive and enduring this association was, and therefore how likely it was to have influenced the roles she played in post-classical antiquity.

The place of Hekate's origin is uncertain; majority opinion places it in western Asia Minor,[2] probably in Caria. Information about her early worship in Asia Minor is slight; there are some indications, however, that she was a deity connected with passage through liminal points.[3] Several scholars place her among the company of

---

[1] The following scholars and their works are cited and discussed in the Introduction. Kroll understood Hekate's general prominence in the Oracles to be due to her syncretization with other goddesses and also to the "oriental origin" of the Oracles (p. 68); Lewy suggested that she became the Cosmic Soul because of her syncretization with other goddesses and also because of her previous role as a magicians' goddess or a goddess able to control "demonic Fate" (pp. 361-66); Wallis implied that the identification was due to Hekate's role in ritual magic (p. 106). Other scholars of the Oracles, who agree that Hekate is the Cosmic Soul, make no guess as to the reason for the equation.

[2] See most recently F. Graf, *Nordionische Kulte* (Rome 1985), pp. 257-9 (hereafter, "Graf, *NK* "). Also W. Burkert, *Griechische Religion* (Stuttgart 1977; Eng. trans. by John Raffan Oxford 1985), pp. 265-66 (hereafter "Burkert, *GR* " with pages numbers referring to the German edition); Th. Kraus, *Hekate* (Heidelberg 1960), *passim*, esp. pp. 24, 55-6 (hereafter "Kraus"); Nilsson *Geschichte der griechischen Religion* 2 vols. (vol. I Munich 1940, 3rd ed. Munich 1967; vol. II Munich 1950, 2nd ed. 1961), I.3 722 (hereafter "Nilsson, *GGR*). In contrast Farnell, *Cults of the Greek States* 5 vols. (Oxford 1896-1909), II 502-7, suggests Thrace as her place of origin. On Hekate in Asia Minor, see also W. Fuchs, "Unerkannte Hekate-Heiligtümer," *Boreas* 2 (1979).

[3] See Graf, *NK*, p. 258. See also Kraus, pp. 11 ff., 77 ff. Kraus suggests that Hekate's connection with liminal points in Asia Minor was an ancient one. She is linked in Western Asia with Apollo, who was himself there a guardian of entrances (Kraus, p. 13), and who in the Greek mainland, as Apollo Agyieus, was guardian of roads (cf. schol. Pl. *Lg.* XI, 914 b: "[Hekate and Apollo Agyieus] fill the roads with light; he in the day, she in the night"). Later evidence includes the cult regulations of the Molpoi from about 100 B.C., which tell of a great procession to Didyma, in which two γυλλοί (probably cubes of stone, Hesychius s.v. γυλλός) were carried, festooned with garlands and sprinkled with wine. One was laid down "in front of Hekate who is before the gates" and the other "upon the threshold" (of the Hekate temple?). The first paean in the procession was

Anatolian "Great Mother" figures. Although there probably is some truth in this suggestion, it signifies little about the origin of Hekate herself, as virtually all goddesses, especially those of eastern origin, can be allied with the "Great Mother" to some degree.

Her debut in Greek literature is the "Hymn to Hekate" at *Theogony* 411-52, a passage that long has mystified interpreters seeking a reason for Hekate's exaltation in the poem beyond all deities but Zeus. J.S. Clay has suggested that Hesiodic Hekate's participation in many of the relationships between men and gods implies that she is the "crucial intermediary between gods and men," having a "critical mediating function."[4] Line 444 would indicate that she *conveys* the herdman's prayer to Hermes, for example. This analysis, however, probably imposes too unified a theology on Hesiod; the temptation to find here certain traces of Hekate's role as a goddess who aids in the conveyance of material or persons from one realm to another must be resisted. We can say, more generally, however, that Hekate's portrayal in the *Theogony* indicates her potential interest and participation in virtually every aspect of the relationship between humanity and divinity.

Hekate's next, rather brief, appearance is in the *Homeric Hymn to Demeter;* it too has puzzled scholars, because of its seeming intrusiveness. The passages in the Hymn should be interpreted, however, as the earliest clear allusions to Hekate's role as a guide at times and places of transition. Hekate enters the story at l. 24, as one of the two creatures who hear Persephone's cry as Hades snatches her away (Helios is the other).[5] Later, at ll. 51-59, she approaches Demeter and is described as announcing (ἀγγελέουσα) something to her. Finally, Hekate re-enters the story immediately after the reascension of Persephone (l. 438) and embraces her. "From that time," says the Hymn, "Queen Hekate was the 'preceder' (πρόπολος) and the 'follower' (ὀπάων) of Persephone."

---

sung to Hekate; see F. Sokolowski, *Lois Sacrées de l'Asie Mineur* (Paris 1955), pp. 129 ff. See also the discussion of her later worship in Stratonicean Lagina at pp. 41-42.

[4] J.S. Clay, "The Hekate of the *Theogony* " *GRBS* 1984 pp. 27-38. Clay offers summary and critique of previous explanations. Notable opinions and their adherents include: M.L. West, ed., *Hesiod, Theogony* (Oxford 1966) pp. 276-8 (Hekate as the special goddess of Hesiod's family; Hesiod expresses his personal, zealous beliefs); Pfister, "Die Hekate-Episode in Hesiods Theogonie" *Philologus* (1928) pp. 1-9 (Hesiod celebrates a goddess popular among the local peasant class of which he is a member); P. Mazon, *Hesiode* (Paris 1928) pp. 24 ff. (Hekate was the local Boeotian version of the πότνια θηρῶν and therefore deserving of special mention). An analysis by Deborah Boedeker, "Hecate: A Transfunctional Goddess in the *Theogony* ?" *TAPA* 113 (1983) 79 ff. makes use of G. Dumézil's theories; Patricia A. Marquardt, "A Portrait of Hecate" *AJP* 102 No. 3 (1981) 243-60, argues for the goddess' close, personal involvement in many spheres of men's lives but offers no guess as to her underlying nature.

[5] It is interesting that Helios and Hekate are connected throughout antiquity in passages dealing with magic: the earliest mention of her in connection with magic, in S. *Rhiz. TrGF* 492 Radt, allies her with Helios; Helios and Hekate are mentioned together in late magical hymns.

In the Hymn, Hekate is present at, or least witness to, both the descent and the return of Persephone. The language used to describe the appointment of Hekate as Persephone's companion is interesting; certainly πρόπολος and ὀπάων can be used to mean simply "attendant;" if they are interpreted literally, however, their use in combination is contradictory. But the very contradiction of the words creates a picture of circumspicuity; by being both behind and in front of Persephone, Hekate thoroughly protects or guides her. The literal meanings of the words also imply that Hekate accompanied Persephone on a physical journey, logically the one to Hades and back; this supports the hypothesis that Hekate traditionally was involved more intimately in the descent and return than the Hymn tells us, escorting Persephone on one of the most difficult and significant journeys imaginable.[6] The fact that Hekate "from that time" of the original return of Persephone played these roles implies that she continued to accompany Persephone annually as she passed from Hades to upper world or vice versa. Vase paintings portray Hekate as accompanying Persephone.[7] Hekate's role in the story of Persephone is that of an escort across a very important boundary; in later literature, as mistress of souls, she regularly guided the dead back and forth across this same line.[8]

Other references show Hekate to be connected with liminal places of a more mundane nature, such as crossroads and doorways. "Enodia" ('Evoδία) is an adjective regularly applied to her as early as Sophocles (*TrGF* 492 Radt), and often thereafter, although it could be used to describe other persons and things as well.[9] In

---

[6]This is supported by Callimachus (fr. 466 = Orph. fr. 42 Kern), who involves Hekate in Persephone's return more directly than the Hymn does. Hekate is described as the daughter of Zeus and Demeter, sent by her father to retrieve Persephone from Hades. There is a related problem with ll. 51-56 of the Hymn, where Hekate is described as "announcing" (ἀγγελέουσα) something to Demeter. Hekate actually announces nothing to Demeter that Demeter does not know already; rather she *asks* Demeter who kidnapped Persephone. An "Orphic" version of the rape (Kern fr. 49) does not involve Hekate at all and places ll. 54-56 of the Hymn in Demeter's mouth (she speaks them to the Eleusinians at ll. 103 ff.). Hekate's role in the extant Homeric Hymn seems to be a confused reflection of an earlier version or versions.

[7]See N.J. Richardson, ed. and comm., *The Homeric Hymn to Demeter* (Oxford 1974) pp. 294-5; F. Graf, *Eleusis und die orphische Dichtung Athens in vorhellenistischer Zeit* (Berlin 1974) pp. 73 ff.

[8]As the subject of Hekate as a guide of the dead or leader of disembodied souls is one that has been discussed frequently by previous scholars, I will not undertake it in depth here. The reader is referred to the following authorities, who provide ancient citations: Graf, *NK*, pp. 257-59; Kraus, *passim* but esp. pp. 60 and 87; Nilsson, *GGR* L3 724 ff. and *Griechische Feste* (Berlin, 1906), pp. 394-98 (hereafter Nilsson *GF*); Heckenbach, "Hekate," *RE* VII.II, Halbband XIV, 2769-82; Roscher, "Hekate," *Lex.* II.1, 1885-1910; Rohde, *Psyche*, trans. W.B. Hillis (1894; Eng. ed. London 1925), discussed frequently throughout, but see esp. pp. 297 ff. and accompanying notes and pp. 593-95. The role will be discussed briefly below, pp. 144-47.

Hekate's role as a birth goddess also should be remembered here; she oversaw not just the transition of the soul out of the body but its transition into the body. For citations describing her as a birth goddess and discussion see Graf, *NK*, p. 257; Kraus, p. 86; Rohde p. 322 ff.

[9]Cf. *Il.* 16.260, where it is used of wasps, and Theocr. *Id.* 25.4, where it is used of Hermes, whose statue stands at the entrance to an estate.

connection with Hekate, it is used not only as a modifying adjective, but also a substantive name;[10] e.g., E. *Hel.* 569-70. "Enodia" expresses Hekate's connection with roads--specifically places where three roads meet. Another adjective frequently used with Hekate's name is τριοδῖτις;[11] she often is described in other ways, too, as dwelling at the crossroads.[12] In Rome she became identified with Trivia--representing the crossroads *(trivium)* themselves.[13]

Further evidence of Hekate's association with liminal places such as doors and other entrances includes Aeschylus (*TrGF*. 388 Radt), where she is invoked as "Despoina Hekate, πρόδομος of kingly palaces," and Aristophanes, *Vesp.* 804, which asserts (surely with some exaggeration) that a hekataion stood before every door in Athens. She had a place in cult at the propylaia of the acropolis in at least one place--Athens--where, Hesychius tells us, she was worshipped as Hekate Propylaia (Hesyc. s.v. προπύλα). Pausanias II.30.2 tells of a Hekate ἐπιπυργιδία worshipped on the Acropolis near the temple of the wingless Nike at the time Alcamenes carved the first statue of her in triple form (c. 430 B.C.);[14] she may be the Hekate Propylaia to whom Hesychius refers. Kraus (p. 96) suggested that Hekate was regularly the guardian of acropolis entries in pre-Periklean times.

The performance of rituals or the worshipping of deities at liminal places such as crossroads, doorways and gates reflect one or more of several concerns. Some customs associated with liminal places--especially political frontiers--express a desire to establish territorial limits and protect what is within them; Burkert has suggested that this desire explains why Hermes, a deity often connected with frontiers and other

---

[10] Although "Enodia" most frequently is used either with Hekate's name or in circumstances where it clearly replaces "Hekate," other goddesses came to use it as well, notably Artemis, Selene, and Persephone, also Brimo and Bendis. Hesychius calls her the daughter of Admetus, which would connect her with the goddess of Pherai, herself possibly a "road" goddess. See Droysen, "Enodia" *RE* V.II, Halbband X, 2635; Schreiber, "Artemis" *Lex.* I.1, 571. Such goddesses, all of whom are connected with Hekate in other ways, probably borrowed the epithet from her. Enodia also was the name of an independent goddess worshipped by the Thessalians, about whom we know very little (see Kraus, ch. III). Polyaenus (VIII.43) tells an interesting story about a priestess of Enodia from Thessaly, who was an expert on drugs. This not only echoes the pervasive view during antiquity that Thessaly was the home of witches and others versed in the use of drugs, but indicates that Enodia herself was considered to be the patroness of such activities. Many of the references to Enodia connecting her with other goddesses reflect this as well; "Enodia" frequently is used in passages about magic, madness, supernatural appearances and the dead (e.g., S. *Rhiz. TrGF* 492 Radt, E. *Hel.* 569-70). The sculptural evidence for Enodia is not certain; in all cases, the goddess assumed to be Enodia could be identified as others, as well, such as Hekate or Persephone. Ultimately, little can be said about Enodia except that she was the "goddess in the road," and had a chthonic character, probably concerned with magic and the Underworld.

[11] E.g., Corn. *ND* 34. Plutarch uses it of the Moon at *De Fac.* 937 f.

[12] S. *TrGF* 535 Radt; Theocr. *Id.* II.36.

[13] See also S.I. Johnston, "Crossroads," forthcoming, 1990, *ZPE* (hereafter cited as Johnston, "Crossroads").

[14] For the dating of Alcamenes' statue, see Kraus, p. 84.

liminal points, is represented ithyphallically.[15] In other cases, significance is attached to liminal places or boundaries because they represent "beginnings"--points at which one departs from one place to another. Passage through a door or gate can initiate an earthly journey, for instance, or reflect the symbolic passage from one mode of life to another, just as passage into the earth initiates Persephone's yearly journey to the Underworld and the annual renewal of her marriage to Hades. The Roman bridegroom, like his modern counterpart, carried his bride across the threshold in order to insure that her passage into a new life was not marred by a stumbling step.[16] If a transition was to be completed successfully, it must be undertaken auspiciously,[17] cautiously, with the help of the gods.

Other rituals associated with liminal places reflect a third concern--they address the dissociation of the liminal place itself. Every *limen*--the threshold, the crossroads, the gate, the frontier--is by definition detached from its surroundings. A threshold is neither inside nor outside of the house, a frontier belongs to neither country, the crossroads are the junction of roads A, B and C but belong to none of them; liminal places, especially crossroads, offer varied options but no reassuring certainties.[18] If the violation of a boundary and the accompanying disregard of limits

---

[15]Burkert, *Structure and History in Greek Myth and Ritual* (Berkeley 1979), p. 40, suggests that the ithyphallic herms, which the ancient Greeks used to mark and protect areas, reflect a primitive instinct, still seen in some primates, of the males of a group to encircle their territory, facing outwards with erect phalli, as if to proclaim their masculinity and ability to protect females and young. A less primitive example of the rigor with which boundaries are established is the care taken by Roman surveyors to divide farmland into parcels as square and equal as possible, by means of the surveying lines called the *cardo* and the *decumanus,* leaving small boundaries of untilled land between portions to facilitate access. A small altar to the Lares Compitales would be set up where four such plots met, to protect the rights of all four landholders at once. Boundary markers *(termini)* were sacred to the Romans; special ceremonies were connected with their establishment and a yearly ritual, the Terminalia, was held to fortify their *numina.* Similarly, boundary stones (ὅροι) were set up by the Greeks to establish the limits of sacred precincts, delineating the property of the god. All these examples show a strong desire in ancient man as an individual to define and protect--through religious and legal means--what is his own. See also C. Faraone, "The Protection of Place: Talismans and Theurgy in Ancient Greece" in *Magika Hiera: Ancient Greek Magic and Religion,* ed. C. Faraone and D. Obbink (Oxford forthcoming 1990) for discussion of protective measures at liminal points, especially doors and gates.

[16]Cat. 61.159-60 implies, however, that the bride could step over the threshold herself as long as she did so auspiciously: *"transfer omine cum bono limen aureolos pedes."*

[17]Omens seen at the outset of a journey, which is itself an act of transition, are especially significant; Thucydides tells of the importance the Spartans placed on omens taken at the beginning of a journey or campaign; three times bad omens prevented them from going forth (5.54-55; 116). The tension surrounding the crossing of limits was not found only among the Greeks. The Romans, whose Janus was in many ways similar to Hekate, were particularly cautious about such things. Even taking into consideration the Roman proclivity to divide any sphere of divine control into myriad smaller ones, the number of Roman gods attached to the doorway is notable; it was watched over not only by Janus but also, for example, by the god and goddess of the threshold, Limentius and Lima, and the goddess of the hinges, Cardea.

[18]Hence their proverbial use to express doubt and confusion, e.g. Thgn. *Eleg.* I.911, Pi. *P.* XI.38, Pl. *Leg.* 799 c, *AP* 7.694.

threatens to bring on the chaotic disorganization or even the destruction of established areas, then the boundary itself must be regarded as a sort of permanent, chaotic Limbo; associated with neither of the two extremes it divided, it eludes the categorization and control applied to them--it belongs to no one. Indeed, because of their dissociation, crossroads became the realm of ghosts (and, in a more literal, immediate sense, of other *personae* who were dispelled from society, such as prostitutes). These feelings of dissociation attached to liminal places give rise to rituals intended to protect the individual who passed through them.

Hekate's presence at terrestrial liminal places primarily reflects the second and third of these concerns. Just as she guided Persephone and the disembodied souls across the boundary between life and death, she helped men cross the more mundane boundaries that they faced daily.[19] This is not to say, of course, that ancient man was consciously grateful to Hekate every time he traversed the threshold or the crossroads--Theophrastus' Superstitious Man is parodic proof of the norm. But at some level he believed that she, or what she represented, was there, just as he felt the presence of "Zeus Horkios" to some degree whenever he swore oaths. Her triplicate statues--placed here and there at liminal places around the landscape--further insured that he could never forget her completely.

Hekate also escorted men through temporal *limines*. Several sources say that Hekate "suppers" (δεῖπνα) were taken to the crossroads each month at the time of the new moon; that is, on the night the old month ended and the new one began (the νουμηνία). The goddess who eased transitions was supplicated at the crossroads--- the liminal point *par excellence*---on the night between old month and new--a temporal *limen,* a time of potential dissolution.[20] An illuminating parallel to this monthly ritual is found in Burkert,[21] who cites Arist. *Ath. Pol.* 56.2:

> the new archon begins the year by proclaiming that "whatever possessions anyone had before his entry into office, he shall have and keep until he (the archon) steps down from office."

---

[19]This is not to argue that Hekate never served the role that Hermes did at liminal points--protecting what was within a boundary from that which was without. The two functions could co-exist. Conversely, Hermes' connection with liminal points, like Hekate's, could include protecting during transitions; he was, after all, a traveller's god and a messenger god. As Psychopompos, he aided men in crossing the boundary between life and death.

[20]Schol. Ar. *Plut.* 594; the third-century Apollodorus, *FrGH* 244 F 109. There are other references to Hekate meals that do not specify the time at which they were offered; see Johnston, "Crossroads." The third-century playwright Theopompos, *ap.* Porph. *de Abst.* 2.16, mentions that hekataia (and herms) also were crowned and cleansed on this day.

Burkert *Homo Necans,* Eng. trans. Peter Bing, (Berlin 1972; trans. Berkeley 1983) (page numbers in this book refer to the Eng. ed.) *passim,* discusses the sense of dissociation felt at the end of temporal units by ancient man. See especially pp. 142-143 for discussion of the Buphonia as an end-of-year act of dissolution.

[21]*Ibid.*, p. 142.

Chaos was felt to lurk in the break between old year and new: "whatever one could seize, one could keep," as Burkert expresses it; it is likely that the break between old month and new evoked similar feelings, although on a lesser scale.[22]

Hekate's association with liminal points remained one of her prominent features in the literature of later periods, which expressed it in many ways.[23] To take but a few examples, the scholiast on Lycophron 1180, discussing the name of the Thessalian Pheraia (commonly an epithet for Artemis) says that Hekate, new-born daughter of Pheraia and Zeus, was thrown out onto the crossroads, from which she was rescued and raised by shepherds. This Hekate was given the name Pheraia, too.[24] Arnobius, writing at the end of the third century A.D., gives a genealogy in which Janus, the Roman deity associated with liminal places, was the child of Hekate and Sky (*Adv. nat.* 3.29). Proclus also connects these two deities in his sixth hymn, which is addressed to Janus and Hekate. In that hymn, she twice is called προθυραία. In Chariclides (fr. 1) she is τριοδῖτις, in magic hymns she is called Ἐνοδία and described as τριοδῖτις (*PGM* IV.1434; IV.2563; IV.2724, 2728).[25]

This brief summary of Hekate's titles and duties has shown how pervasive and long-lived was her association with liminal points.[26] It has been suggested that she served as a guide or escort across these points, facilitating the transition and protecting against the chaos--sometimes literally conceived of in the form of ghosts-- that lurked within them. As subsequent chapters will show, the role of escort or guide across liminal places naturally brings with it the role of mediator or intermediary. The guide must move easily from one realm to the other and thus, like the intermediary principles that later philosophers posited, must partake to some extent of both. Hekate's location in a cave, in the *Homeric Hymn to Demeter* (l. 25), expresses this fact succinctly: Persephone's escort makes her home neither above the

---

[22]Indeed, time, at least originally, was reckoned by this cycle in most of Greece, although the lunar month later was complicated by additional civic and political divisions of time.

[23]Her connection with one expression of this--keys--will be discussed below, pp. 39 ff.

[24]Pheraia herself is called "λιμενοσκόπος," "watching the harbour," at Call. *Dian.* 259; harbours are another liminal point. Hekate is called λιμενῖτι at *PGM* IV.2563. Artemis, because of her association with Hekate, borrowed several epithets that express her connection with liminal points, among them "Λιμενοσκόπος" (schol. Lyco. 1180). This or a similar story seems to be alluded to by Stephanus of Byzantium, in his explanation of the title τριοδῖτις; he states that Hekate was called "τριοδῖτις" and "Enodia" because she was found as an infant, by Inachus, *in the road.*

[25]In one of these hymns (*PGM* IV.2708-84), which is an appeal for Hekate to send a loved one home to the worshiper, she three times is asked to send the loved one specifically to the lover's door or threshold itself. In Theocr. *Id.* II.60, a love philtre, which Hekate is called on to empower, is to be smeared on the lintel of the loved one's door. The importance of liminal places in magic is discussed briefly in Chapter X and in Johnston, "Crossroads."

[26]Graf, *NK* p. 258, offers a slightly different explanation of Hekate's attachment to doors and other liminal points, deriving it from her character as "goddess of the outdoors:" "Dass die Göttin des Draussen den Durchgang ins Innen schützt und bewacht (so wie sie der Geburt vorsteht) ist verständlich...."

earth nor below it but intermediarily between the two. The guide acts to bridge--either literally or figuratively--two distinct realms in order that the individual may pass from one to the other. So, too, that which is intermediary acts to close the gap between two discreet entities and provide continuity.[27]

As the next two chapters will show, in late literature, as a cosmic κλειδοῦχος, as Mistress of the Moon, or as Cosmic Soul itself, Hekate continued to provide passage between the worlds of men and gods or between otherwise detached spheres, such as the Sensible and Intelligible Realms.[28]

---

[27]Cf. the conclusions of L. Kahn, "Hermès la frontière et l'identité ambiguë," *Ktema* 4 (1979) pp. 201-211.

[28]For the moment I have not addressed evidence connecting Hekate with magic; this will be taken up in detail in Part II, which discusses theurgy in the Chaldean Oracles, and in particular in the final chapter, "Hekate and Magic."

Chapter III
Hekate's Later Roles as Guide or Intermediary

The previous chapter reviewed Hekate's roles as a goddess associated with liminal points in traditional literature and cult; it was argued that her association took the form of guiding or escorting individuals at places or times of transition. In later philosophical or mystic literature, Hekate's guiding roles became increasingly similar to those of the Cosmic Soul as outlined in the first chapter.

This chapter will provide a general, comparative context for the forthcoming examination of Chaldean Hekate's cosmological roles[1] by examining similar evidence selected from those systems that usually are referred to by the terms "Orphic," "Neopythagorean" and "Neoplatonic." The examination is divided into two sections. "The Mistress of the Moon" concentrates on evidence just prior to or contemporaneous with the emergence of the Chaldean Oracles, taken from sources which may have had some influence on them. "Hekate Κλειδοῦχος" discusses evidence somewhat later than (and probably influenced by) the Oracles.

The Mistress of the Moon

The Middle Platonic school popularized the idea that the Moon was both a liminal point and a transmissive or mediating entity between the Sensible and Intelligible Worlds, an idea that persisted throughout later antiquity in philosophical and mystical thought.[2] The earliest extant expression of the idea is found in Xenocrates (*ap.* Plut. *De Fac.* 943 f = fr. 56 Heinze), who connects the Moon and lunar air with the second and middle of his three πυκνά or densities (the Sun and stars belong to the first and the Earth and its waters to the third). The Moon and the lunar air are the interpositive layer in his three-tiered universe. The transitional nature of this πυκνόν is illustrated by Xenocrates' attachment to it of the daemones, who he says mediate between gods (who inhabit the first layer) and men (who inhabit the third); the daemones are similar to both in nature (*ap.* Plut. *Obs. Orac.* 416 c-d = fr. 23 H., with comments at Dillon, p. 32). Of similar significance is Xenocrates' postulation of a double Zeus, one of whom rules the sphere above the Moon, one the

---

[1] For the moment, discussion of Hekate's roles as Soul or anything else in the Chaldean system itself will be postponed; the fragmentary nature of the evidence for that system, and the fact that its explication is the primary goal of this study argue for treating it separately, in the next chapter.

[2] There is some evidence that the concept of the Moon as a mediator or boundary between two opposites may have begun earlier. For example, the Hippocratic Περὶ Ἑβδομάδος, which connects various human organs with astral bodies, equates the Moon and the centrally located diaphragm. Plato, *Smp.* 190 b, makes the Moon the parent of hermaphroditic creatures (whereas males are descended from the sun and females from the earth).

sphere below (*ap*. Plut. *Plat. Quaest.* IX, 1007 f = fr. 18 H.); the Moon marks the point at which a division of cosmic realms is made.

Further illustrations of the Moon's function as both a *limen* and a conducive principle abound in post-classical antiquity.[3] Calvenus Taurus, for example, writing in Athens in the mid-second century, makes the Moon the point of division between the world of the ever-changing and that of the constant (*ap.* John Philoponus, *De Aet. Mund.*, p. 145, 13 ff. Rabe). By the end of antiquity, the emperor Julian could satirically situate a banquet of the Caesars in the air around the Moon. These semi-divine souls were between gods and men in nature: they belonged above the earthly realm but were not quite worthy of the heavens (*Caes.* 307 c).[4]

One author who had a lot to say about the nature of the Moon--and who addressed the question in connection with a wide variety of subjects--was Plutarch, whose active life slightly preceded the emergence of the Chaldean Oracles. In several passages Plutarch described the Moon as marking the boundary between the Sensible and Intelligible Worlds. He also attributed to it a variety of mediating or transmissive powers; at *De Is.* 368 e, for example, Plutarch, who himself connects the Moon with both Isis and Osiris, explained the seemingly contradictory Egyptian belief that the Moon was the Mother of the World, yet bisexual. According to him, this bisexuality reflected the fact that the Moon, like a woman, was filled or impregnated by the Sun above, but in turn, like a man, emitted or sowed generative principles into the air below. In other words, the Moon was the intermediary transmitter of life-giving principles, much in the same way as the Cosmic Soul was the transmitter of the Ideas.[5] At *De Fac.* 928 c, Plutarch compared the Moon's position between the Sun and Earth to that of the liver or "another of the soft viscera" (tr. Cherniss), which lay between the heart and the bowels. This Moon, he said, conducted downwards the warmth of the Sun and conducted upwards the exhalations of the Earth, refining them in the process.

The picture of Hekate as a Moon goddess is familiar to classicists--too familiar perhaps. It is important to remember that although Hekate's association with the

---

[3] The intermediary nature of the Moon is discussed throughout Dillon and Wallis. Especially in its role as a intermediary entity, it came to play a big part in eschatological doctrines. See also discussion in H. Goergemanns, *Untersuchungen zu Plutarchs Dialog De facie in orbe lunae,* Bibliothek der klassischen Alterwissenschaften neue Folge II Reihe Band 33 (Heidelberg 1970) and F. Cumont, *Afterlife in Roman Paganism* (New Haven 1922; rpt. New York 1959), pp. 96 ff.

[4] See also Tardieu, pp. 209 ff.

[5] Interestingly, the divinity to whom Hekate specifically is compared in *De Is.* is not the bisexual, intermediary Moon, but rather Anubis, the jackal-headed god. According to Plutarch, Anubis represents the horizon, which lies between the visible realm of Isis above the earth and the invisible realm of Nephthys below the earth (368 f). The specific reason given for the comparison is that Anubis and Hekate are gods of both the Underworld and the Heavens, but the intermediary nature of Anubis' physical position (as well as his canine aspects) must have encouraged the analogy. In other works of Plutarch Hekate is connected with the Moon (see discussion below).

Moon became commonplace in late antiquity,[6] verifiable associations between the two do not survive from earlier than the first century A.D.,[7] after the Moon's role as an liminal or transmissive entity had been established and fast was becoming one of its dominant traits. Shared possession of intermediary or transmissive functions probably was not the *sole* basis of the association between Hekate and the Moon; Hekate's connection with Artemis undoubtedly was a contributing factor.[8] But the importance of these shared traits in cementing the association is supported by three observations. First, Hekate's associations with the Moon did not begin until the first century A.D. (see n. 7), at least two centuries after those of Artemis with the Moon began (see n. 8). Second, these associations of Hekate and the Moon closely followed the enthusiastic development of the Moon's liminally transmissive roles in philosophical and mystic literature. Third, the first associations of Hekate with the Moon appear in philosophical literature (Plutarch) and in a drama written by a philosopher (Seneca) (see n. 7); these are authors likely to have been influenced by the philosophical/mystical sources that made the Moon an intermediary principle. Finally, the Plutarchan associations (which will be examined below) link Hekate and the Moon specifically *because* of their common role as intermediary or transmissive principles. Taken together, these observations suggest that the intermediary or transmissive nature shared by Hekate and the Moon strongly contributed towards their eventual identification. In particular, as will be shown, they shared the eschatological function of transmitting or guiding disembodied souls or daemones across the boundary between the earthly and celestial spheres; this is analogous to Hekate's earlier role as the guide of disembodied souls on their way to Hades.

Obs. Or. 416 c-f. is one of the Plutarchan passages in which the Moon both is portrayed as an intermediary entity and is associated with Hekate. In general, it discusses daemones, whose nature is said to combine the natures of men and gods (416

---

[6] E.g., Porphyry (*ap.* Eus. *PE* III.11, 113 C) and Eusebius himself (*PE* III.16, 126 C) call her the Moon; Porphyry (*ap.* Eus. *PE* V.10, 193 D) places her in the aether, the traditional place of the Moon. In the magical papyri, "Selene" and "Hekate" seem to be used interchangeably.

[7] The earliest references I am able to find are Sen., *Med.* 790, and the references from Plutarch, which will be discussed in this section. Roscher's article, "Hekate" (*Lex.* II.1, 1897 ff.) cites nothing earlier. I do not consider the classical connections between Hekate and νουμηνία offerings (discussed above in the chapter on Hekate's earlier nature, p. 26, and in Johnston, "Crossroads"), to signify any attachment to the Moon itself; the attachment is expressive of her help at the time of transition from old month to new.

[8] There is evidence for Hekate's identification with Artemis as early as the fifth century (A. *Suppl.* 676, fr. 158; E. *Phoen.* 110). Artemis' identification with the Moon precedes that of Hekate with the Moon; the first certain evidence for the idea is found in the second-century B.C. Stoics (e.g., Diog. Bab. Diels *Doxogr.* 549 b 7; Apollod. Stoic. fr. 40 *ap.* Suid. v. "ταυροπόλος") (the Stoic identification of Artemis and the Moon probably began as a logical development of their identification of Artemis' twin brother, Apollo, with the Sun). By the time of Plutarch (e.g., *Quaest. Conv.* 659 a) the identification of Artemis with the Moon was so commonly held an assumption that it could be used as supportive evidence in making another point.

c-d). Xenocrates, Plutarch said (416 d), set up a system comparing gods, men and daemones to three types of triangles. Xenocrates equated gods with the equilateral triangle, which is equal in all its lines, men with the scalene, which is unequal in all its lines, and daemones with the isosceles triangle, which is "partly equal and partly unequal." Plutarch himself, however, suggests a better analogy: the Moon is a "mixed" (μεικτόν) body mimicking the daemonic race; in fact, the Moon's alternate waxing and waning is a cycle in harmony with the varying circumstances of the daemones.[9]

Next there follows a passage discussing Hekate (416 e-f). The entire passage reads (Babbitt's translation with slight revisions):

> But there is a body with mixed characteristics that actually parallels the daemones--namely the Moon. And when men see that [the Moon], by being consistently in accord with those cycles through which the daemones pass, is subject to apparent wanings and waxings and transformations, some call her an earth-like star, others a star-like Earth, and others still the lot of Hekate, who is both earthly and heavenly. Now if someone withdrew or removed the air that is between the Earth and the Moon, he would destroy the unity and communion of the Universe, for there would be an empty and unconnected space in the middle. In just the same way, those who refuse to leave us the race of daemones make the relations of the gods and men remote and alien.

> μεικτὸν δὲ σῶμα καὶ μίμημα δαιμόνιον ὄντως τὴν σελήνην, τῷ τῇ τούτου τοῦ γένους συνᾴδειν περιφορᾷ, φθίσεις φαινομένας δεχομένην καὶ αὐξήσεις καὶ μεταβολὰς ὁρῶντες, οἱ μὲν ἄστρον γεῶδες οἱ δ' ὀλυμπίαν γῆν οἱ δὲ χθονίας ὁμοῦ καὶ οὐρανίας κλῆρον Ἑκάτης προσεῖπον. ὥσπερ οὖν ἂν εἰ τὸν ἀέρα τις ἀνέλοι καὶ ὑποσπάσειε τὸν μεταξὺ γῆς καὶ σελήνης, τὴν ἑνότητα διαλύσειε καὶ τὴν κοινωνίαν τοῦ παντός, ἐν μέσῳ κενῆς καὶ ἀσυνδέτου χώρας γενομένης, οὕτως οἱ δαιμόνων γένος μὴ ἀπολείποντες, ἀνεπίμεικτα τὰ τῶν θεῶν καὶ ἀνθρώπων ποιοῦσι καὶ ἀσυνάλλακτα.

---

[9]Frank Babbit, in the notes to his Loeb edition of *Obs. Orac.* (London 1937), explains this with reference to *De Is.* 361 c. There Plutarch quotes a passage of Empedocles (Diels I, p. 267, 115), in which the daemones are described as being driven up and down between Sun and Earth in recompense for their actions. When they have been purified, they take the position proper to them--logically this would be the Moon, lying between the two extremes of the area they are driven across during their punishment. In this passage, too, Plutarch stresses the mediating nature of daemones, citing Plato's description of them as an interpretive and ministering race; they convey prayers and petitions of men to the gods, and oracles and gifts of the gods to men (probably referring to Pl. *Smp.* 202 e).

The Moon, described by some men as a star-like Earth or an earth-like star,[10] also is called by some the lot (κλῆρος) of Hekate, who is described herself as both an earthly and a heavenly goddess. The original source for Hekate's reputation as both earthly and heavenly is impossible to determine; it recalls, perhaps, Hesiod's description of her as the daughter of Asteria or as receiving shares on the earth, in the heavens and in the sea, and also, perhaps, her associations with the Olympian Artemis. But whatever the original provenience of the idea, Plutarch introduces it here because he believes it supports the arguments he is making about the Moon and the daemones. His logic can be reconstructed as follows: he wishes to show that the removal of the daemones from the cosmic scheme would make communication between men and gods impossible. In support of this he adduces, as an analogue, the fact that the removal of the lunar realm, where the daemones dwell, would cause the disunification of the Universe: there would be no communion between the earthly and heavenly realms without the Moon and lunar zone that lie between them.[11] In support of *this* (and also, more generally, in support of his argument that the Moon is the proper home of the daemones, who have a nature half-way between those of men and gods), he reminds his audience--other men of philosophical tendencies, perhaps?--that current conceptions of the Moon make it an entity whose nature is half-way between that of the earth and that of the heavens: it is an "earth-like star," "star-like earth," or the "lot of Hekate, who is both heavenly and earthly." For Plutarch, the fact that the Moon's *nature* partakes of both the earthly and the heavenly lends support to the idea that its position is between them.

What does this tell us about Hekate and her relationship to the Moon? Primarily, that it was the place assigned to her, was her "lot," was the portion in the universe most suited to her. The immediate succession of the phrase describing her as both earthly and heavenly implies that, for Plutarch and his contemporaries at least, the reason it was her lot was that *like it,* she partook of both realms and lay halfway between them.

The foregoing discussion brings to mind another connection commonly made in post-classical antiquity--that between Hekate and daemones. She often was called

---

[10]Cf. Plutarch's other descriptions of the Moon as a "mixed body:" *De Fac.* 943 e (composed of Earth and Star); *ibid.* 945 c (created by a god as a compound of that which is above and that which is below). See further H. Goergemann, above, n. 3, pp. 83-86, in particular Goergemann's discussion of how seriously Plutarch took this "myth" of the soul's ascension to the Moon and his citations for the possible Neopythagorean origins of the Moon's mediating role.

[11]Here it seems it is the air between the Moon and Earth, not the Moon itself, that is portrayed as essential to mediation. However, the resulting picture is actually the same. Removing this air pulls the Moon down to the Earth (as, in fact, Thessalian women inadvisedly attempt to do, Plutarch complains in the next section) and pushes out the sublunar zone in which the daemones commonly were imagined to function. On the Thessalian trick, see P.J. Bicknell, "The Dark Side of the Moon," in *Maistor. Classical, Byzantine and Renaissance Studies for Robert Browning*, ed. Ann Moffatt (Canberra, Australia 1984) pp. 667-75.

their queen or controller.[12] The mediating nature of daemones has been alluded to in the previous paragraphs. It began with Diotima's description of them in Plato's *Symposium*--or perhaps even earlier, with Hesiod's description of them as the immortal, yet not divine, spirits of the golden race that watched over men.[13] Mediation between the human and the divine became their dominant trait in late philosophical and mystical thought,[14] and was almost certainly the impetus behind their connection with the Moon, which began with Xenocrates and was common throughout late philosophy and mysticism. Even in later contexts in which daemones took on a threatening character, they lost none of their intermediary nature. In fact, their unpleasant characteristics were intensified by it; philosophers such as Plutarch, in putting them between gods and men also made them responsible for all the divine misrepresentations, demands for unpleasant sacrifices, etc., that formerly were blamed on the gods. As the concept of "divinity" became more detached, philosophy and mysticism called for something to fill the roles that the gods, now completely severed from the material world, no longer were permitted to fill; the daemones stepped in.

Hekate's ascendance to the daemonic throne was promoted by her earlier nature. From classical times Hekate was the mistress of phantoms (φαντάσματα) and similar creatures.[15] Although creatures of this sort were not called "daemones" specifically until Plutarch (*Dio* 2), they shared with later daemones both an ability to harm or frighten men if they so wished and a nebulous existence between man and god, life and death.[16] Traditionally, they were understood as the restless souls denied entrance to Hades for lack of proper burial rites, the souls of those who died

---

[12] E.g., Porphyry's beliefs as expressed at Eus. *PE* III.16, 126 c (Eusebius asks how Porphyry can assert that Hekate is the Moon, a celestial body, if he also says that she is the ruler of evil daemones); at *PE* IV.23, 174 a ("[Porphyry says] that Hekate and Sarapis are the rulers of the evil daemones"), and in V.24, 202 c,d (the symbols of Hekate's telestic statue are called "symbols of the daemones' power"). The adjective "evil" in the first two examples seems to have been applied to the daemones ruled by Hekate by Eusebius, not by Porphyry; Porphyry's own words at IV.23, 174 b, make Sarapis alone the ruler of *evil* daemones. Judging from remarks in Augustine (*De Civ. Dei* X.9-11), Porphyry regarded daemones in general not as bad but rather as simply subordinate in rank to gods--mediators who could be bad or good. See also Chapter IX, "The Chaldean Daemon-Dogs."

[13] Hes. *WD* 122-28. Platonists certainly understood Hesiod's daemones this way; see, for example, Calcidius *In Plat. Tim.* 129-36.

[14] Daemones are from their earliest philosophical/mystical portrayals creatures of mediation or creatures in transition (e.g., *Smp.* 202 d ff., Empedocles Diels I p. 267 115 = *ap.* Plut. *De Is.* 361 c). It is with Xenocrates, however, that this idea first finds full expression and that daemones become by definition the class between gods and men; after Xenocrates, the idea was accepted universally, e.g., Apul. *ap.* Aug. *De Civ. Dei* VIII.18; Iamb. *Myst.* I.5-6; 16,6-20,19; Plut. *De E.* 394 c, *De Is.* 360 e; consistently throughout Christian commentators such as Eusebius (*PE*). See also the discussion in Nilsson, *GGR* II.2 540.

[15] Classical examples are E. *Ion* 1048 ff.; *Hel.* 569-70; Hipp. *Morb. Sacr.* 6.362; Trag. Incert. fr. 375.

[16] Hipp. *Morb. Sacr.* 6.362; E. *Ion* 1049.

before their time--"ἄωροι"--or the souls of those who died violently--"βιαιοθάνατοι."

Such creatures naturally gathered around Hekate. Hekate was a goddess of birth and a goddess of death, accompanying souls across the greatest boundaries they crossed.[17] Those who were not permitted to complete these transitions were fated to wander with her in a sort of Limbo. Moreover, her role as a goddess of crossroads and other liminal points brought her into contact with these creatures, who traditionally dwelt at such places.[18] She was the goddess who protected the living against these potentially harmful spirits, but by the same token, she was also the goddess who could lead them on.[19]

Of course, other factors encouraged her coronation as the daemonic queen as well. The defining characteristic of the daemones of Platonic philosophy and mysticism was their ability to travel from one realm to another, even to escort others across the boundary between two realms--those in the *Phaedo* (107 d ff.) are given the task of guiding the souls of the dead to their proper places. The fact that Hekate shared these traits would have encouraged the affiliation that already had begun to grow from her earlier relationship with the daemones' ancestors--the φαντάσματα. The Moon may enter into the equation, as well. The daemones already had begun to be associated with the Moon by the time of Xenocrates; Hekate's election as a Moon goddess at some later point made it easier for her to add the lunar daemones to her ranks.

Although it is difficult to chart with exactitude the development of Hekate's role as queen of the daemones, it is clear that her role as a guide across liminal points contributed to it in several ways and at several stages. Two further points should be made. First, whatever the factor(s) behind Hekate's initial connection with daemones, the intermediary and transmissive roles of daemones in late philosophy and mysticism were widely and well enough accepted to reflect, in turn, upon their queen, strengthening her existing reputation as a guide across liminal points. Second, just as the increasingly negative traits of the daemones never completely obscured their roles as mediators, so the potentially frightening traits of many of Hekate's earlier supernatural associates should not obscure their intermediary nature. Whatever

---

[17] See n. Chp. II, n. 8 for references.

[18] See Johnston, "Crossroads," for discussion of the reasons these souls lingered at crossroads and other liminal places.

[19] She is not identified with truly horrific supernatural creatures, such as Gorgo, Mormo and Empousa, until late Hellenistic times (examples in Rohde, *Psyche*, app. VI and VII). However, she herself can take on grim aspects earlier (e.g., Theocr. *Id.* II.12). and her classical control over phantoms often is linked to unpleasantness--they are described as frightening men or causing mental sickness, especially at night (Trag. Incert. 375; Hipp. *Morb. Sacr.* 6.362) and the chorus at E. *Ion* 1048 ff. asks Hekate and her νυκτιπόλοι ἐφόδοι to help guide the cup of Gorgon poison to Ion's lips; E. *Hel.* 569, in contrast, does imply that Hekate could send pleasing (εὐμενῆ) phantoms.

"phantoms" were exactly (however closely they can be associated with daemones), any creature that wandered between Earth and Hades, or Earth and Heaven, was intermediary. Trapped between realms, they were condemned to roam with the goddess who had refused to allow them to complete their passage. Indeed, this very element of marginality may have helped to make these creatures frightening; they were of a uncategorized, dissociated nature, and, it would be assumed, were unhappy and vindictive because of their enforced and fruitless wandering. As early as Elpenor, disembodied spirits not allowed entry into Hades complained of their lot.

A topic closely related to that of Hekate and daemones, and also to that of Hekate and the Moon, is Hekate's power over disembodied souls. In fact, although some Neoplatonists made careful distinctions between daemones and disembodied souls, the difference between the two categories is slight or non-existent in archaic, classical and Hellenistic sources. Hesiod's daemones are the souls of his golden age men (*WD* 122-8); in Plutarch, the two terms seem to be used interchangeably.

De Fac. 943 a ff.[20] discusses the double release of the soul. First, the soul is separated from the body in the "realm of Demeter"--that is, on earth; then, the soul is separated from the mind in the "realm of Persephone"--on the Moon.[21]

Plutarch continues with details of the process (944 c ff.). There are three special lunar crevices (βάθη...καὶ κοιλώματα). The biggest one (μέγιστον) is called the "Gulf of Hekate" ('Εκάτης μυχόν). In this one the souls give or receive punishment for crimes they suffered or committed while they were "daemones" (apparently in contrast to crimes experienced while they were embodied). The other two are deep (μακρά) and are called "The Gates" (accepting Cherniss' emendation in his Loeb edition). Through these two crevices the souls pass, according to merit, now to the side of the Moon that faces Heaven and is called the Elysian plain, then to the side facing Earth--"the house of ἀντίχθων (lunar) Persephone."

The passage is obscured by textual problems; it also is made more difficult by the fact that throughout this dialogue, Plutarch seems to regard Persephone and Hekate as different manifestations of a single goddess (see n. 21). What can be said with certainty, however, is that the Moon's crevices are the places where two things

---

[20] For analysis of this passage and the theory of the descent of the soul through celestial bodies in general, see J. Dillon, "The Descent of the Soul in Middle Platonic and Gnostic Theory," in *The Rediscovery of Gnosticism*, vol. I, *The School of Valentinus*, ed. Bentley Layton (Leiden 1980) pp. 358 ff.

[21] Interestingly, the adjective Plutarch applies to Persephone here--μονογενής--characteristically is applied to Hekate (e.g., at Hes. *Th.* 426 and 448 and A.R. III. 847 and 1035) and would not seem to be appropriate to Persephone herself at all. Although Plutarch separates the two goddesses in this passage, his application of the adjective to Persephone implies that a softening of the line between the two was already well underway by this time, especially with respect to their shared association with the Moon. Further evidence of this is found in the fact that before this passage, at 937 f, Plutarch tells us that the Moon is called "τριοδῖτις," a title given exclusively to Hekate, yet at 942 e ff. says that the Moon is called "Kore" and "Phersephone."

happen to disembodied souls: earlier injuries suffered or committed meet with retribution, and the daemones pass from "heavenly" blessedness to "earthly" embodiment or back again. The two actions are actually parts of the same process--passage from one state of existence to the other, passage from one portion of the universe to the other. Hekate's gulf, and therefore Hekate, is involved with this passage of souls because it is the site of at least the first part of the process--retribution of previous wrongs (it seems that the souls then proceed to one of the other crevices for actual transportation).

The passage that follows this one (944 c-e) describes the further behavior of the daemones or disembodied souls. The daemones do not necessarily remain on the Moon forever; they descend to Earth and take charge of oracles, attend to and participate in mystic rites, and act both as the chastisers of men and as their saviors in war or on the sea--all the things, in fact, that gods traditionally were said to do, but which the new philosophy taught was inappropriate to divinity. We circle back to the conclusions reached above after the examination of Plutarch's *Obs. Orac.* 416: one function of the Moon was to provide links between the divine and human worlds and also to provide a transitional way-station from which those links--in the form of disembodied souls or daemones--could move up or down the cosmic ladder.

Plutarch's description of the ultimate fate of the disembodied soul (*De Fac.* 944 f, ff.) also illustrates his understanding of the Moon as an intermediary, transmissive body. The Moon is the proper "element" (στοιχεῖον) of souls, he says, for they are, in the end, resolved back into the Moon just as bodies are resolved into the Earth. Assumedly this resolution of souls into the Moon occurs when the mind is released from the soul (943 a). When, eventually, the Sun sows new minds in the Moon, The Moon creates new souls and sows them in the Earth, which furnishes bodies.

Thus, the Moon receives, nurtures and sends forth souls. Plutarch emphasizes this transmissive role by closing his dialogue with remarks about how each sphere--Earth, Moon, Sun--aids in the creation of a new man (945 c):

> In truth, when after the death of a man the Earth ⟨gives back⟩ all those things that she took for his creation, she actually contributes nothing [to the creation of a new man]. And the Sun takes nothing [to use in the creation of men] except for taking back again the minds that he once gave. But the Moon both takes and gives, and both joins together and divides, according to her various powers....Indeed, the inanimate [body] is itself powerless, and liable to be harmed by other things. And the mind, reigning supreme, is unable to suffer. But the soul is a mixture, an intermediate thing, just as the Moon was created by god as a compound and blend of the things that are above and those that are below.

> οὐδὲν γὰρ αὕτη δίδωσι μετὰ θάνατον ὅσα λαμβάνει πρὸς γένεσιν (ἀποδιδοῦσα,) ἥλιος δὲ λαμβάνει μὲν οὐδὲν ἀπολαμβάνει δὲ τὸν νοῦν διδούς, σελήνη δὲ καὶ λαμβάνει καὶ δίδωσι καὶ συντίθησι καὶ διαιρεῖ [καὶ] κατ' ἄλλην καὶ ἄλλην δύναμιν...τὸ γὰρ ἄψυχον ἄκυρον αὐτὸ καὶ παθητὸν ὑπ' ἄλλων, ὁ δὲ νοῦς ἀπαθὴς καὶ αὐτοκράτωρ, μικτὸν δὲ καὶ μέσον ἡ ψυχὴ καθάπερ ἡ σελήνη τῶν ἄνω καὶ κάτω σύμμιγμα καὶ μετακέρασμα ὑπὸ τοῦ θεοῦ γέγονε.

The intermediary Moon, known to some as the "lot of half-heavenly, half-earthly Hekate" to some as "τριοδῖτις" and to Plutarch himself as the site of the Gulf of Hekate, played an essential role in the fluid career of the disembodied soul or daemon, itself an intermediary creature.

Soteriologically minded philosophers and theurgists, who wished to assure the rising of their own souls, later advanced the idea that Hekate, by controlling the crossing of the boundary between humanity and divinity, either could aid the ascent or could force the descent of the soul. This subject will be explored more completely in the chapters on theurgy, but mention of it belongs here as well, for it indicates how important Hekate's role as a guide became in a personal sense; the special abilities and good will of this goddess were important for those seeking salvation. Porphyry (*ap.* Eus. *PE* III.11, 113 c-d), describing the symbols of the Moon/Hekate, says that a "multitude of souls" dwell within her,[22] and Proclus (*Hymn to Hekate and Janus*, quoted pp. 147, n. 19) asks both her and the Roman patron of liminality to "lift up his soul from its wanderings in error below."

---

[22]The passage occurs during Porphyry's discussion of the various symbols found on gods' statues. The portion about the statue of Hekate/Moon, in its entirety, reads:

> But, again, the Moon is Hekate, and is the symbol of her varying phases and of her power, which is dependent on those phases. For this reason, her power appears in three forms, the figure in white robes, golden sandals and lighted torches being the symbol of the new Moon. The basket, which she bears when she has mounted high, is the symbol of the cultivation of crops, which she causes to grow according to the increasing amount of light she gives. The symbol of the full Moon is the goddess wearing brazen sandals. Or, one might judge, from the branch of olive she carries, that she is of a fiery nature. [One might also judge], from the poppy, that she is productive and that a multitude of souls dwell within her, just as if within a city, for the poppy is the symbol of a city.

It is impossible to evaluate the validity of some of Porphyry's interpretations of these symbols-- would most people really think of "a fiery nature" when they saw an olive branch? But his attempted interpretations do reflect the genuine attachment to Hekate/Moon of the properties he lists, if not in common belief then at least in such mystic/philosophical belief as Porphyry represents (i.e, she was believed to be the dwelling place of souls, whether or not the poppy truly symbolized that fact).

Hekate Κλειδοῦχος

Proclus, a mid-fifth-century Platonist and student of the Chaldean Oracles, comments on Hekate's cosmological roles at *In R*. II.121.8. The passage occurs within his exegesis of *Rep*. 614 b, in which Er describes for the first time the marvelous meeting place between earth and heaven of souls who are on their way to a new incarnation, to reward or to punishment.

In his lengthy exposition of 614 b (II.113-122), Proclus gives various information relevant to the story of Er. The comments concerning Hekate arise almost at the end of the exposition, during his discussion of the number Twelve (II.120-121). Why, Proclus asks, did Plato specify that Er spent *twelve* days seemingly dead, while his soul gathered information? After rejecting the attempts of previous exegetes to elucidate the significance of this number, he offers his own. Twelve, he says, "has the ability to bind together and harmonize diverse elements, whether they be of the individual body or the Cosmos; Twelve is the most complete boundary, resembling the causes that roll together the limits of the Cosmos" (II.121.4-5). He continues a few lines later (II.121.7-8):

> Therefore [in view of the powers of Twelve just stated], in the *Laws* [828 d], [Plato] allotted the twelfth month to the worship of the chthonian deities, and [therefore, in view of the powers of Twelve just stated], the theologian[23] says that the greatest goddess Hekate, who closes the boundaries of "things within the Cosmos" ("τῶν ἐγκοσμίων"), and who, on account of this, is called "Key-holder" ("κληδοῦχος"), was allotted the twelfth portion [of the Cosmos].
>
> διὸ καὶ μῆνα τὸν δωδέκατον ἐν Νόμοις ἀπένειμε ταῖς τῶν χθονίων θεραπείαις καὶ τὴν μεγίστην θεὸν Ἑκάτην τὰ πέρατα τῶν ἐγκοσμίων συγκλείουσαν καὶ διὰ τοῦτο κληδοῦχον ἀποκαλουμένην τὰ δωδέκατά φησιν ὁ θεολόγος τοῦ κόσμου κληρώσασθαι.

Proclus then concludes his arguments: Er was revived on the twelfth day because it was only by then that he had seen everything he was supposed to have seen, including the souls who had established a life separate from that of the body, in accordance with the dictates of the number Twelve, the delimiter of all the Cosmos and of all the boundaries in the Cosmos, which are "folded together into their proper sources."

---

[23] By this Proclus means Orpheus, to whom the term θεολόγος regularly was applied. This portion of Proclus' statement is included as part of Orph. fr. 316 (Kern). For Proclus' respect for and study of the works of "Orpheus," see M.L. West *The Orphic Poems* (Oxford 1983) pp. 227 ff.

CHAPTER III

The logic of his arguments and some of Proclus' allusions are not altogether clear, at least to a modern mind, but four points come forth: 1) Orpheus, "the theologian," called Hekate "the Closer of the boundaries of things within the Cosmos;" 2) because she closed these boundaries, he also called her "Key-holder;" 3) Orpheus allotted to Hekate the twelfth portion of the Cosmos (seemingly the Moon, whose associations with Hekate, disembodied souls and the delimitation of cosmic space have been discussed above) and 4) according to *Proclus himself*, the powers of Twelve--and by extension those of the Moon and Hekate, too--included the ability to "close" or establish the limits of the Cosmos, to harmonize and bind together diverse elements both of individuals and the Cosmos as a whole and to bring its souls to fulfillment outside the body. These powers and responsibilities closely resemble some of those of the Middle Platonic Cosmic Soul, who by mediating between the Sensible and Intelligible Worlds, divided them and all the opposing forces that they symbolize, who "closed the boundaries of things within the Cosmos" by standing between the Sensible and Intelligible Worlds (the cosmic and hypercosmic realms), and who received unto herself disembodied souls. Proclus, then, worked from a set of assumptions according to which Hekate played the same roles as the Cosmic Soul herself.

One of the important words in this passage is "key-holder," "κλειδοῦχος." From archaic times this word often was used metaphorically to express the fact that someone was "mistress" or "master," of whatever the key in question unlocked: the mistress of a household held its key.[24] Alternatively, the key-holder controlled

---

[24]The term is fairly common in everyday or cultic use; gods as well as men hold it. It is used of wives and slaves who are given responsibility over the house (e.g., E. *Troades* 492). In most cases where "κλειδοῦχος" is used of a deity, "holding the key" clearly is a way expressing the fact that he or she has control over a physical or emotional realm: e.g., at Ar. *Thesm.* 1143, Athena holds the keys to Athens; at E. *Hipp.* 538, Eros is the tyrant who "holds the keys to the bedchambers of Aphrodite;" at P. *P* VIII.4, Hesychia holds the keys of wars and councils. Paus. V.20.3 mentions a statue of Plouton at Olympia holding keys, which the Olympians explained by saying that Plouton locked up Hades so that none might return from it. Keys and key-holders are mentioned several times in the Orphic Hymns: Proteus is the god who holds the keys of the seas (XXV.1), Plouton has the keys to the entire earth (XVIII.4); Eros has the keys to aether, sky, sea and earth (LIV.4); and Daimon has the keys to joy and sorrow (LXXIII.6). Hekate herself is called the "Key-holding Queen of the entire Cosmos" at I.7. The only other deity in the Orphic Hymns actually called "κλειδοῦχος" is Prothuraia, (II.5) whose hymn immediately follows that of Hekate. What she is keyholder of is not specified. However, as A.A. Barb, "Diva Matrix" *Journal of the Warburg and Courtauld Institute* 16 (1953) 193-238, has shown in detail, the key--either as a physical object or as an inscribed or engraved sign--was used in later antiquity as a magic charm to "unlock" the uterus, i.e., to bring about swift and safe childbirth, or to protect the uterus against the "manifold ailments of the female sex organ" (p. 94; cf. now also Robert Ritner, "A Uterine Amulet in the Oriental Institute Collection," *Jnl. Near East. Studies* 43 (1984) 209-221). As this rather short Orphic Hymn also addresses Prothuraia with numerous other titles unmistakably related to childbirth (e.g., "Eileithuia," "ὠκυλόχεια"), it is possible that the key she holds is of the type Barb discusses. The generality with which the idea of key-holding deities regularly is treated in the Orphic Hymns should not preclude understanding individual examples to indicate more specific duties.

access to another's realm: a priestess held the key to a goddess' temple, Aeacus held the keys to Hades,[25] Janus held the keys that allowed Jupiter to enter and exit from Heaven.[26] But in mystic literature, especially of post-classical antiquity, the word κλειδοῦχος took on additional significance. Examination both of Hekate's associations with the key throughout antiquity and of later associations of the word "key-holder" will help to elucidate the meaning of this title in Proclus' passage.

The key was one of Hekate's symbols at least from Hellenistic times onwards. Generally, the keys held by Hekate were those that opened Hades,[27] which agrees with her duties as the guide of disembodied souls. For example, at *PGM* IV.2292, Hekate's key is said to open the "bars of Cerberus." At *PGM* IV.2335 and LXX.10, it is referred to as the key of "she who rules Tartaros" or of "the Lady of Tartaros." At Orph. *Argo*. 986, Hekate is said to "unbar" the gates of Hades; the implement necessary to unlatch the ὀχῆες would be a key. Other literary passages describe Hekate as providing--or prohibiting--access into and out of Hades;[28] although these passages do not mention keys specifically, they contribute to the picture of her as the goddess who opened the gates of the Underworld. The importance of this role to the magician or witch is explored in more detail in Chapter X; briefly, the success of traditional magic depended on the aid of the daemonic souls that Hekate could release by unlocking the gates of Hades.

There are some references in which Hekate's key has no stated connection with Hades[29] or in which its significance is difficult to discern.[30] Most importantly, inscriptions from Lagina in Stratonice, the Asia Minor site of one of Hekate's cults, tell of a priestess called the κλειδοφόρος--the key-bearer--who walked in a yearly procession called the κλειδὸς πομπή or κλειδὸς ἀγωγή.[31] These inscriptions date from the first century B.C. to the third century A.D. Literary mention of Hekate's

---

[25]*IG* 14.1746. Cf. Ar. *Ra*. 465 ff., Luc. *de Luctu* 4 and *Cata*. 4; cf. also *AP* 7.391, in which Hades tells his key-holders (κλειδοῦχοι) to bar the gates.

[26]Ov. *F*. I.125-28: *"praesideo foribus caeli cum mitibus Horis: it, redit officio Iuppiter ipse meo. inde vocor Ianus."*

[27]This has been argued, for example, by Köhler "kleiduchos" *RE* XI.1 Halbband XXI, 598; Heckenbach "Hekate" *RE* VII.2 Halbband XIV, 2773; Laumonier, p. 398.

[28]E.g., Ov. *Meta*. VII.234; Sen. *Oed*. 568 ff.; Ap. *Meta*. XI.2; Lucian *Philops*. 22; Verg. *A*. VI.258.

[29]E.g., Orph. *Hymn* I.7 (Quandt).

[30]Starting in Hellenistic times, Hekate's statues sometimes are shown with keys as well as other objects. See E. Petersen, *Die dreigestaltige Hekate* I and II (*AEM* 4, 1880 and *AEM* 5, 1881) particularly II 65 ff. for examples. Petersen himself suggested that these keys represented the keys to Hades, but Kraus, p. 50, argues that there is no cogent reason for accepting this.

[31]The pertinent inscriptions first were published by J. Hatzfeld "Inscriptions de Lagina en Carie" *BCH* 44 (1920) 70-100, numbers 2, 6, 9, 15, 17, 18, 53, 56; Charles Diehls and Georges Cousin, "Inscriptions de Lagina" *BCH* 11 (1887) 5-39, numbers 6, 7, 14, 37, 41, 45. Further discussion of the inscriptions and cult are found in Kraus, pp. 48-50; Laumonier, *Les Cultes Indigènes en Carie* (Paris 1958) pp. 344-418; Nilsson, *GF* pp. 400-401.

sanctuary there is found in Strabo (XIV.660, 663), who calls it "very famous;" Tacitus (*Ann.* III.62) reports that Stratonicians petitioned Tiberius in 22 A.D. to grant them a sanctuary for "Trivia" and "Jupiter." How old the cult or the κλειδὸς πομπή actually was, however, is uncertain. Unfortunately, just as little is known about the office of the κλειδοφόρος as about the cult itself. Judging from the inscriptions, it usually was held by the daughter of the priest of Hekate and apparently was a position of honor; inscriptions and dedicatory statues commemorate the year-long service of various girls who held the office.

Although Hatzfeld, one of the first editors of the inscriptions,[32] suggested that the key the girls carried was simply a key used to unlock the precinct of Hekate, such as any priestess might carry, most scholars have argued that the apparent festivity of the procession and the stature of the office of κλειδοφόρος indicate greater significance. They understand this key, like others, to be a symbol of Hekate herself, expressing the nature of the goddess.[33] Specifically, Laumonier suggested that the key was the key to Hades;[34] given the absence of other clear associations between Hekate and keys at the time of the inscriptions, this suggestion makes the most sense.[35]

Hekate's title "Key-holder," as reported by Proclus, undoubtedly had some roots in these previous associations with the infernal key.[36] But the context in which Proclus used the term, and its meanings in other philosophical or mystic literature, suggest that his use went beyond a mere reflection of Hekate's earlier roles. Proclus himself indicates this when cites Orpheus' statement that Hekate's title "Key-holder" was based on her ability to "close the boundaries of all things within the Cosmos"

---

[32]*Ibid.*, p. 83.

[33]Thus Kraus, pp. 48-50; Laumonier, pp. 398, 412, 416-17; Nilsson, *GF* p. 401; Köhler, above, n. 27; Diehls-Cousin, p. 36.

[34]Laumonier pp. 398, 412, 416-17. Kraus, however, warned that the study of Hekate's known connections with keys can offer only hints about the possible significance of the κλειδὸς πομπή; to draw conclusions about the Laginetan festival based on Greek and Roman literary evidence alone is dangerous (p. 49). Kraus notes that the issue is complicated further by the fact that no other evidence from Lagina--such as coins, inscriptions, frieze reliefs--connect Hekate with the key.

[35]Three works that are helpful in understanding the symbolism of keys and key-holding deities in antiquity as a whole are Siegfried Morenz "Anubis mit dem Schlüssel" in *Religion und Geschichte des Alten Aegypten* (Wien/Cologne, 1975) pp. 510-20; W. Köhler "Die Schlüssel des Petrus" *ArchRW* VIII (1904) 214-243; and H. Diels, "Antike Türen und Schlösser," Chp. II of *Antike Technik* (Leipzig 1914).

[36]Proclus' use of the term may refer most immediately, however, to Orphic Hymn I.7 (Quandt), in which Hekate is called the "Key-Holding Queen of the Entire Cosmos." In the hymn itself, the title may have been used metaphorically to mean "mistress," rather than "key-holder" in the more precise sense (see n. 24above). The phrase in the hymn is meant to praise her power over the whole world (cf. l. 2, which describes her as "celestial, earthly and of the sea"). Proclus, however, did not necessarily understand the phrase in the way the author of the hymn intended, and was free to develop the idea of Hekate as a "key-holder of the Cosmos" in any way he liked, using other Neopythagorean, Neoplatonic or Chaldean ideas about Hekate, key-holders and the cosmos.

("τὰ πέρατα τῶν ἐγκοσμίων συγκλείουσαν") and when he gives his own opinion, in turn, that this ability is dependent on the power she shared with Twelve to bind together and harmonize diverse elements, on her status as "the most complete boundary," and on her participation in the fulfillment of disembodied souls. Examination of uses of "κλειδοῦχος" in post-classical Platonic and Pythagorean literature takes this argument further; long before Proclus, the word "κλειδοῦχος" had acquired similar mystic and cosmological associations, of which he probably was aware.

The earliest extant such use of "κλειδοῦχος" is found in Plutarch, *De Gen. Socr.* 591 b. The context of the passage in which it arises makes it an excellent *comparandum* for the Proclean use of κλειδοῦχος. Plutarch tells about the soul-journey through the sublunar region of the heavens of a certain Timarchus, described as a friend--and later, tombmate--of Socrates' son. Thus, the Plutarchan myth is given a Platonic setting from the outset. Like the Platonic Er, whose soul-journey Proclus discusses at *In R.* II.121.8, Timarchus learns how the universe is constructed. Indeed, much of what he sees or hears--the music of the spheres, the wailing of lamenting souls, the three Fates, daughters of Necessity--is drawn from Plato's story of Er.

There are four regions within the universe, a daemon tells Timarchus (Lacy and Einarson's trans., slightly modified):

> The first is of life, the second of motion, the third of birth and the last of decay; the first is linked to the second by Unity at the invisible [the surface of the celestial sphere], the second to the third by Mind at the Sun, and the third to the fourth by Nature at the Moon. A Fate, daughter of Necessity, is the key-holder ("κλειδοῦχος") of and presides over each link: over the first Atropos, over the second Clotho, and over the link at the Moon, Lachesis. The turning point of birth is at the Moon.

> τέσσαρες δέ εἰσιν ἀρχαὶ πάντων, ζωῆς μὲν ἡ πρώτη, κινήσεως δὲ ἡ δευτέρα, γενέσεως δὲ ἡ τρίτη, φθορᾶς δὲ ἡ τελευταία· συνδεῖ δὲ τῇ μὲν δευτέρᾳ τὴν πρώτην Μονὰς κατὰ τὸ ἀόρατον, τὴν δὲ δευτέραν τῇ τρίτῃ Νοῦς καθ' ἥλιον, τὴν δὲ τρίτην πρὸς τετάρτην Φύσις κατὰ σελήνην. τῶν δὲ συνδέσμων ἑκάστου Μοῖρα κλειδοῦχος Ἀνάγκης θυγάτηρ κάθηται, τοῦ μὲν πρώτου Ἄτροπος, τοῦ δὲ δευτέρου Κλωθώ, τοῦ δὲ πρὸς σελήνην Λάχεσις, περὶ ἣν ἡ καμπὴ τῆς γενέσεως.

The passage then goes on to explain that the Moon is the portion of the universe given over to the daemones and also the site to which souls rise after death and from which they descend again into birth. The passage paints, in fact, exactly the same picture of the Moon's eschatological significance as was painted by the passages of Plutarch examined in the last chapter, and the same picture as was sketched by Proclus at *In R.* II.121.8.

At the moment, however, our specific concern is not with the Moon itself but rather with Plutarch's use of the word "κλειδοῦχος" He says that each Fate sits at the boundary between two realms and acts as a key-holder--that is, she restricts access into and out of two adjacent realms. This agrees with Plutarch's description of the Fates in other passages;[37] indeed, Plutarch's portrayal of the Fates as cosmic gate-keepers is not innovative--the idea that the Fates or similar goddesses marked the divisions between cosmic realms was an enduring Platonist concept, which found its justification in Er's vision (*Rep.* 617 c). Moreover, the meaning that Plutarch attached to the word " κλειδοῦχος" was essentially the same as it traditionally held-- it described the guardian of an entrance. But the combination of the concept and the word is notable: it shows that at least as early as Plutarch, deities that controlled passage across cosmic boundaries--as well as those who controlled access across earthly or infernal boundaries--could be described as "κλειδοῦχοι." In fact, the developmental link between this passage from Plutarch and Proclus' portrayal of Hekate as "κλειδοῦχος" seems a strong one not only because their common philosophical source (*Republic* X), but also because Hekate was often equated with Fate or the Fates in later antiquity.[38]

The Proclean attachment of the term "κλειδοῦχος" to Hekate, then, drew not only on her traditional portrayal as a key-holder, but also on Plutarch's use of the word "κλειδοῦχος" and more generally on the Platonic concept of celestial gate-keepers. The word was used similarly by Eusebius' student Basilius of Cappadocia, who preceded Proclus by a few decades, to describe Saint Peter, the doorkeeper who admitted souls to Heaven (*Serm. Contub.*, *PG* 30, 816.11).

A different Neoplatonic connotation of "κλειδοῦχος," found in texts discussing numerology, offers a third basis from which we can elucidate Proclus' use of the word. The sixth-century A.D. Byzantine scholar Joannnes Lydus (*de Mens.* I.15 = p. 9, 4 Wünsch = Orph. fr. 315), addresses the significance of the Decad in the Pythagorean and Platonic systems; in the latter part of the discussion he offers information about Ten that he attributes to the fifth-century B.C. Pythagorean philosopher Philolaus and to Orpheus:

---

[37] *Quaest. Conv.* 745 c 1, *de Fac. Lun.* 945 d 3.

[38] E.g., Schol. Hes. *Th.* 411; *PGM* IV 2795 and 2858. A particularly interesting passage comes from a second-century pseudo-Plutarchan dialogue. *De Fato* 568 e ff. describes Fate as the "Soul of the Cosmos," which, the author says, has three subdivisions that correspond to celestial divisions-- Clotho, Atropos and Lachesis. The last of these, Lachesis, who represents the sub-lunar portion of the Soul, receives what her celestial sisters send forth and transmits it to the terrestrial regions. Here we find the Cosmic Soul--which had become equated with Hekate at about the time this dialogue was written--identified with the Fates in their Plutarchan roles as celestial "κλειδοῦχοι."

Philolaus was correct when he called [this number] by the name "Ten" (δεκάς), as it is the "receiver (δεκτική) of the unlimited;" and Orpheus correctly called [Ten] the "One having branches" (κλαδοῦχος), for from [Ten] grow forth all the numbers just like branches.

ὀρθῶς οὖν αὐτὴν ὁ Φιλόλαος δεκάδα προσηγόρευσεν, ὡς δεκτικὴν τοῦ ἀπείρου, Ὀρφεὺς δὲ κλαδοῦχον, ἐξ ἧς ὡσεὶ κλάδοι τινὲς πάντες οἱ ἀριθμοὶ φύονται.

There is a textual problem in this passage. One manuscript of Lydus uses "κλειδοῦχος" rather than "κλαδοῦχος," as Kern notes. Lydus misunderstood the Dorian form of the word "κλειδοῦχος," which is " κλαδοῦχος," to mean "The One having branches" ("κλάδοι"); hence his explanation that the numbers grow forth from Ten like branches. The scribe who wrote "κλειδοῦχος" recognized Lydus' misreading for what it was and substituted the correct Ionian equivalent, restoring the meaning of the original quotation: Orpheus called Ten the "key-holder."[39] Similarly, the fourth-century, pseudo-Iamblichean *Theologum. Arithmet.* calls Ten and Four (which, in its guise as the Tetractys, bears a close, engendering relationship to Ten) "key-holders" (28.13, 81.14 de Falco; cf. Phot. *Bibl.* 144 a 6).[40]

Lydus and pseudo-Iamblichus both give evidence that Ten was called the keyholder; Lydus, and an earlier Pythagorean source he used, call it the number that receives unto itself the unlimited and produces all other numbers. Lydus expands on these ideas immediately before the passage given above: he calls Ten the encompasser of all other numbers, the giver of limit to all unlimited things, and the compiler, constricter and encompasser of all such things as either the "noetic Physis" or "sublunar

---

[39]Lydus' mistake is useful, in that it offers some substantiation of his attribution of the quotation to "Philolaus." Lydus' misunderstood source was Dorian; it must belong to the milieu of Dorian pseudo-pythagorica--that is, to the same background as Philolaus himself. Whether the quotation itself can be attributed to Philolaus or rather belongs to some Dorian "pseudo-Philolaus" cannot be determined, but at any rate, Lydus' information indeed comes from approximately the source to which he attributes it. We know that Philolaus particularly was interested in numbers and how they related to the concept of limited and unlimited; this would make him a tempting name on which to hang later statements about the cosmic significance of numbers.

The authenticity of fragments of Philolaus, and of the theories attributed to him in general, long have been questioned. A good discussion is found in W. Burkert, *Lore and Science in Ancient Pythagoreanism.* (Nürnberg 1962; English edition, Cambridge, Mass. 1972) Chp. III. At the least it can be said that Lydus' statement about Philolaus reflects an idea traditionally attributed to earlier Pythagorean/Platonic cosmology. Burkert concludes (pp. 267; 276) that the nature of many of the Philolaean fragments concerning numbers and harmony rules out post-Aristotelean forgery.

[40]The eleventh-century antiquarian George Cedrenus (*Hist. comp.* I p. 297.7 ff. Bekk. = Orph. fr. 316 Kern) offers almost the same information as Lydus (and makes the same mistake): "Ten is called the receiver as [it is] receptive of the unlimited, and it is called the One having branches [i.e., the key-holder] because all the numbers grow forth from it like branches."

Physis" embrace (i.e., Ten encompasses the physical world).[41] Other such descriptions of Ten's powers can be found throughout later antiquity.[42]

Clarification of these statements about Ten must come from Pythagorean number theory, according to which the primary function of numbers in general was to organize and limit space. Ten was considered to be the most perfect of numbers, from which the others grew forth. Ten, therefore, was an especially effective limiter or organizer of what would otherwise be disorganized space and chaotic matter. Ten was the number of dots in the Tetractys, the perfect triangle symbolizing the kernel of wisdom;[43] within the proportions of this triangle, philosophers found such universally significant formulas as the harmonic ratios (the musical intervals of fourth, fifth, octave and double octave) and the Platonic pattern of point, line, plane and solid.[44]

Ten and the Tetractys were called "κλειδοῦχοι" because they contained the force that physically limited (or "closed") the Cosmos by imposing boundaries on previously unlimited matter, and the force that organized matter within the Cosmos by providing the delimiting numbers, ratios and harmonies by whose rules the Cosmos worked. Without number, the universe would have been a formless mass. The roles

---

[41] Ten is said to have been born from Four; probably this refers to the sacred figure of the Tetractys, formed of ten dots arranged in four tiers. Cf. Lucian *V. Auct.* 4.
    Cf. also Proclus' comments on this passage (*In R.* II. 169.20 Kr. = Orph. fr. 315 Kern). In the midst of his discussion of the significance of the number 1,000, the cube of ten (II.168-171). Proclus calls her the all-receiving, venerable Mother of all because she contains and embraces all that is in the Cosmos; he says that she who places a boundary around all things is said to be unchangeable and untiring because the Nature that maintains the Cosmos is in effect eternal and indissoluble; he also says that she is called chaste because she limits all things without having been involved in the process of engenderment herself. The Decad, or Ten, he goes on to say (170.9-10), is the subsistence of the Cosmic forms and is the sum of the Cosmos; in fact, the Decad is the Cosmos (170.13).

[42] The fourth-century B.C. Platonist Speusippus spent half of his book *On Pythagorean Numbers* discussing the number Ten; Aristotle (*Met.* 986 a 8; *Probl.* 910 b 31) called it the perfect number that comprises the whole nature of numbers and determines cosmic structure. Moderatus said (*ap.* Porph. *VP* 48) that the Decad was called the Receiver because it enclosed all the numbers preceding it. Orph. fr. 315 also includes comments by Philolaus and Iamblichus on the nature of Ten (although not, it seems, specifically on the Orphic *Hymn to Number*) Philolaus (fr. 11 Diels I.313,5) says "It is necessary to contemplate the activities and the existence of numbers with consideration of the power that is within the Decad; for the power of the Decad is great and all-perfect and all-effective and a source and guide sharing in the life of men. Without her all is limitless and indistinct and unrevealed." Pseudo-Iamblichus (*Theologum. Arithmet.* 59) provides more allegorical information: "the Pythagoreans, speaking theologically, name [Ten] Cosmos, or Ouranos, or Pan, or Fate ('Ειμαρμένη) or Aion, and Strength (Κράτος) and Faith (Πίστις) and Necessity ('Ανάγκη), and Atlas and Untiring One ('Ακάμας) and simply God and Phanes and Helios." According to the fifth-century Neoplatonist Syrianus (*In Aristotel. Metaphys.* 106, 14 ff. Kroll = Orph. fr. 315), the Orphic *Hymn to Number* called Ten the "all-receiving venerable Mother of all, who placed a boundary around all things." The significance of Ten, the Decad, and the Tetractys in Middle-Platonic authors is discussed throughout Dillon and Burkert.

[43] The remarks that follow on the Tetractys are taken in large part from Burkert, pp. 72 ff.

[44] The Pythagoreans were said to swear their greatest oath by the Tetractys, in fact (Lucian *V. Auct.* 4; cf. Iamb. *VP* 85).

played by Ten and the Tetractys are similar to some of those that the Cosmic Soul played in the *Timaeus* and throughout Middle Platonism.[45] Soul also was composed of, and in a sense gave birth to, numbers, harmony and cosmically significant ratios; Soul, as the boundary between the Sensible and Intelligible Realms, also "encompassed the Sensible World," thus dividing the Universe into distinct and meaningful realms.

These roles played by Ten and Four complement the roles played by some of the other key-holders that have been discussed in this section. Some key-holding deities guide or transmit individuals and material across liminal points--their keys "open doors." But other key-holders *establish and retain* the liminal points and boundaries that structure space--their keys "close doors." Indeed, expressions of mediation or liminality always carry two implications, although usually only one is verbalized at a time. Implicit in Hekate's portrayal as a guide across the boundary between life and death, for example, is the threat that in some case, at some time, she will refuse to allow passage. Those that she treats thus are doomed to remain, with her, eternally at the point of passage.[46] Implicit in the portrayal of Ten and Four as structurers of the universe, similarly, is the possibility that an individual with the proper numerological and philosophical learning could devise a way to cross the cosmic boundaries they establish. As Chapter VII will show, for example, an understanding of the music and motion of the spheres, which finds its basis in the *Timaeus'* outline of the Soul's possession of all significant numerical ratios, was essential to the theurgist's success.

The word "κλειδοῦχος," then, carried at least three sets of connotations at the time that Proclus used it to describe Hekate: 1) it alluded to Hekate's traditional role as the key-holder who opened the gates to Hades in order to receive or release souls; 2) its use had been extended, especially by Platonist authors, to apply to the guardians of celestial boundaries as well, particularly those who controlled the passage of disembodied human souls; and 3) it expressed the power of Number-- specifically Ten and Four--to create boundary and organize chaotic matter by means

---

[45]Some authors took the role of Ten a bit further; understandably, if Ten controlled the very structure of the Cosmos, or was the boundary that defined the Cosmos, then in a sense Ten was the Cosmos. Pseudo-Iamblichus (see previous note) gives the most eclectic--almost hymnic--definition of Ten, associating it with a varied group of divinities taken from several mystic and philosophical systems.

[46]Cf. the monograph by Britt Haarløv, *The Half-Open Door. A Common Symbolic Motif within Roman Sepulchral Sculpture* (Odense 1977). Haarløv, discussing the door as a symbol for the division between life and death in funerary contexts, argues (p. 100) that "The half-open door, the door with one or both door-leaves (usually one) ajar...[is not] a motif that represents something static, but a *motif that stands for action*. What is thus given expression to is that the door can be opened...." This expresses the point I make above from a different angle: the passageway between life and death could be opened or shut. On funerary monuments of the Hellenistic and Imperial ages, Haarløv suggests, its openess probably indicates not only its readiness to admit the soul but the possibility that the soul later will return from death.

of establishing limits. Whatever his original "Orphic" source intended to convey by attaching the adjective "κλειδοῦχος" to Hekate, Proclus seems to have understood it to draw most directly on the latter two connotations; for *him,* the Orphic title "key-holder" described aspects of Hekate that agreed with his portrayal of her as having the ability to bind together and harmonize diverse elements, to close the boundaries of things within the Cosmos, to bring individual souls to fulfillment--in short, as an entity much like the Cosmic Soul. Proclus' key-holding Hekate stood not on the threshold between Hades and the upper world, as an earlier key-bearing Hekate had, but on the threshold between the Sensible and Intelligible Realms. Her station there, as Chapter IV and Part II will show, was just as important to the theurgist, who depended on celestial intermediaries, as her earlier station at the infernal gates was to the traditional magician or witch, who depended on chthonic spirits.

The preceding sections, "Hekate Κλειδοῦχος" and "The Mistress of the Moon," have discussed some of the roles Hekate was allotted in the philosophy and mysticism from which the Chaldean Oracles developed and in the philosophy and mysticism that was, in turn, influenced by the Oracles. Now that some groundwork has been laid, the next chapter will examine in detail the cosmological importance of Chaldean Hekate's role as Soul itself.

Chapter IV
Hekate and the Chaldean Cosmic Soul

The Chaldean Oracles were composed towards the end of the Middle Platonic period, by which time ideas about the Cosmic Soul and its functions were fairly well established. The time of their composition also was one during which Hekate's role as a guide across liminal points was taking on new philosophical and mystical significance. One way in which this significance was expressed was shown in the section entitled "The Mistress of the Moon."

The Chaldean system apparently was the first to equate Soul and Hekate, as Lewy has noted, p. 364.[1] Chapter V, "Hekate Μεταξύ," will suggest some reasons that the Chaldean system might have been motivated to do so. First, however, this chapter will examine in detail the cosmological roles bestowed on Hekate/Soul by the Oracles.

The cosmological roles filled by Hekate/Soul can be broken into three categories: 1) transmitter of the Ideas and thereby structurer of the physical world; 2) dividing bond between the Intelligible and Sensible Worlds; 3) source of individual souls and enlivener of the physical world and of man. It is artificial to separate these roles sharply, for they really are interrelated facets of a larger one that in the end can be defined only as that of link between the Sensible and Intelligible realms, between man and god. For purposes of analysis, however, it is convenient to address the variations individually.

Transmission of the Ideas

Fragment 35 (Kr. 20 = Dam. II.133.3-6)[2] describes the emergence of several Chaldean entities:

> From him leap forth the implacable thunderbolts,
> And the lightning-receiving womb of the splendid light
> Of Father-born Hekate, and the girding flower of fire,
> And the strong *pneuma* [situated] beyond the fiery poles.
>
> Τοῦδε γὰρ ἐκθρῴσκουσιν ἀμείλικτοί τε κεραυνοὶ
> καὶ πρηστηροδόχοι κόλποι παμφεγγέος αὐγῆς
> πατρογενοῦς Ἑκάτης καὶ ὑπεζωκὸς πυρὸς ἄνθος
> ἠδὲ κραταιὸν πνεῦμα πόλων πυρίων ἐπέκεινα.

---

[1] The evidence supporting a Chaldean equation of Hekate and Soul is reviewed in the Appendix.
[2] Note Des Places' correction to his original text in *Delebecque* (above, Introduction, n. 1), p. 324. Hereafter, all references to Des Places' corrections will be cited as "Des Places, *Delebecque*, p. ***."

CHAPTER IV

The Oracle says that a certain divinity sends forth thunderbolts and also a womb[3] to receive those thunder/lightning bolts; the womb belongs to Hekate, who is born of the Father, the Supreme God of the Chaldean system.[4] Probably, the emitter of all these things is the Paternal Intellect (Πατρικὸς Νοῦς),[5] a hypostasis of the Father that is related closely to Him[6] and represents His intellectually creative powers. According to several Oracle fragments (e.g., 3, 4), the Paternal Intellect is one means through which the absolutely transcendent and untouchable Father works upon the Intelligible and Sensible worlds.

Kroll, p. 20, suggested that in the Oracles, the terms "lightnings" and "thunderbolts" represent the Platonic Ideas or Forms, which sometimes were equated in Middle and Neoplatonic doctrine with numbers; Lewy argued this as well, p. 85 n. 72; p. 119 n. 201. All other scholars of the Oracles, including Des Place, accept the premise. The premise is supported by the fact that intellectual powers, or Intellects, generally are symbolized by fire or fiery phenomena in the Oracles. Fragment 35, then, describes the womb of Hekate as receiving the Ideas from the Paternal Intellect and, one presumes, becoming "pregnant" with them.

Fragment 34 (Kr. 20 = Proc. *In T.* I.451.19-22) further discusses this procedure (Kroll suggested that it may be a fragment of the same oracle):

> From here springs forth the genesis of varied matter;
> From here the sweeping lightning obscures its flower of fire
> As it leaps into the hollows of the Cosmoi; for from here all things
> Begin to stretch forth towards that place beneath the wondrous rays.

---

[3] "Κόλποι," in the plural, refers to the sinuses within the womb (e.g., Hipp. *Nat. Puer.* 31 and frequently elsewhere in medical texts) or, poetically, to the womb as a whole (e.g., E. *Hel.* 1145). For the sake of consistency and concision, I have chosen to translate κόλποι throughout this study as "womb."

[4] I will not discuss here the significance of the "girding flower of fire" and the "*pneuma* beyond the poles," both of which also are emitted by this source; see Lewy, p. 122, for a possible explanation.

[5] Des Places, p. 75, makes no certain identification, suggesting tentatively that it may be Kronos or the ἅπαξ ἐπέκεινα. In this he follows the source, Damascius, who cites the Oracle in his discussion of whether the Hebdomad properly is called "Kronos." Later commentators often conflated the ἅπαξ ἐπέκεινα or Kronos with the First Intellect (Theiler is helpful in understanding such Neoplatonic manipulations of the Oracles and their gods). Lewy, p. 121 n. 209, also refrains from certain identification, but notes that a less complete source of the Oracle (Proc. *In Cr.* 58.19-22) makes the subject the Pure Intellect or ἅπαξ ἐπέκεινα, whom Lewy identifies here with the First Intellect. Fr. 81 (Kr. 42) mentions the "noetic lightning-bolts of the Intellectual Fire," alias the First Intellect; fr. 82 talks about the bestowal of certain tasks on the lightnings; Lewy, p. 131 n. 247, suggests that the bestower--the controller of the lightnings--is the Paternal Intellect. For discussion of the ἅπαξ ἐπέκεινα and δὶς ἐπέκεινα and their substitution for the Paternal Intellect and Second (demiurgical) Intellect by the ancient commentators, see in addition to Theiler the discussions in Kroll, p. 27, and (more theoretical, less helpful) Lewy, p. 77.

[6] Cf. fr. 20 *bis* (not in Kr. = Dam. II.16.18): "[The Father is]...noetic, having the Intelligence within Himself" ("...νοητόν, ἔχων τὸ νοοῦν ἐν ἑαυτῷ").

"Ενθεν ἀποθρῴσκει γένεσις πολυποικίλου ὕλης·
ἔνθεν συρόμενος πρηστὴρ ἀμυδροῖ πυρὸς ἄνθος
κόσμων ἐνθρῴσκων κοιλώμασι· πάντα γὰρ ἔνθεν
ἄρχεται εἰς τὸ κάτω τείνειν ἀκτῖνας ἀγητάς.

It is probable that the source from which all springs forth in line 1 is the Paternal Intellect, as in fr. 35.[7] The action described is this: from the Paternal Intellect spring the basic seeds of the material world (the genesis of varied matter); these seeds are identified with the "lightnings," which again, as in fr. 35, can be understood as the Ideas. The Ideas enter the hollows--i.e., the κόλποι or womb--of the Cosmoi,[8] becoming in the process less distinct, more muddied by contact with the lower, increasingly hylic strata of the universe and less reflective of the noetic truth (a typical Platonic concept). From there (from the Cosmic womb[9]) "all" begins to stretch forth towards the place beneath the wondrous rays; in other words, from the Cosmic womb, the Ideas--the models for "all" physical existence--proceed into the hylic world, where genesis is completed as physical structures are created.

The two fragments present a picture in which the transmission of the Ideas from the Intelligible to the Sensible World and thus the formation of the physical world depends upon the nurturing mediation of a womb. The womb is that of Hekate; in the latter case its sinuses are called the hollows of the Cosmoi in reference to the fact that it is through them that the Cosmoi emerge into physical existence--the adjectival possessive is displaced. Thus, in these fragments, Hekate, by means of her womb, plays the same role as does the Cosmic Soul in other Middle Platonic doctrines.[10] She receives the noetic Forms or Ideas and brings them forth anew for use in structuring--indeed creating--the physical world.[11] This Chaldean idea surely

---

[7] Proclus makes the subject "Source of sources" ("πηγὴ πηγῶν"), which he identifies with the "greatest god" ("μέγιστος θεός"). As the Supreme Father of the Chaldeans was conceived of as absolutely transcendent, however, it is unlikely that he participates in creation even to this extent. The phrase "Source of Sources," used several times by Proclus and other commentators, regularly refers to Paternal Intellect, one of the two entities (with the Paternal Power) who, second on the cosmological ladder, enacts the Father's will (see Lewy, p. 82 and nn. 58-59).

[8] Here the plural is used; this usually implies the planets and/or stars as well as Earth.

[9] In agreement with Des Places, who refers the ἔνθεν in this sentence to κόσμων...κοιλώμασι of l. 3, not the original ἔνθεν of l. 1.

[10] See Chapter I.

[11] Lewy, pp. 120 ff., understands this process somewhat differently. He suggests the material that Hekate's womb receives is part of the Cosmic Soul: "Hecate being the Cosmic Soul, the 'Wombs' of her 'all-illuminating ray' may be conceived as receptacles destined to receive the effluence of this Soul" (Lewy translates κόλποι as wombs throughout his book). He supports this contention with a line from another fragment (DP 96.3 = Kr. 47 = Psell. *PG* 122, 1141 c 9): "[The Soul] possesses many plenitudes of Cosmic wombs" (his trans.) and with the hypothesis that the wombs of the Cosmic Soul must be in the Cosmic "Body" (although such an entity does exist, e.g. in fr. 37, it is not necessary to understand its presence here). Lewy suggests that the formation of the latter required its being "ensouled" by having the effluence of the Cosmic Soul poured into its hollows.

lies behind Psellus' statement (*PG* 122, 1141 d, discussing fr. 96) that the plenitude of Hekate/Soul's full womb (πολλῶν πληρώματα κόλπων [ψυχῆς]) symbolizes her power over the orderly arrangement or regulation (διακόσμησις) of the Cosmos; when her womb helps to turn the Ideas into structured matter, it arranges and regulates the previously formless physical world.

Another fragment gives information that fits into the scheme just described. Fragment 38 (Kr. 24 = Proc. *In Prm.* 895.12) reads:

> These are the thoughts of the Father, after which is my enwrapping fire.
>
> Ἔννοιαι πατρὸς αἵδε, μεθ' ἃς ἐμὸν εἰλυμένον πῦρ.

Lewy, Dodds[12] and Des Places agree that the speaker of this Oracle is Hekate/Psyche, based on the assumption that her place on the cosmological ladder is after or below that of the Paternal Intellect, who emits the Ideas (the "thoughts of the Father").[13] Lewy has argued convincingly that Hekate's fire is described as "winding" (his trans.) or "enwrapping" in accordance with the typical Platonic picture of the Cosmic Soul, who encloses the Sensible World.[14] It should be noted that the Oracle is in the first person; the goddess herself describes this scheme. One of Hekate's duties as an oracular goddess was to describe the cosmological system to inquiring theurgists; understanding the scheme had soteriological significance in Chaldean doctrine.

The "fire" or "lightning" poured into the womb of Hekate, then, represents the Ideas; Hekate is involved in their transmission to the material world. The Ideas originate in the Paternal Intellect and are sent forth from there. The Paternal Intellect also is called the "First" Intellect. There is a Second Intellect as well, understood to be "lower" on the cosmic ladder. Both Intellects, and their emissions, are portrayed as "Fires" or fiery substances in the Oracles.

He conflates two processes here with unfortunate results. Certainly, as I shall discuss below, the ensouling or enlivening of the physical world, or Cosmic Body, depended upon the mediating action of the Cosmic Soul, alias Hekate. And that ensouling could be represented as the pouring out of the Soul into or onto the Body. But the wombs or womb of the Cosmic Soul are not necessarily those of the Cosmic Body; it apparently was this identification that led Lewy to the illogical suggestion that the Cosmic Soul/Hekate pours her *own* substance into her *own* wombs (or womb).

[12]Lewy, p. 91; Dodds, "New Light," p. 273 n. 34.

[13]Proclus himself, in the lines immediately preceding his quotation of this fragment, tells us that the "Paternal Thoughts" are the Ideas.

[14]This part of Lewy's suggestion makes sense; the subsequent portions of his analysis, pp. 91-93, however, in particular his remarks on the snaky hair of Hekate, are not persuasive.

Fragment 6 (Kr. 22 = Simplic. *In Arist. de Caelo* II.1 p. 375.19-21 Heib.) discusses these two Intellects:[15]

> Like some girding, noetic membrane (s)he divides
> The First Fire and the Second Fire, which are eager to mix.
>
> ὡς γὰρ ὑπεζωκώς τις ὑμὴν νοερὸς διακρίνει,
> πῦρ πρῶτον καὶ πῦρ ἕτερον σπεύδοντα μιγῆναι.

The Intellects "are eager to mix;" that is, the more transcendent First Intellect is in danger of being polluted by the Second Intellect, who comes into closer contact with the Sensible World and therefore is more hylic than the First. They are kept in their respective places, and the structured order of the universe thereby is retained, by an unidentified, liminal entity resembling a "girding, noetic membrane."

The identity of this girding membrane is uncertain. The ancient sources give little help, and Festugière and Kroll (see n. 15) suggest only that it was involved in dividing the Intelligible from the Sensible World. Lewy mentions this fragment only briefly (p. 92 n. 101), but his comments imply that he considers it to represent Hekate/Cosmic Soul in her role as boundary between the Sensible and Intelligible Worlds. Des Places (trans. and comment. of fr. 6) also suggests that the membrane is Hekate/Soul.[16]

Lewy and Des Places are correct. Because they overlooked some connections between fr. 6 and other Oracle fragments, however, they missed important implications about Hekate's cosmological functions.

The role of the First Intellect is to emit the Ideas. Hekate is involved with "nurturing," regenerating and moving those Ideas towards the Sensible World. But how, exactly, do the Ideas make the final leap into materialization? How are the

---

[15] The sources for this fragment give no help in identifying the Fires or the entity described as a girding membrane. Simplicius uses the verse to exemplify the function of Atlas in myth; Atlas divides yet unifies the earthly and heavenly realms as does this noetic membrane. Festugière, who first identified the quotation in Simplicius as a Chaldean fragment ("Un Vers Méconnu des Oracles Chaldaïques dans Simplicius," *Symb. Osl.* 26 [1948] 75-77), suggested that the two fires represent the First and Second Intellects. To explain the membrane he adduces Proc. *In R.* II.224.28 ff. and Dam. II.131.27, which identify the ὑπεζωκώς ὑμήν with the power of division, and quite correctly suggests that this girding membrane serves as a link yet divider between the Sensible and Intelligible Worlds. Kroll, p. 22, was aware of only the first line of the fragment, which appears in Dam. II.131.27. Without the rest of the fragment to guide him, Kroll suggested this membrane divided the mundane sphere from the transmundane.

[16] Des Places ("Notes Complémentaires," p. 125) points out that in the *Corpus Hermeticum*, Treatise X.11, the soul is said to reside in the membrane (ὑμήν) surrounding the brain--that is, between the mind and the body, which accords with the traditional Middle Platonic placement of the soul between the corporeal and the noetic. See Festugière's remarks on the hermetic passage in A.D. Nock and A.-J. Festugière, ed. and trans. *Corpus Hermeticum* (Paris 1946; rpt. 1983) I.128 n. 47 (he cites the Chaldean fragment as a *comparandum*).

specific objects of the World created? These are the responsibilities of the Second Intellect, or Second "Fire."[17]

The Second Intellect is identified by commentators with the Demiurge of the *Timaeus*. The Oracles themselves give evidence that such an entity held a position in their pantheon, although extant fragments never use the word "Demiurge" itself. According to Proclus (*In T.* II.50.23 = DP 67[18] = Kr. 35), the Chaldean fragment speaking of the creation of the World from "fire, water, earth and all-nourishing aether" credited the Demiurge with this accomplishment; Lewy, p. 119, and Kroll, p. 35, accept Proclus' attribution as accurate. Fragment 33 mentions an "artisan" (ἐργοτεχνίτης) of cosmic fire whom Proclus also identifies with the Demiurge.[19] Fragment 68 (Kr. 35 = Proc. *In T.* II.50.25-27) describes an "other" or second mass of fire that "by itself works all things" (τὰ πάντα αὐτουργῶν) in order to bring the body of the Cosmos to completion and prevent it from remaining inconspicious and "membrane-like." Proclus identifies this second mass of fire with the Demiurge; Kroll, p. 35, understands this to mean the Second Intellect. At *In T.* I.408.14-15 Proclus identifies the δὶς ἐπέκεινα, alias the Second Intellect, with the Demiurge, and at II.61.19-24 specifically ascribes belief in a demiurge to the Chaldeans. Speaking more generally, it makes sense that a demiurge should be included in the Chaldean system, which relied so heavily on the *Timaeus* for the rest of its cosmology. In short, it is likely that the Second Fire or Intellect, from whom Hekate separates the First in fr. 6, is the Chaldean version of Plato's Demiurge.

Realization that the complete materialization of the Ideas in the Hylic World requires three entities[20] in Chaldean doctrine--an emitter, a transmitter and a final, receptive "moulder"--is important for understanding a series of other fragments, which discuss triads. Triads, and the triadization of entities and substances, became very popular in later philosophical and mystical thought. At the time of the Oracles' composition, however, overuse of the principle was not yet rampant; indeed, the presence of triads in Chaldean system, so greatly reverenced by the Neoplatonists, probably encouraged later uncontrolled triadization. Triads in the Oracle fragments

---

[17]Fragment 7 says, "The Father perfected all things and handed them over to the Second Intellect, Whom all of you, race of Man, call the First." ("Πάντα γὰρ ἐξετέλεσσε πατὴρ καὶ νῷ παρέδωκε δευτέρῳ, ὃν πρῶτον κληΐζετε πᾶν γένος ἀνδρῶν.")

[18]Cf. Des Places, *Delebecque*, p. 326.

[19]Des Places points out (fr. 33 n. 1) that Proclus uses the same word at *In T.* I.142.23 to describe Hephaestus, who "belongs" to the "demiurgical chain" of entities (for misuse of "chains" (σειραί) in Oracle exegeses, see Kroll, p. 22). Cf. *In T.* II.89.25: "The Oracles call the Demiurge of All the "ἐργοτεχνίτης."

[20]Lewy, pp. 105-120, develops the theory of the Ideas and their materialization further than I have done here. He finds two levels of Ideas--primordial and particular. Some of his arguments for this theory depend on his other premises concerning the triad and its members, with which I disagree. Although the theory of two levels of Ideas existed among the Middle-Platonists, I do not interpret the evidence that Lewy adduces as demonstrative of their presence in Chaldean doctrine.

HEKATE AND THE CHALDEAN COSMIC SOUL 55

themselves (as opposed to exegeses of the Oracles) should not be explained away lightly.

The Oracles do not describe in full measure the components of the triads they mention. Three fragments, however, give specific information about one of the triads. Fragment 23 says,[21]

> ...so that the triad might hold together all things in the process of measuring them.

> ὄφρα τὰ πάντα τριὰς συνέχῃ κατὰ πάντα μετροῦσα.

fragment 28,

> In the womb of this triad, all is sown.

> Τῆσδε γὰρ ἐν τριάδος κόλποις ἔσπαρται ἅπαντα.

indicates that this triad, or part of it, had a role in engenderment. Fragment 31,

> From the two of these flows the band of the first triad,
> Which is not really the First, but that triad where the noetics are measured.

> Ἐξ ἀμφοῖν δὴ τῶνδε ῥέει τριάδος δέμα πρώτης
> οὔσης οὐ πρώτης, ἀλλ' οὗ τὰ νοητὰ μετρεῖται.

reveals that one of the elements of this triad confined or bound together other things-- probably the two other elements. Furthermore, this triad, although thought to be the First, wasn't; rather, it was the place where noetic substances were "measured."[22]

---

[21] According to Lewy this fragment was followed immediately by fr. 24: "[Nature separates the cohesion]...into the beginning and the middle and the end in accordance with the dictates of Necessity" (the first four words are supplied from the source, Dam. I.291.11-13). He gives no compelling evidence for this, however. See also Des Places, *Delebecque,* p. 324.

[22] The phrase "which is not really the first, but that triad where the noetics are measured," refers to the fact that another triad exists in the Chaldean system, the Triad of Supreme Father, Paternal Intellect and Paternal Will. Misguided men reverence the demiurgic triad as if it were the "First," or "Paternal" Triad. This "First" Triad is referred to in some other fragments mentioning triads. For example, fr. 27 (Kr. 18 = Dam. I.87.3; II.87.14): "For the Triad shines in every world, the Triad that the Monad commands" ("Παντὶ γὰρ ἐν κόσμῳ λάμπει τριάς, ἧς μονὰς ἄρχει"), indicates that the Triad's influence and works pervaded the Cosmos, but that despite its importance, it was in the end the tool of the Monad, or Supreme, Transcendent Father. Hadot first suggested that the Monad meant the Father here (P. Hadot, *Porphyre et Victorinus* [Paris 1968] I 96 n. 2 and 261 n. 1). Similarly, fr. 26 (= Lydus *De Mens* II.6, 23, 12 W; not in Kroll; cf. Des Places, *Delebecque,* p. 324) "...For the Cosmos, O Triadic Monad, upon knowing you, revered you " ("Μουνάδα γάρ σε τριοῦχον ἰδὼν ἐσεβάσσατο κόσμος"), indicates again the crucial role the Triad played in cosmological--even soteriological--thought, but also again indicates that the Triad was in the end composed of differing portions of the Monad. The Triad is but an attribute of the Monad, which reflects the Chaldean notion that all creation ultimately was only the hypostasized effluence of the Father--the "Triadic Monad" is the Father in his guise as Triad.

This "measuring," also mentioned in fr. 23, is an important function of this triad. In the context of Platonism, "measuring" means dividing material substance into significant proportions. Specifically, in Middle Platonism, the Ideas are thought to be "measured" and divided as they proceed into the hylic world. This measurement or division of the Ideas enables them to enform the previously chaotic mass of matter, thus creating a structured physical world. If it is in this triad that this important measuring of the Ideas occur, then it is logical to assume that this triad has some connection with the Paternal Intellect, who emits the Ideas, with Hekate/Soul, who transmits them, and with the demiurgical Second Intellect. In fact, this triad must comprise just these three entities.[23]

The triad that measures or divides also holds together or retains (συνέχω) according to fr. 23--in fact, the two processes are ineluctably linked. Thus, the triad performs a function very similar to that of the Cosmic Soul in the *Timaeus* and later Platonic doctrine; the Soul divides yet links the Sensible and Intelligible Worlds, enclosing the Sensible World in the process, and also links disparate portions of the hylic world by transmitting the Ideas.[24]

To elucidate the functions of this triad further it is necessary to concentrate once more on its middle element. It was suggested that this element was Hekate/Soul; this agrees with the strong similarity the roles of the triad bear to those of the Cosmic Soul. Fragment 28, quoted above, mentions that this triad possesses a womb, into which "all" is sown. It has been suggested already that in the Oracles, "womb" regularly[25] refers to that of Hekate, and that Hekate's womb serves as the

---

[23]The differing view of Lewy will be summarized in n. 26 below. Support for my position includes the remarks of Lydus (*De Mens.* II.8), who, introducing fr. 28, also makes this Triad enclose (περιέχω) all noetic things and serve as the source from which all divine number emerges in proper order. Considering the role of number in Middle and Late Platonic thought, especially its equation with the Ideas and its importance in structuring the physical world, it is likely that a triad responsible for numbers would be involved with the Cosmic Soul and Demiurge.

[24]What the Triad holds together yet divides or delineates is not specified by extant fragments--the "all" of fr. 23 is, of course, open to interpretation. But certainly "all" must include the physical world, and probably includes the universe as a whole--Sensible and Intelligible Worlds together.

[25]The only possible exception is fr. 30 (Kr. 19 = Dam. II.67.1-3), "Source of sources, Womb containing all things." The subject of the phrase, according to Damascius, is the Paternal Intellect (Kroll concurs). However, it should be noted that Kroll created this fragment from two distinct portions of a sentence in Damascius, which reads in its entirety: " Διόπερ οὐδὲ πηγὴ μία τῶν πολλῶν αὕτη γε, ἀλλὰ πηγὴ τῶν πηγῶν, καὶ πηγῶν ἁπασῶν, κατὰ τὸ λόγιον, μήτρα συνέχουσα τὰ πάντα....." Ruelle, the most recent editor of Damascius, cites only the last phrase of the sentence, "συνέχουσα τὰ πάντα," as part of the actual Oracle fragment, indicating that the word "μήτρα" was added by Damascius himself to describe, metaphorically, the manner in which the "Source of sources" contained all things. The word "μήτρα" as far as I have been able to discover, does not appear elsewhere in Chaldean lore, nor is any word meaning "womb" elsewhere used to describe the Paternal Intellect or the Source of Sources. Lewy (p. 82 and notes) suggests that the original subject of the Oracles was the Paternal Power (Δύναμις). In short, it is difficult to assign a subject to the original Oracle with any certainty.

nurturing transmitter of the Ideas towards the hylic world. Therefore, fr. 28 confirms what has been hypothesized about this triad--as a whole it is concerned with processing the Ideas; individually, its component parts (Paternal or First Intellect, Hekate or Cosmic Soul, and the Second or Demiurgical Intellect) emit, transmit and mould those Ideas.

In conclusion,[26] this triad's middle entity, Hekate/ Soul, stands between the two other members--the Paternal Intellect or emitter of the Ideas and the Demiurgical Second Intellect who uses those Ideas to create the physical world.[27] She is in fact the "bond" ("δέμα") of the triad mentioned in fr. 31, joining together its other members. Hekate, within her womb, performs the important role of "nurturing" the basic Ideas and then sending them forth, altered, to the Demiurge for his creative use. One of the ways in which she nurtures and alters the Ideas is to measure or divide them. In doing this, she helps to provide the delineation, boundaries and structures from which the physical world is built.[28] In addition to these functions, she serves

---

[26]My analysis of the identity of this triad and of the functions of each of its members is aided by that of Lewy, pp. 106-117, but differs from it significantly in the following ways: 1) He leaves Hekate/Soul out of the triad and its functions altogether, which 2) leaves her out of the process of measuring and delineating. 3) He makes the womb of the triad belong to the Demiurge or Second Intellect (p. 116) who 4) in effect constitutes the entire triad (p. 116). Finally, 5) he attaches no special importance to the "bond" of the triad mentioned in fr. 31, which I understand to represent Hekate in her role as the middle entity of the triad or her role as an enclosing, limiting entity (p. 115). In sum, his errors in interpreting the significance of this triad stem from his failure to include Hekate as one of its members.

[27]The preceding discussion elucidates fr. 50 (Kr. 27 = Dam. II.164.19): "In the middle of the Fathers, the center of Hekate is borne on" ("μέσσον τῶν πατέρων Ἑκάτης κέντρον πεφορῆσθαι"). Lewy, p. 142, who placed too much stress on the fact that φορεῖσθαι was used in late antiquity to describe astrological movements, interpreted this fragment as referring to the Moon, "Hekate's abode." Through a complex identification of the "Fathers" with other astrological symbols, and specifically by identifying the midmost "Father" with the Sun, Lewy implies that the fragment is to be explained by a close connection in Chaldean doctrine between Sun and Moon--a connection he does not substantiate (on the astrological system of the Chaldeans, see now Tardieu, pp. 220-225).

More logical is Festugière's suggestion that the Fathers are actually the Intellects--First and Second--although no where else in the Oracle fragments are the Intellects called "Fathers." Kroll, p. 27, implicitly identifies them with the Intellects, pointing out that the commentators explained that the Fathers were the ἅπαξ ἐπέκεινα and δὶς ἐπέκεινα, who usually were associated with the Intellects. The explanation of the Fathers as Intellects makes sense in light of what is known about Hekate's role in Chaldean doctrine. Ancient commentators called the triad formed by the ἅπαξ ἐπέκεινα, Hekate and the δὶς ἐπέκεινα the "Source Fathers;" although this term is not found in the extant Oracles, it is the clue to understanding this fragment.

[28]Fragment 37 is a continuous description of the process this section has discussed (cf. Lewy, pp. 109-112; Des Places' notes on the fragment):

> The Father's Intellect, thinking with its vigorous Will, whirred forth the Ideas of varied forms. All of these [Ideas] sprang from a single source; for Will and Accomplishment both are born from the Father. But [the Ideas] were divided into other noetic [portions], having been apportioned by noetic Fire. For, beforehand, the Lord set before the polymorphous Cosmos an imperishable noetic model, along whose disorderly track the cosmos hastened and became visibly enformed,

as the intermediary principle between the two Intellects, dividing yet linking them. "Girding membrane" of fr. 6 is a particularly apt term for Hekate in this role, because a membrane, although it separates, is usually thin, pliable and diaphanous; it divides, yet allows some contact between the two substances it divides.[29]

Hekate's roles in the Chaldean Oracles, as presented so far, closely match portions of the picture of Hekate in late mystic/philological thought that was painted in the last chapter. Like the Proclean Hekate Κλειδοῦχος, the Chaldean Hekate/Soul is relied upon to define or structure the world, and fulfills this duty by "mathematical" means--by measuring or dividing the Ideas, which are themselves

---

engraved by the varigated Ideas. These [Ideas] have one source, from which whir forth other mighty, divided Ideas; these break upon the bodies of the Cosmoi, and, like bees, move about in the awesome womb, flashing all around nearby, hither and thither, [they are] the noetic thoughts from the Paternal source, who pluck the flower of fire with the vigor of tireless time. The first source of the Father bubbled forth these primordially generated Ideas.

Νοῦς πατρὸς ἐρροίζησε νοήσας ἀκμάδι βουλῇ
παμμόρφους ἰδέας, πηγῆς δὲ μιᾶς ἄπο πᾶσαι
ἐξέθορον· πατρόθεν γὰρ ἔην βουλή τε τέλος τε.
᾽Αλλ᾽ ἐμερίσθησαν νοερῷ πυρὶ μοιρηθεῖσαι
εἰσ ἄλλας νοεράς· κόσμῳ γὰρ ἄναξ πολυμόρφῳ
προὔθηκεν νοερὸν τύπον ἄφθιτον, οὗ κατ᾽ ἄκοσμον
ἴχνος ἐπειγόμενος μορφῆς μέτα κόσμος ἐφάνθη
παντοίαις ἰδέαις κεχαραγμένος· ὧν μία πηγή,
ἐξ ἧς ῥοιζοῦνται μεμερισμέναι ἄλλαι ἄπλατοι
ῥηγνύμεναι κόσμου περὶ σώμασιν, αἳ περὶ κόλπους
σμερδαλέους σμήνεσσιν ἐοικυῖαι φορέονται
στράπτουσαι περί τ᾽ ἀμφὶ παρασχεδὸν ἄλλυδις ἄλλῃ,
ἔννοιαι νοεραὶ πηγῆς πατρικῆς ἄπο, πουλὺ
δρεπτόμεναι πυρὸς ἄνθος ἀκοιμήτου χρόνου ἀκμῇ.
᾽Αρχεγόνους ἰδέας πρώτη πατρὸς ἔβλυσε τάσδε
αὐτοτελὴς πηγή.

Some of the things that fr. 37 says must remain obscure here for reasons of space; see Kroll, pp. 23-24; Lewy, pp. 109-112; Des Places' notes to the fragment. The general picture, which agrees with the one I have presented in this section, is this: the Paternal Intellect "thinks" [emits] Ideas. They break on the bodies of the Cosmos (enter into material existence) and move about in the awesome womb, which should be understood as Hekate/Soul's womb; "flashing" reflects the common portrayal of the Ideas as lightning. The first of these actions does not necessarily precede the second--the Ideas logically move about in the womb before they break on the bodies of the Cosmos. Additionally, the Oracle says that the Ideas had to be divided and apportioned; this procedure is related to--perhaps fulfills--the setting up of an imperishable "model" from which the physical Cosmos is to be developed.

[29]Lewy, p. 92, already has noted in part the aptness of the word "membrane" (ὑμήν), suggesting that a membrane is a boundary, but an intangible one. He proceeds from analysis of the membrane symbol to a supposedly related but unpersuasive analysis of Hekate's snaky hair. "Girding" probably reflects the original portrait of the Cosmic Soul in the *Timaeus* as περικαλύψασα the Sensible World: in dividing the Sensible and Intelligible Worlds, the Cosmic Soul also encloses or girds the Sensible World. See also n. 16, above, for a hermetic use of the word ὑμήν.

numerical in nature. Like the Mistress of the Moon (and like the traditional Hekate), she transmits entities or material across a liminal point, from one place to another.

Hekate as Dividing Bond

The previous section already has presented some of the arguments for regarding Chaldean Hekate as an intermediary and transmissive entity between the Sensible and Intelligible Worlds.

In this section, that role will be discussed further. Representative evidence from the ancient commentators that presents her not only as the intermediary between the two worlds, but also as a sort of "principle of mediation"--the entity depended upon to link together almost any two disparate but juxtaposed spheres or states of existence--will be reviewed as well.

Fragment 189 (Kr. 30 n.1 = Proc. *In T*. II.130.23) is but a single word: "ἀμφιπρόσωπος," "with a double face." Des Places makes it an epithet of Chaldean Hekate, following Lewy, p. 93, and Kroll, p. 30 n. 1. There is no doubt that they are correct in assigning the adjective to Hekate/Soul; the exegetes regularly use it and the related adjectives "ἀμφιφαής" and "ἀμφίστομος" in connection with Hekate/Soul. At *In T*. II.129.25-130.23, Proclus calls Soul "ἀμφιπρόσωπος" and "ἀμφιφαής" and alludes to the Chaldean description of Hekate's statue in frs. 51 and 52. At *In T*. II.246.19 and II.293.23 Proclus says that Soul is "ἀμφιπρόσωπος" and "ἀμφίστομος." Damascius (I.315.20 and II.152.23) calls Hekate "ἀμφιφαής."[30]

The adjective "ἀμφιπρόσωπος" expresses an ability to face in two directions;[31] it also is applied to Janus (Plut. *Numa* 19.11), seemingly as a translation of

---

[30] "Ἀμφιφαής" also is used in fr. 1.4, where "...the Power (Δύναμις) of circumsplendent strength (ἀλκή), flashing in noetic divisions" is introduced as one of the predicates of the Supreme Father. Lewy, p. 86 and p. 94 n. 112, suggests that ἀλκή here is a predicate of Hekate as the Cosmic Soul. Other uses of ἀλκή in the Oracles support its connection with Soul/Hekate: fr. 2.2 (Soul is armed with triple ἀλκή); fr. 32.4 (Hekate pours forth the great ἀλκή of the powerful and vivifying fire); fr. 117 (the theurgist is saved by the Soul's ἀλκή--accepting Des Places' reading) fr. 119 (ἀλκή provides for the soul's ascension). Two uses, fr. 49.1 and fr. 82.2, bear no clear relation to Soul/Hekate; fr. 118.2 may refer to the Soul/Hekate's power to convey to the theurgist by dreams the symbols necessary for ascension (see Des Places' comments on this fragment and on the relation between ἀλκή and Hekate/Soul in the hymns of Synesius, pp. 36-37).

[31] The word "ἀμφιπρόσωπος" theoretically can mean "with faces all around," rather than "facing both ways," just as "ἀμφιφαής" can mean "visible all around" rather than "visible in two directions." However, that the more restricted meanings "facing both ways" and "visible in two directions," are intended can be assumed for the following reasons. 1) Although the third word used in connection with these two by the exegetes to describe Hekate/Soul, "ἀμφίστομος," theoretically *could* mean "with mouths all around," according to LSJ it is never used that way--it means "with two mouths" and is applied to things such as a "two-mouthed ichneumon," a tunnel, or an army facing in two directions." 2) The contexts in which these three "ἀμφι" adjectives appear argues for the more

his Latin epithet "*bifrons*." The other adjectives, "ἀμφιφαής" and "ἀμφίστομος," express an ability to interact with two different realms. The fact that these adjectives differ from the "triple" adjectives found in connection with Hekate from classical times (e.g., τρίγληνος, τριοδῖτις) should be stressed: in Chaldean contexts, the goddess is given only two faces because she is expected to view two specific realms, the Intelligible and the Sensible Worlds, between which she stands as Cosmic Soul. The adjective draws not so much on her previous reputation as a many-headed or many-bodied goddess as it does on this particular cosmological role. Conversely, for this same reason, "double" adjectives such as those used by Proclus and Damascius are not applied to Hekate until Middle and Late Platonic times, and even then appear only in mystic and philosophical contexts.[32]

The fact that Chaldean Hekate must do more than look to both realms--must *interact* with both of them--should be stressed. The contexts in which the exegetes use these adjectives give details as to how she interacts. At *In T*. II.129.25-130.23, Proclus says that "ἀμφιπρόσωπος" and "ἀμφιφαής" Soul is placed between "The Fathers" (the transcendent god and the demiurge), receiving into her womb all "noetic emissions" and sending forth the "bodily channels of life." In other words, he describes Soul's role in transmitting the Ideas across the boundary between the Intelligible and Sensible Worlds, as was discussed in Chapter I. At *In T*. II.293.23, he says that "ἀμφιπρόσωπος" and "ἀμφίστομος" Soul stands between between Eternity and the generated world, between the divided and the undivided, participating (μετέχω) in both. At *In T*. II.246.19 ff., Proclus discusses "ἀμφιπρόσωπος" and "ἀμφίστομος" Soul's relation to "that above" and "that below" and her abilities to divide and to unify the Intelligible and Sensible spheres and to transmit material from the former to the latter. Damascius (I.315.20 and II.152.23) refers to "ἀμφιφαής" Hekate's transmissive placement between the two "Fathers," i.e., the transcendent god and the demiurge. By facing in both directions and reacting to both the Sensible and Intelligible spheres, Hekate/Soul bridges the gap between them that she herself, as Soul, establishes and guards.

---

restricted meanings; the adjectives occur when Hekate/Soul's position between the *two* spheres (Sensible and Intelligible) and her power to mediate between them is described. The exegetes are concerned with the way in which Hekate/Soul interacts with these two spheres, and, in any case, these are only two spheres with which Hekate/Soul *can* interact.

[32] In disagreement with Kroll, p. 30, who suggests that the adjective refers to the three- or four-headed statue of the goddess, and Lewy, p. 93, who follows Kroll. Lewy later, p. 355, mentions the more philosophical connotations of the adjectives, but makes no suggestion that these gave rise to its use in the Oracles. Des Places specifically translates the adjective as *"à double face"* and, judging from his brief comments (fr. 189 n. 1), leans towards a explanation such as I have offered here. Cf. also Tardieu, p. 217.

Fragment 189 supports the idea that Chaldean Hekate was a goddess who served as an transmissive intermediary between the Sensible and Intelligible Worlds. This intermediary function greatly interested ancient scholars of the Oracles, who enthusiastically developed it far beyond its original Chaldean limits; it seems that whenever a link between two disparate principles was required, Hekate was pressed into action and some bit of Chaldean doctrine was twisted into support. Some examples of this have been adduced during discussion of her role in transmitting the Ideas--her placement between the ἅπαξ ἐπέκεινα and the δὶς ἐπέκεινα, equated with the Transcendent Father and the Demiurge, is especially popular among later commentators. Psellus mentions this Triad of ἅπαξ ἐπέκεινα, Hekate and δὶς ἐπέκεινα several times during his exegeses of the Oracles; he probably follows Proclus in sometimes referring to the whole group as the "πηγαῖοι πατέρες" ("Source Fathers"), or "κοσμαγοί" (e.g., *PG* 122, 1152 a; *Hyp. Keph.* 74, 12 K). He also refers to Hekate simply as having the middle place among the gods and being the center of all Powers (*PG* 122, 1136 b; cf. Tardieu, p. 217). Finally, he makes Hekate the source of dreams; specifically, her girdle is understood as the symbol of this power (*Hyp. Keph.* 74, 41 K) As Lewy remarked, p. 93, dreams commonly were believed to be sent by means of daemons, the mediators between god and man. Psellus' eagerness to place the Chaldean Hekate in control of this process may be based in part on his understanding of her as a intermediary goddess, particularly one who stood between the divine and human worlds and controlled the messengers between them.

Damascius often mentions Hekate's intermediary position, too. At II.43.27 he places her between the First Father, who represents for him the "Undivided," and the Second Father, who is the "Much-divided;" he makes a similar statement at I.315.20 and at II.89-90 discusses the idea in depth. Proclus (*In T.* II.129.25) gave Hekate/Soul the middle place among the gods; his rearrangement of the Chaldean system of gods to suit his Platonic ideals (see Lewy, pp. 481-5) jettisoned many Chaldean ideas, but adamantly retained Hekate as the middle member of the "πηγαῖοι πατέρες" or "κοσμαγοί."

Do what they might to other aspects of Chaldean doctrine, the ancient commentators insisted on presenting Hekate as a deity or entity that stood between two others, usually an active entity who transmitted material or forces from one to the other. This indicates that Hekate's position as a intermediary in the genuine Chaldean system was too important and well known to dismiss, and also that this role of intermediary, particularly as Hekate played it, was important to the theories of the commentators themselves. The growing importance of mediating principles in general was discussed in Chapter I; this, certainly, encouraged the commentators. Some reasons for the popularity of Hekate herself as a mediator, in the Oracles themselves and in later times, will be discussed in Chapter V.

Hekate as Ensouler and Enlivener

Some Middle Platonic doctrines gave the Soul responsibility for sending down--even creating--the individual souls of men and also for ensouling the world as a whole. The first idea originated in the *Philebus'* description of the Cosmic Soul creating individual souls; it was linked to the connection between the Soul and daemones, who were disembodied souls. The second originated in the Middle Platonic interpretation of the *Timaeus* and was regularly one of Soul's duties in Middle Platonism and Neoplatonism. Chaldean doctrine followed suit, giving Hekate/Soul responsibility for the ensouling of men and the world.

Fragment 51 (Kr. 28 = Proc. *In R.* II.201.14-16; cf. Des Places, *Delebecque*, p. 325) describes part of a cult statue of Hekate:[33]

> For all around the hollows of the cartilage of [Hekate's] right flank,
> The abundant liquid of the Primal Soul gushes unceasingly,
> Completely ensouling the light, the fire, the aether and the Cosmoi.
>
> Δεξιτερῆς μὲν γὰρ λαγόνος περὶ χήραμα χόνδρων
> πολλὴ ἄδην βλύζει ψυχῆς λιβὰς ἀρχιγενέθλου
> ἄρδην ἐμψυχοῦσα φάος πῦρ αἰθέρα κόσμους.

Hekate (or, to be specific, her "λαγών") is the source of the liquid[34] of the "Primal" or "Cosmic" Soul. This fragment comes from the same Oracle as fr. 52 (Kr. 28 = Psellus *PG* 122, 1136 a 11-12):

> In the left flank of Hekate resides the Source of Virtue,
> Which completely remains within, not sending forth its virginity.
>
> Λαιῆς ἐν λαγόσιν Ἑκάτης ἀρετῆς πέλε πηγή,
> ἔνδον ὅλη μίμνουσα τὸ παρθένον οὐ προϊεῖσα.

Let us turn now to the interpretation of fr. 51. The fragment says that Hekate/Soul ensouls the light, the fire, the aether and the Cosmoi, to each of which Lewy assigns specific meanings, pp. 88-9;[35] the general implication of the line--and its primary importance--is that Hekate is charged with ensouling virtually everything.

---

[33] It is known that the fragment describes a statue of Hekate because of the extensive ancient testimonia for the fragment (see Des Places' edition) and also because fr. 52, which is a part of the same Oracle, specifically names Hekate.

[34] Procl. *In T.* III.256.32-257.2, with this Oracle in mind, says that water is the proper home of the Soul because it is the symbol for Life. Therefore, he continues (257.2), Soul is called the "spring" (λιβάς) of all ζῳογονία in the Oracles and Plato calls the Soul a πηγή at *Phaedr.* 245 c.

[35] Light=Aion, the "Father-begotten Light (but. cf. Des Places, *Delebecque*, p. 325); Fire=the Empyrean; Aether=region of fixed stars; Worlds=zone of planets, including Earth.

The "liquid of the Primal Soul" pours forth from her abdomen; she herself is the Primal, or Cosmic, Soul. Fragment 53 (Kr. 28 = Proc. *In T.* I.408.16-17; II.61.24-25) similarly says [36]

...I, Psyche, dwell below the Paternal thoughts,
Ensouling All with my warmth,

...μετὰ δὴ πατρικὰς διανοίας
ψυχὴ ἐγὼ ναίω θέρμῃ ψυχοῦσα τὰ πάντα.

and Porphyry (*Phil. Orac. ap.* Eus. *PE* V.7, 191 c = Wolff 122) quotes Hekate as saying "I am such a one as is able to ensoul the highest world."[37]

The basic idea is straightforward--one entity or deity is responsible for dispersing Soul and souls throughout the universe. But how does Hekate accomplish this and what was the significance of "soul" to the Chaldeans?

The previous section of this chapter showed that a womb--or the sinuses of that womb--(κόλποι, κοιλώματα) within Hekate's body served as nurturing transmitters of the Ideas. As fr. 51 shows, from hollows within her abdomen--probably from the sinuses of her womb[38]--also pours forth soul (from Soul comes souls). Fragment 96 (Kr. 47 = Psellus *PG* 122, 1141 c 7-9) says:

---

[36] Kroll, p. 28, suspects this fragment of being a Neoplatonic forgery, but it is accepted by all other scholars of the Oracles.

[37] Lewy, pp. 47-8, argues that this oracle is actually a Chaldean Oracle. Dodds, "New Light," p. 267, is dubious about this, as he is about most of Lewy's newly identified "Chaldean" fragments. For further discussion of Porphyry and the Oracles, see pp. 4-5; 79; 130-32; 141-42; 154-56 and nn.7, 14; 161-62. Cf. also *Phil. Orac. ap.* Eus. *PE* III.11, 113 c-d , quoted above, p. 38 n. 22.

[38] The use of λαγών in frs. 51 and 52 has a distinctly sexual or reproductive tone, for in post-classical Greek, particularly in poetic or oracular describing the birth of children, the *plural* of λαγών regularly is used to refer to a single, specific organ within the abdomen--the womb. E.g., Heliod. *Aeth.* II.26.2, III.2.4 (= *AP* IX.485.6); Naumach. *ap.* Stob. 4.22.32; arg. E. *Ph.* (solution to the Sphinx's riddle); *AP* I.44.2, VII.168.4, XIV.125 2 and 6, XIV.58.4 (metaph. in a riddle), XV.31.1 (metaph. of the earth's womb); *Orac. Sibyl.* 457; Luc. *Podagr.* 106. Cf. also the interesting story at Philostr. *VA* 3.39, where a woman in childbirth is aided by her husband's act of releasing a rabbit (λαγώς); as the rabbit jumps from his arms, her womb releases the child. The husband is warned to release the rabbit at just the right moment, without delay; otherwise, the womb would be extruded with the child. Philostratus refers to the woman's womb in this passage by the term μήτρα, which is found more commonly in medical texts than λαγών, but it seems clear that what is going on here is a bit of sympathetic magic based on the similarity of names (as well as on rabbits' well-known fecundity).

It also should be noted that at *In T.* III.248.5 ff., when Proclus wanted to show how "the theologians, speaking in the secret ways that they do, invent stories about the marriages and parturitions of the gods in order to symbolize and explain the same process that Plato describes as taking place in the mixing bowl," he adduced the "Orphic" story of how Zeus and Hera mated to give birth to the "All," the Hesiodic story of Rhea bringing forth from her womb the children fathered by Cronos, *and Chaldean fr. 51*. Clearly, Proclus understood the process described by fr. 51 to have sexual or reproductive overtones

> Soul, being a brilliant fire by the Power of the Father,
> Remains immortal and is the Mistress of Life
> And holds the plenitude of the full womb of the Cosmos.
>
> "Ὅττι ψυχή, πῦρ δυνάμει πατρὸς οὖσα φαεινόν,
> ἀθάνατός τε μένει καὶ ζωῆς δεσπότις ἐστὶν
> καὶ ἴσχει [κόσμου] πολλῶν πληρώματα κόλπων.

This fragment provides several pieces of information. It indicates, first, that Soul/Hekate possesses the womb of the Cosmoi; second, that the Soul is the "Mistress of Life" ("ζωῆς δεσπότις") and, third, that her "fire" or potency, is endowed by the Power (Δύναμις) of the Father.

Fragment 32 (Kr. 19 = Proc. *In T.* I.420.13-16) helps to elucidate these ideas. It says:

> Workwoman, she is the bestower of life-bearing fire,
> And filling the life-giving womb of Hekate.............
> ....(s)he spills on the "Maintainers"
> The force of [the] vital and powerful fire.
>
> Ἐργάτις, ἐκδότις ἐστὶ πυρὸς ζωηφόρου [αὕτη],
> καὶ τὸν ζῳογόνον πληροῦσ' Ἑκάτης........κόλπον
> ....ἐπιρρεῖ τοῖς συνοχεῦσιν
> ἀλκὴν ζειδώροιο πυρὸς μέγα δυναμένοιο.

Half a foot (two short syllables) is missing from the second line; two feet from the third. The fragment's message is clear, however; Hekate's womb is filled with a "life-bearing" fire by a superior power. In turn the womb becomes "life-giving," which implies that it passes the fire along to others. Hekate or her womb is probably the subject missing from l. 3 that spills forth this fire upon the "Maintainers" or "Connectives"--minor, daemon-like entities of the Chaldean system, who seem to be involved with the final, demiurgical stage of the world's creation (on this, see Lewy, pp. 129-31, 155-56, 345-53). It is possible that the missing portion of the fragment listed other entities or other portions of the Cosmos that received this outpouring of life from Hekate's womb.

But who is the "workwoman" and "bestower" of line 1? Most previous commentators have taken insufficient note of the fact that the two nouns are feminine, going so far as to suggest that they refer to entities with masculine names.[39] Rather, the terms refer to the Paternal Power--Πατρικὴ Δύναμις--an entity whose name is feminine.[40] The Πατρικὴ Δύναμις, like the Πατρικὴ Νοῦς, is a hypostasis of the Supreme Father. The hypothesis that the workwoman is the Paternal Power may seem to contradict the preceding analysis of fr. 34 and 35, in which the Paternal Intellect impregnates Hekate's womb (pp. 49 ff.). Actually, two slightly different processes are taking place; the Paternal Intellect, naturally, conveys the Ideas--represented as lightning/thunder or the Father's thoughts--through Hekate's womb; the Paternal Power, on the other hand, conveys an enlivening (ζωηφόρος) substance; similarly, fr. 96 ascribed the Soul's "fire," or life-giving potency, to the Paternal Power. The two processes are analogous and closely related; it is artificial to separate them, for separation implies that the bestowal of life/soul was absolutely distinct from the bestowal of the Ideas. These two predicates of the Father, Intellect and Power, co-operate in the transmission of essential noetic materials through Soul/Hekate; the Intellect is concerned more with the creation of physical form in the world, the Power with endowing those forms with soul.[41]

---

[39]Lewy, p. 83, equates this workwoman with the Paternal Intellect (Νοῦς), whose name, of course, is grammatically masculine. Proclus does introduce the fragment with a feminine noun, "τριάς": "the third noetic triad is τὸ αὐτοζῷον, concerning which the Oracles say that it is the 'workwoman' and 'bestower.'" But it was undoubtedly Proclus' own idea, some three centuries after the Oracles, to equate the "workwoman" with the third noetic triad (whom Proclus himself identifies with Νοῦς), and thus the gender of "triad" alone cannot account for the feminine noun. Kroll, p. 19, seems at a loss and only briefly mentions the line. Although he admits some possibility that the Second Intelligence (the male "Demiurgical" Intelligence) may be the subject of l. 1, he argues there is no convincing evidence that it refers to either of the Intelligences. Des Places offers no suggestion, but at least uses feminine nouns *("ouvrière," "distributrice")* in his translation. Festugière's edition and translation of Proclus' *In T.* suggests that the fragment refers to the *"Pensée pensante."* P. Hadot in his translation and commentary of Marius Victorinus' *Adversus Arium* (Paris 1960) p. 862, finds influence of this entity in Victorinus' term *"operatrix,"* which is at least feminine.

[40]Lewy argues, pp. 87, 106 and 342 n. 116, that Δύναμις should be understood as the feminine predicate of the Supreme Father. Elsewhere, pp. 262-3, he also argues that she represents Hekate. His arguments are not convincing. In the second case, he interprets fr. 136 "...It is for no other reason that God turns away man and with life-giving δύναμις sends him on an empty path," as referring to Hekate's role as queen of the daemones who mislead men--Hekate, alias the life-giving δύναμις, is the tool through whom the Father works. The phrase may well refer to Hekate (the adjective "life-giving," often used of Hekate, supports this), but there is no reason to assume that this Hekatean δύναμις is the same as the Paternal Δύναμις.

An additional reason for understanding "workwoman" and "deliveress" to refer to Δύναμις rather than to Νοῦς as Lewy suggests, is the nature of the term "workwoman." Νοῦς, being pure Intellect never "works;" in fact, fr. 5 specifically states that it is not through works (ἔργα) but through mind (νοῦς) that he accomplishes his goals. Δύναμις, understood as the assembly of all of the Supreme Father's abilities, is a much more logical candidate for the term "workwoman."

[41]Ultimately, like everything else, Soul/souls come from the Supreme Father. Cf. fr. 115 (Kr. 52 = Psellus *PG* 122, 1144 d 1-2; cf. Des Places, *Delebecque,* pp. 327-8),

It is necessary to hasten towards the light and towards the rays of the Father,
from where the Soul/soul is sent, clothed in much Intellect.

Other information from the Oracles about Δύναμις confirms the idea that one of her duties is to aid in the transmission of noetic substances, particularly "life-giving" substances, through Soul/Hekate. Fragment 56 says:

> Rhea truly is the font and stream of the blessed noetic [substances]
> For she is the first of all in power and
> having received into her marvelous womb
> She pours forth a whirling generation upon All.

> Ῥείη τοι νοερῶν μακάρων πηγή τε ῥοή τε·
> πάντων γὰρ πρώτη δυνάμει κόλποισιν ἀφράστοις
> δεξαμένη γενεὴν ἐπὶ πᾶν προχέει τροχάουσαν.

It generally is agreed that Rhea means Hekate here.[42] This Rhea/Hekate is "first of all" in δύναμις, i.e., she possesses or uses more of it than other entities.[43] The statement confirms or explains that of the first line--Δύναμις enables Rhea/Hekate to be a font and stream--and implicitly explains line 3--the δύναμις enables her to pour forth a whirling generation on All.[44]

> Χρή σε σπεύδειν πρὸς τὸ φάος καὶ πρὸς Πατρὸς αὐγάς,
> ἔνθεν ἐπέμφθη σοι ψυχὴ πολὺν ἐσσαμένη νοῦν.

fr. 25 (Kr. 46 = Procl. In T. III.316.10),

> For the Father conceived these things and man was ensouled by him.

> Ταῦτα πατὴρ ἐνόησε, βροτὸς δέ οἱ ἐψύχωτο.

and fr. 94.1 (Kr. 47 + Procl. In T. I.318.17-18 and 408.19-20),

> The Father of men and gods put intellect into the soul and the soul into a lazy body.

> ...νοῦν μὲν ψυχῇ, [ψυχὴν δ'] ἐνὶ σώματι ἀργῷ
> ἡμέας ἐγκατέθηκε πατὴρ ἀνδρῶν τε θεῶν τε.

Psellus (PG 122, 1152 c 5 ff.) gives two sources for the human soul--the Paternal Intellect and the πηγὴ ψυχῶν (i.e., Hekate).

[42] Kroll, p. 30, and Des Places agree that Rhea here is to be identified with Hekate; Kroll has suggested some reasons for the equation, based on Hekate's syncretism with many goddesses by the second century. Festugière (Proclus, Timée V, 117 n. 1) agrees as well. A more important consideration when discussing the equation between Hekate and Rhea is the attempt of the Middle and Neoplatonists to find some underlying harmony between the three great theological/cosmological systems they revered--the Orphic (or Hellenic), the Chaldean and the Platonic. Rhea is important in some versions of the Orphic system. Proclus--and others--apparently tried to juggle the positions of Rhea and Hekate within their respective systems and place them on parallel "rungs" of the cosmic ladder; this act influenced those such as Psellus and Damascius who relied on Proclus. This "juggling" probably was not completely without basis, however. It is likely that the Chaldean system itself sought to validate itself by means of affiliating its divinities with those of other system. For more on this subject, see Lewy, pp. 481-5, and Theiler, pp. 252-301.

To return to fr. 32, the substance that Δύναμις delivers into Hekate's womb is described as "ζωηφόρος" and Hekate's womb, in turn, becomes "ζῳογόνος." The "Mistress of Life" (fr. 96) also is called its disperser (fr. 32). The connection between Hekate/Soul and Zoë in the Oracles is a close and logical one, based on the belief that the soul was the animator: without soul, life is gone. Even when "soul" took on increased eschatological and soteriological significance, the connection between life (as opposed to death) and soul remained, especially as it pertained to the entry of the soul into a body, including a Cosmic Body (cf. *Tim.* 30 b ff.). Fragment 174 (not in Kroll = Hermias *Phaedr.* 110, 5 c) says:[45]

[The Self-moving Soul] provides life to other things, rather than to herself

ἡ δ' ἑτέροις παρέχει τὸ ζῆν, πολὺ μᾶλλον ἑαυτῇ.

supporting the idea that Chaldean Hekate/Soul animated all things.[46]

The connection between Soul and life was taken up enthusiastically by a variety of ancient commentators; Hekate/Soul constantly is described by the name "ζωογόνος" or similar titles.[47] Psellus and Damascius, as usual, are among the richest sources of examples: at *PG* 122, 1141 d 1-2, Psellus gives Soul, the

---

Lewy, pp. 84-5, argued that "'Ρεία" should be understood as an adverb, "easily," in fr. 56-- this is wrong, as Des Places points out (fr. 56, n. 1).

[43] "Δύναμις" and "δύναμις" cannot be separated from one another very strictly. "Power" supplies "power," just as in Plato all good things come from "The Good." It is sometimes unclear, as in this case, whether "δύναμις" means the entity, "Paternal Power," or the power she bestows.

[44] Fr. 5 (Kr. 13 = Proc. *In T.* II.57.30-58, 2) gives a slightly different picture of the role of Δύναμις in transmission:

> For the First Transcendent Fire does not close up his Power in matter by
> Works but by Mind (Νοῦς); For the Intellect from the Intellect
> Is the artisan of the fiery Cosmos.

> ...οὐ γὰρ ἐς ὕλην
> πῦρ ἐπέκεινα τὸ πρῶτον ἐὴν δύναμιν κατακλείει
> ἔργοις ἀλλὰ νόῳ· νοῦ γὰρ νόος ἐστὶν ὁ κόσμου
> τεχνίτης πυρίου.

The fragment is concerned with the respective roles of the First (Paternal Intellect) and the Second (demiurgical) Intellect in the creation of the material Cosmos. The "First Transcendent Fire," or First Intellect does not physically "work"--that is the job of the Second. Rather, he helps to transmit power into matter by thinking (perhaps this represents the use of the Ideas, often called "thoughts").

[45] Accepting Des Places' conjecture (which is based on the context of Hermias' quotation) that the subject of the fragment is Hekate/Psyche.

[46] The fragment is introduced during Hermias' treatment of Pl. *Phaedr.* 245, which discusses the fact that soul is the self-moving, or animating, ingredient in all living creatures.

[47] The Chaldean association of Life and Soul is well accepted by modern scholars. Kroll, p. 28, referred to Hekate as *"vivifica."* Lewy, p. 356, suggests the association originated in Plato's *Phaedrus.*

"mistress of life," the ability to animate even the dead; at *Hyp. Keph.* 74.10 K he says that she fills all things with life and noetic light and at 74.19 refers to her as "ζωογόνος;" at *Hyp. Keph.* 75.3 he makes Hekate the highest member of the "life-giving sources" (above the ψυχὴ ἀρχική, which comes second). Damascius II.154.18-19 says she sends forth "life-bearing streams;" at II.235.12 ff. he calls her ζωογονική.

Fragment 56 (Kr. 30 = Proc. *In Cr.* 81.6-8 P.) must be examined again before leaving discussion of Hekate's life-giving role:[48]

> Rhea truly is the font and stream of the blessed noetic [substances]
> For she is the first of all in power and
> having received into her marvelous womb
> She pours forth a whirling generation upon All.
>
> Ῥείη τοι νοερῶν μακάρων πηγή τε ῥοή τε·
> πάντων γὰρ πρώτη δυνάμει κόλποισιν ἀφράστοις
> δεξαμένη γενεὴν ἐπὶ πᾶν προχέει τροχάουσαν.

It is particularly appropriate that Hekate be identified with Rhea, the Mother of the Gods, in this fragment, because the fragment portrays her as a life-giving, generative goddess. Fragment 56 supports the portrait of this goddess as a bestower of life, for the "whirling[49] creation" that pours forth upon all things emanates from her, and her womb is called "awesome" or "unspeakably marvelous" ("κόλποι ἄφραστοι"). She is truly a "ζωογόνος θέα," as Proclus says, discussing the fragment.

Why do the Oracles regularly couch descriptions of Hekate's transmissive abilities in procreative or nurturing language? The Chaldean equation between Hekate and Rhea, and the more general syncretism of Hekate with Rhea and other "Mother Goddesses" during the second century must be considered first. Kroll and Lewy argue that such syncretism was the primary basis for Hekate's exaltation in the Oracles. This seems unlikely, as does the assumption that such syncretism would be a strong motivation for describing mediation and transmission in "motherly" terms, although syncretism may have been a contributing reason, as the second century was a time at which Rhea, Cybele and other versions of the "Mother Goddess" gained wider popularity.

The real answer lies in the fact that biological imagery such as is found in the Oracles regularly was used in mythological cosmogonies and theogonies--one has only to think of Hesiod's *Theogony* for examples.[50] Such a use of mythological

---

[48] Already considered briefly above, p. 66.
[49] The significance of the word "τροχάουσαν" will be discussed in Chapter VII, "Hekate's Top and the Iynx-Wheel."
[50] Another example, providing an interesting analogy to the Chaldean description of the Paternal lightning-bolts entering Hekate's womb is the cosmogony of Pherecydes of Syros (Kirk, Raven,

imagery accords with the general trend of the Oracles--and of the second century as a whole--to sanctify philosophy by allying it with religion, which will be discussed in Chapter V.

Additionally, and more specifically, the reproductive terms under consideration here were introduced because of the way in which the Chaldean system viewed mediation, particularly mediation as it involved transmission of noetic materials to the Sensible world. Mediation was not a cold, scientific process; Soul and the Ideas were necessary for the creation and animation of the world, which otherwise would have remained a formless mass. God's bestowal of the Ideas on the world was a vitalizing act. She who aided in that bestowal by receiving and then transmitting the "seed" of these blessings naturally would be understood as His partner in creation--the Mother of the world--and described in appropriately "fertile" terms.

To sum up: Hekate's responsibilities as Cosmic Soul in the Oracles include the conveying of noetic material--specifically the Ideas and the animating liquid of the Soul--across the cosmic boundary into the Sensible World.[51] This role of transmitter had a complementary side, however; her position made her the "girding membrane" that served as a limit between the Intelligible and Sensible realms. Her role as creator and retainer of limits is expressed also by her participation in the conveyance of the Ideas, for the Ideas endow previously formless matter with structure and boundary. The Soul, or Hekate, is where those Ideas are "measured" or divided into significant proportions; until this is accomplished, the demiurgical Second Intellect cannot use them to construct the physical world.

Chaldean Hekate's characteristics are very similar to some of those that Hekate possesses in late philosophical and mystical literature such as was examined in Chapter III. In all cases, Hekate is concerned with the bridging of boundaries on a cosmic scale; in some cases, she also is concerned with the establishment or retention of those boundaries. But the overwhelming importance of Hekate to the Chaldean

---

Schofield, *The Presocratic Philosophers* [Cambridge 1984] pp. 56 ff.). Here, the Supreme God masturbates and places his semen into five recesses ("μυχοί"). From this seed the lesser gods are born. Cf. also the remarks of J. Dillon, "The Descent of the Soul in Middle Platonic and Gnostic Theory," in *The Rediscovery of Gnosticism,* vol. I, *The School of Valentinus,* ed. Bentley Layton (Leiden, 1980), pp. 357-364. Dillon points out that in Gnosticism, the feminine element usually is portrayed as disruptive, as a "principle of negativity, boundlessness and lack, and provokes the generation of the multiplicity of creation" (p. 357). Certainly, as this chapter has shown, Hekate/Soul is an essential element in the act of creating the material world; she is not, however, presented as "negative," or "boundless." In the same volume, U. Bianchi, "Observations on Valentinianism" (pp. 103-117), discusses "Sophia"--a specific example of this Gnostic tendency.

[51] My aim in Part I primarily has been to study the intermediary and transmissive roles that Hekate played in late literature; thus, my interest here in her responsibilities as a giver of Soul and Life has centered on the fact that she acts not as its originator, but its transmitter. It would be remiss not to remark, however, that the role has other implications; as the chapters on theurgy will show, Hekate's control over souls had important soteriological implications.

system in particular *is* unusual. Although a full analysis of this topic must await the end of this study, after the theurgical elements of the Oracles are examined, Chapter V can begin to solve the puzzle by addressing two questions. First: by Middle Platonic times, Hekate had begun to be syncretized with other goddesses; her personality grew to include other traits. Why was her role as a liminal guide and guard important enough to late mysticism and philosophy that it not only was retained but was expanded? Second (and conversely): given that mediation was an important concept in late mysticism/philosophy, why was it necessary for the Chaldean system and related schools of thought to represent it in the guise of a deity?

Hekate Μεταξύ:
How She Became What She Did

Both of the questions posed in the last chapter can be addressed by placing the Chaldean Oracles in the context of other, contemporaneous philosophical or religious movements.

The answer to the first question has been mentioned already: a growing interest in mediating deities and principles in general. As the gods increasingly were portrayed as transcendent, as detached from the world of men, the need for intervening principles or entities increased. Eventually, intermediary entities entered into almost all philosophical or mystic expressions of the relationship between divinity and humanity, as they did into relationships between other opposing concepts or entities, such as "divided" and "indivisible" or "time" and "eternity." The "Principle of Mediation" was at least in part responsible for the burgeoning philosophical interest in daemones and the intermediate position of the Moon.

Certainly, the Chaldean Oracles were the products of a system that utilized Platonic doctrines. Their creators, be they the Juliani or others, were men well aware of the trends in contemporary philosophy, including the increasing popularity of intermediaries. Indeed, although Hekate was the most important intermediary in the Chaldean system, and the one whose role was elaborated in the widest variety of ways, she was not the only one; Chaldean Eros, who seems to have grown directly from the Eros of Diotima's speech in the *Symposium*, and the Chaldean daemonic system, which will be discussed in Part II, also have mediating and transmissive functions. Other movements that similarly combined religion and philosophy posited similar mediators: the variety of Gnosticism promoted by Valentinus (*fl.* 135-60), for example, included a deity called Ὅρος ("Boundary"). When another Gnostic deity, Sophia, intruded disastrously upon the previously transcendent Paternal Abyss, Ὅρος saved the entire universe from chaotic destruction by his literal intervention. Ὅρος represented the separating or delineating side of the cosmic mediator; from what little can be deduced about him, the Christos of Valentinian Gnosticism probably was the transmissive principle, able to help souls ascend.[1]

In short, during the first and second centuries A.D., the roles of cosmic intermediaries and transmitters became ever more important, especially in those systems that, like the Chaldean one, were drawn from philosophical as well as religious sources. It was essential to the belief in an absolutely transcendent God that a gulf between divine and human be established, yet also essential that prayers,

---

[1] On mediation in Valentinian Gnosticism, see F. Sagnard, ed. and trans., *Clement d' Alexandrinus* (Sources chrétiennes 23) (Paris 1948). See also Tardieu, *passim*, for a comparison of the Chaldean and Gnostic systems.

salvation and the creative force necessary to enform and ensoul the physical world be transported across it. It is not difficult to understand, then, why the Chaldean system so greatly exalted Hekate/Soul, who both performed these cosmological roles, and who also, as Part II will show, was a personal mediator, able to bring the theurgist closer to divinity.

The second question posed at the beginning of this chapter remains: given that mediation, transmission and the establishment of boundaries were important concepts in late mysticism/philosophy, why was it necessary for the Chaldean system and similar schools of thought to represent them in the guise of a deity or to personify them?

By the time of the Oracles, philosophers long had felt compelled to retain some of traditional religion's validity by explaining religious "truths" in philosophical terms or allegory. Plutarch's treatment of Isis and Osiris is one example of this. Alternatively, philosophy and religion could be combined more or less harmoniously into a single doctrine. It was during the late second and early third centuries, as well as anyone can judge, that the group of hymns collected under the term "Orphic" were composed; probably the first thing that impresses the modern reader of these hymns is the vast number of deities and epithets that have been gathered together, but philosophical ideas, which have been identified variously as Stoic or Platonic, also are present in abundance. The century preceding the Oracles' composition gave birth to Apollonius of Tyana, who followed a Pythagorean/Platonic creed, but who also performed traditional magical or shamanistic feats.

Such was the general atmosphere. An article by Philip Merlan[2] provides specific help in understanding the Oracles themselves. Working from the assumption that religion constantly was challenged by Greek philosophy in ways such as those described above, he asks whether religion ever retaliated; his answer is yes. Initially, he notes, the retaliation arose in foreign religions. As examples, he gives Egyptian religion, particularly as expounded by Chaeremon, and Judaism, particularly as promoted by Philo. Merlan summarizes Philo's attitude as follows (pp. 171-72):

> ...as [Philo] sees it, the Jews are superior to the Greeks not so much with regard to the results of their pursuit of wisdom as with regard to the sources--human speculation with the Greeks, divine revelation with the Jews....Adherents of Moses are the true philosophers. What philosophers acquired through philosophy, Jews acquired through their νόμοι καὶ ἔθη.

---

[2] P. Merlan, "Religion and Philosophy from Plato's *Phaedo* to the Chaldean Oracles," *Journal of the History of Philosophy* I.2 (1963) 163-176.

The tide had begun to turn; "true wisdom" was asserted to come not from philosophy, but rather from religion.[3]

Philo and Chaeremon flourished in the first century. Merlan argues that Greek religion itself caught up with the rebellious trend begun by foreign religions in the second century. Its primary weapon, he suggests, was the corpus of Chaldean Oracles (pp. 173-75):

> ...in the second century A.D. in the Hellenic world, a very strange work originated, pretending to be a collection of oracles, including particularly oracles by Apollo...What strangely philosophic questions it must have been which the oracle was asked and what strangely philosophic answers they received! The God who gave them obviously was very well acquainted with Platonic and Aristotelean concepts and had read his *Timaeus* very well, in all likelihood also (Ps-?) Plato's *2nd* and *6th Letter*....But what is particularly important: these philosophical doctrines are supposed to be found in oracles-- they represent divine wisdom. The inference is obvious: whatever is valuable in Greek philosophy can be found in documents of divine revelation. Obviously religion is true philosophy.

Merlan's article argues that the Chaldean Oracles attempted to validate philosophical ideas by calling them religious revelations. Would they not, similarly, sanctify philosophical entities and concepts by identifying them with Graeco-Roman gods and goddesses?

If one sought to represent in the terms of traditional divinity the philosophical concepts of cosmic mediation and transmission, what better candidate could be found than Hekate, for whom mediation and transmission of various kinds always had been important roles?[4] Of course, changing times and circumstances, some of which have been pointed out in previous chapters, motivated changes in the specific expressions of these roles: she could be the goddess supplicated at the time of the new moon and the new month, the escort at the palace door and the guide at the crossroads, the conductor to Hades and the queen of the souls that never made it there, the key-holder to the higher realms of the cosmos and the lunar purifier of souls--or all of these things at once. But the concept behind these duties was at heart the same: from early

---

[3] He points out, pp. 170-71, that Philo perhaps opened the offensive with his gnomic statement "philosophy is the handmaiden of divine wisdom," a variation on the belief, found particularly among the Stoics, that τὰ ἐγκύκλια are the servants of philosophy. Cf. also the remarks of Tardieu, pp. 230-1.

[4] I do not argue that Hekate's role as a witches' goddess had nothing to do with her exaltation in the Chaldean pantheon; certainly, the fact that the Chaldean salvation relied on theurgy--i.e., a form of magic--made Hekate all the more appealing. I will suggest in Part II, however, that magic itself is a mediating art, providing means to cross boundaries between Hades and the upper world or Earth and Heaven. Hekate's involvement with traditional magic was another manifestation of her nature as a guide across liminal points (but one that was fairly well established by the time of the Chaldean Oracles).

times, Hekate was the deity who could aid men at points of transition, who could help them to cross boundaries, whether they be of a prosaic, everyday nature, of an extraordinary, once-in-a-lifetime nature or, later, of a theurgical nature. The ancients certainly saw unity within the various expressions of this role--indeed, they used the earlier expressions to validate or clarify the later ones, as a passage from Damascius illustrates (*In Phaed.* [vers. 1 Westerink] 496.1 ff.).

After he reviews Socrates' description of the confusingly divergent paths (σχίσεις and τρίοδοι) that present themselves to disembodied souls on their way to Hades (*Phaed.* 107 e ff.), Damascius explains that there are several ways in which one could express the eschatological doctrine that lies behind it. Speaking philosophically, as Socrates did in the *Phaedo,* one could say that souls need guides after death; after all, if there were only a single path for souls to take, guides would be unnecessary. But, Damascius continues, speaking "hieratically" about this doctrine, one could instead adduce the fact that "honors are paid to Hekate at the crossroads;" for Damascius, the fact that Hekate traditionally was supplicated at crossroads symbolized the circumstances that souls could expect to meet with after death.

Damascius knew well the Chaldean doctrine that equated Hekate with the Cosmic Soul. Among other things, this equation made her responsible for the successful passage of souls into embodiment and also out of embodiment--the same transition that Socrates describes at *Phaedo* 107 d-108 c.[5] Without Chaldean Hekate/Soul's help, an individual soul might not complete the transition, might wander between worlds forever (as, likewise, some of the souls in the *Phaedo* are said to do when they ignore their guides). Hekate traditionally was supplicated at the earthly crossroads to insure safe transition through an uncertain point; she was the factor that bridged the gap imagined to exist there, guiding men through a place that was proverbial for its uncertainty.[6] By using a reference to Hekate's familiar presence at terrestrial crossroads to explicate Platonic doctrines about the soul's experiences after death, Damascius indicates that he--and his audience--considered Hekate's function at earthly *limines* to be analogous to Hekate/Soul's eschatological function at the cosmic *limen*. The scales were indeed different, but the duties were comparable: in either guise Hekate guided individuals through points of transition, smoothing the way.[7]

---

[5] Cf. the remarks of Lewy, pp. 219-226.
[6] See Johnston, "Crossroads."
[7] Cf. also Dam. *In Phaed.* (vers. 2 Westerink) 108.1 ff. for a similar use of Hekate's traditional presence at the crossroads.

Hekate was one of the few Graeco-Roman divinities included in the Chaldean system, and she served it well, both as traditional goddess and as cosmological principle. Part II will examine how she served individual followers of the system--theurgists seeking salvation.

PART II
HEKATE AND THEURGY

Chapter VI
Theurgy and Magic

The previous chapters discussed the philosophical and cosmological facets of Hekate's role as Soul in the Chaldean system. This chapter will address the ways in which Hekate/Soul could aid the individual man--the theurgist--and how they were related to her cosmological duties.

Before describing Hekate's role in Chaldean theurgy it is necessary to describe Chaldean theurgy itself. This, in turn, leads to defining the term "theurgy," a task that has been problematic for ancient and modern scholars alike. In the context of this book, a thorough analysis of the controversy cannot be attempted, but a summary of the problems involved and the recent approaches to their solution is in order.[1]

---

[1] Two good discussions of theurgy in general and of individual Platonists' involvements with it are found in Gregory Shaw, "Theurgy: Rituals of Unification in the Neoplatonism of Iamblichus," *Traditio* XLI (1985) 1-28; and in the second half of A. Smith, *Porphyry's Place in the Neoplatonic Tradition* (The Hague 1974). Some other helpful discussions of theurgy and magic are: Fritz Graf, "Prayer in Magic and Religious Ritual," in *Magika Hiera: Ancient Greek Magic and Religion* ed. C. Faraone and D. Obbink (Oxford forthcoming 1990); G. Luck, "Theurgy and Forms of Worship in Neoplatonism," in *Religion, Science, and Magic: In Concert and in Conflict* ed. Jacob Neusner, Ernest S. Frerichs and Paul V.M. Flesher (New York and Oxford 1989), pp. 185-225; Hans Dieter Betz, gen. ed., *The Greek Magical Papyri in Translation* I (Chicago 1986); Garth Fowden, *The Egyptian Hermes* (Cambridge 1986) *passim*, but esp. Part II; Charles Robert Phillips, "The Sociology of Religious Knowledge in the Roman Empire to A.D. 284," *ANRW* II.16.3 (Berlin 1986), 2677-2773; G. Luck, *Arcana Mundi* (Baltimore 1985), pp. 20-5; Anne Sheppard, "Proclus' Attitude to Theurgy," *CQ* 32 (1982), 212-14; Michael Winkelmann, "Magic: A Theoretical Reassessment," *Curr. Anthr.* XXIII no. 1 (1982), 37-66; S. Breton, "L'homme et l' âme humain," *Diotima* 8 (1980), 21-24; A.-J. Festugière, *Études de philosophie grecque* (Paris 1971); A.A. Barb, "The Survival of Magic Arts," in *The Conflict Between Paganism and Christianity in the Fourth Century* ed. Arnaldo Momigliano (Oxford 1963), pp. 101 ff. Dodds, *G&I;* L. Rosan, *The Philosophy of Proclus* (New York 1949) S. Eitrem, "La Théurgie chez les Néoplatoniciens et dans les Papyrus Magiques," *Symb. Oslo.* XXII (1942), 49-79; Th. Hopfner, "Theurgie" *RE*, VI.1 Halbband XI, 258-70. Books and articles on individual authors' attitudes to theurgy are cited in notes below. Chaldean theurgy is treated throughout Lewy, Kroll and Des Places and in O. Geudtner, *Die Seelenlehre der Chaldäischen Orakel*, Beitr. z. Klass. Philol., 35 (Meisenheim am Glan 1971) and F.W. Cremer, *Die Chaldäischen Orakel und Jamblich De Mysteriis*, Beitr. z. Klass. Philol., 26 (Meisenheim am Glan 1969). Hereafter, all these sources will be cited by the author's last name only, with the exception of Dodds, *G&I* and Graf, *Prayer* (to distinguish these works from others by the same authors that are cited frequently in this book).

Much of the uncertainty concerning theurgy centers on the following interrelated issues: how does theurgy compare with magic (i.e., γοητεία) and, on the other hand, with philosophical or intellectual means of obtaining salvation? Should it be thought of, on one hand, as "white" or beneficent magic, or, on the other hand, as a method of causing the soul's ascension and unification with the divine through ritual rather than through spiritual contemplation? Could philosophic contemplation and ritualistic theurgy be practiced by the same man to complementary purposes? And--a final question that underlies the rest--can lines even be drawn between religious ritual, philosophic contemplation, magic and theurgy, except in the mind of the practitioner himself or his critic?[2]

Rosan was the first scholar to propose a two-fold division of theurgy: "lower" theurgy, he suggested, comprised the use of ritual objects and actions and was appropriate to those men still bound by earthly appetites; "higher" theurgy was a more contemplative and theoretical exercise, somewhat akin to the *theoria* of Plotinus. Smith redefined Rosan's two-fold division of theurgy; his monograph strongly has influenced scholarly work on theurgy ever since. He replaced Rosan's "higher" theurgy with "vertical" theurgy, which linked men to gods through the power of *philia;* "lower" theurgy became "horizontal" theurgy, which acted upon the world of humans and daemones by means of *sympatheia*, much in the way that traditional magic did.[3] Smith argued, against Rosan, that both forms of theurgy included ritualistic action; the important distinction lay in the *direction* in which the theurgy operated.

Unfortunately, Rosan's model, even in Smith's revised form, inevitably seems to imply that the so-called lower theurgy was more ritualistic, more primitive and, thus, inferior to the contemplative "higher" theurgy. As a result, acceptance of

---

[2] On this last question, see (most recently in a long line of scholars who have addressed the question) Graf, *Prayer,* who shows that magic (and perhaps theurgy) by and large used the same rituals and the same form of prayer as did "traditional" religion. It is *what* the magician burns as an offering, for example, not the way in which he burns it, that distinguishes him from the ordinary "religious" man. As Graf suggests, the magician purposely sought isolation from his social group, in order to "move into a sphere removed from his fellow men, where he will converse with the divinity." The many other secondary works on the topic include D.E. Aune, "Magic in Early Christianity," *ANRW* II 23:2 (Berlin 1980) 1507-57; G.E.R. Lloyd, *Magic, Reason and Experience* (Cambridge 1979); J.M. Hull, *Hellenistic Magic and the Synoptic Tradition* (London 1974); H. Geertz and K. Thomas, "An Anthropology of Religion and Magic," *Jnl. of Interdisc. Hist.* VI.1 (1975) 71-109; Mary Douglas, *Purity and Danger: An Analysis of the Concepts of Pollution and Taboo* (London 1966); R. Allier, *Magie et Religion* (Paris 1935); L. Deubner, *Magie und Religion* (Freiburg 1922); and H. Hubert and M. Mauss, "Esquisse d'une théorie général de la Magie," *Année Sociol.* 7 (1902) 1-140. Graf's article includes further citations. Most of the works cited in the previous note also address this issue; see in particular the volume edited by Neusner, Frerichs and Flesher.

[3] Cf. also Sheppard, who adds a third tier to Rosan's and Smith's structure. Festugière and Lewy proposed a similar two-fold division of Neoplatonic soteriological methods. One's soul could be unified with the divine by means of either 1) philosophic contemplation or 2) theurgic ritual. See Shaw for criticism of this approach.

this model and its accompanying implication have led to much scholarly puzzlement and even chagrin[4] over the fact that apparently "spiritual" men, such as Iamblichus for instance, could participate in the "material" rites mentioned at *De Myst.* V.16; 221,1-4:

> We should not be afraid to say this thing as well: that we frequently need to perform rituals on account of pressing bodily needs, to the gods and good daemones of the body.

Aren't such actions the mark of a "lower" theurgist, modern scholars have asked?

More recently, Shaw's excellent study of Iamblichus and theurgy has clarified the picture by showing that not all ancient authors (if any) made the distinction that Rosan and Smith outline. If we immerse ourselves in the Neoplatonic "worldview," Shaw argues, and more closely examine statements that ancient authors--particularly Iamblichus--make about theurgy, we discover not a two-fold distinction but

> ...different theurgies to match the different types of men, who, as Iamblichus said, have different cultic needs....What Iamblichus in fact was pointing out in his discussion of different sacrificial modes for different types of people was that the ritual performed should be suited to the person who performs it. (pp. 25-6)

According to Shaw's reading of Iamblichus, intrinsically "there is nothing better about silent prayer than animal sacrifice" (p. 23). Iamblichus himself says, in a passage cited by Shaw, that:

> Each man performs his service to the Holy according to what he is, not according to what he is not; after all, the sacrifice must not surpass the proper measure of the worshipper. (*De Myst.* V.15; 220,6-9, Shaw's trans., p. 23)

All forms of theurgical worship, when appropriately applied and correctly completed, work "vertically" (to retain Smith's term) to link an individual man to god. Theurgy's "horizontal" axis, according to Shaw's analysis, would be the specific environment in which theurgy's vertical or unifying power was expressed, whether that environment be spiritual or gross (p. 22). Iamblichean theurgy, in short, was an ecumenical discipline, admitting many modes of worship, so long as the practiioner was sincere and correctly focused in his attempts.

The division of theurgy itself into types is only one part of the problem; the scholar of theurgy also must confront the delineation of the difference between "theurgy" as a whole and "magic" in the more traditional sense (γοητεία). On this

---

[4] E.g., Smith, p. 89.

issue, too, Shaw has clarified for us the opinion of Iamblichus, who insists that the *inner disposition* of the performer marks the critical division between γοητεία and theurgy,[5] two disciplines that he adamantly separated.[6] Proper piety and intention, whatever the nature of the ritual, unifies, purifies and prepares the soul of the theurgist in a way that ordinary magic cannot. The pious Iamblichean theurgist *subordinated* himself to the gods, allowing them to work upon him; the traditional magician, of course, was supposed to do precisely the opposite.

Shaw's article takes us much closer to understanding Iamblichus' attitude towards theurgy and magic. Unfortunately, no one has yet systematically applied his standards to other ancient authors who discuss theurgy. To do so would be a challenging task, for the statements of ancient authors often are self-contradictory and constantly conflict with one another, reflecting and defining, as Shaw himself suggests (p. 4), "fundamental differences in the attitude of late antique thinkers toward their place in the world and in their sense of responsibility as embodied souls." Augustine (*De Civ. Dei* X *passim*) for example, as might be expected, rejected using the term "theurgy" to describe a higher or purer form of "magic," considering it instead to be a deceptively attractive and reassuring synonym for what was actually the γοητεία with which demons tempted men away from valid means of reaching God (it should be noted that Augustine's remark implies that the theurgists viewed themselves as practicing something superior to γοητεία). In contrast, Porphyry, from whose works on theurgy Augustine drew much of his own information,[7] approved of theurgy as a means of improving or purifying a lower level of the soul, although he understood contemplation and virtue to be necessary for salvation of the higher level;[8] he also apparently recognized a level of theurgy concerned not at all with spiritual salvation but with more worldly, immediate goals. Still argued are the questions of whether Porphyry's teacher, Plotinus, advocated the use of theurgy or was himself a theurgist. Consensus remains with Dodds' opinion that Plotinus, like any man of his time, recognized the power of theurgy (understanding it to make use of the συμπάθεια that existed throughout the cosmos) but disapproved of it, especially as a means to psychic ascension and mystical union with the divine, which he accomplished by contemplation instead.[9] Iamblichus' follower Proclus[10]

---

[5] Shaw, p. 25; he elucidates and improves a suggestion first made by Smith, p. 99.

[6] E.g., *De Myst.* III.26; 161,10-16.

[7] On this, see particularly Smith and J.J. O'Meara, *Porphyry's Philosophy from Oracles in Augustine* (Paris 1954) as well as discussions in the other general works on theurgy cited in n. 1.

[8] *De Regr. An.* 27*.21-28*.15 (in Bidez, *Vie de Porphyre*).

[9] See Smith, especially the second half of the book; John M. Rist, "Mysticism and Transcendence in Later Neoplatonism," *Hermes* 92 (1964) 213-225; P. Merlan, "Plotinus and Magic," *Isis* 44 (1953) 341-8 with A.H. Armstrong's reply, "Was Plotinus a Magician?" *Phronesis* 1 (1955) 73-79; and Dodds, *G&I*.

[10] For Proclus' attitudes towards theurgy, see Smith, Chp. VIII.

apparently believed that salvation depended on both theurgical practices and personal preparation such as prayer; there had to be spiritual support for theurgical rituals. He also distinguished two levels of theurgical activity, one directed towards the noetic world and the goal of psychic unification and ascension, the other directed towards this world and more practical goals such as normally would be met by traditional magic, e.g., rainmaking (Marinus, *Procl.* 28).

Obviously, much remains to be done towards the clarification of theurgy's development and its representation by individual authors. An exhaustive analysis of these and other ancient sources cannot be undertaken here, of course, but if it were, probably we would learn that, as with so many religious terms, the meaning of the title "theurgist" lay in the user's mind. What *can* be attempted here, however, now that the problems and potential solutions involved in the study of theurgy have been introduced, is a brief analysis of Chaldean theurgy as we glimpse it in the Oracle fragments and in exegetes' comments. Does Shaw's description of Iamblichean theurgy hold good for Chaldean theurgy? If not, how can we describe it instead? It is particularly appropriate to apply these new standards of evaluation to *Chaldean* theurgy, for despite the uncertainty of how to define "theurgy" in general, it is at least certain that if any system of practices and beliefs can claim the title, it is that one lying behind the Chaldean Oracles.[11] According to tradition,[12] the elder Julian, father of the composer of the Oracles, invented the term and developed the practices it described; in support of tradition is the fact that the terms "theurgist" and "theurgy" are not found in literature earlier than the Oracles. But more important than the dubious validity of the tradition is the very fact of its existence. Later commentators and scholars believed that the roots of theurgy lay in the Oracles and in the other works of the Juliani; therefore, their understanding and definition of "theurgy" must have relied heavily on those sources.[13]

The primary issues to be considered are: 1) Does our evidence for Chaldean theurgy indicate an interest in contemplation as well as in ritualistic action? If so, are they mutually exclusive or mutually supportive practices? 2) Is there evidence that a proper "inner disposition," rather than ritual action alone, was requisite for successful Chaldean theurgy? 3) Who is portrayed as being in control of the theurgical process-- gods or men? Finally, 4) what distinction--if any--did Chaldean theurgy make between itself and traditional magic?

---

[11] See Lewy, Excursus IV, for a compilation and analysis of the evidence concerning the word "theurgy" and its cognates.

[12] See pp. 2-4.

[13] See Cremer's discussion of the Chaldean Oracles as the "organized" elements of theurgy, pp. 20 ff., and his general discussion of the roots of theurgy, pp. 19 ff. See also Fowden, above, n. 1, Part II.

Our first question is fairly simple to answer; the extant Oracle fragments describe both rites and actions (most of which are familiar from traditional Greek religion or the magical papyri) and spiritual and intellectual practices necessary for salvation.

In the first category belong fr. 131, "To sing the paean," "τὸν παιᾶνα ἀείδειν," fr. 132, "Keep silent, myste," "σῖγ' ἔχε, μύστα," fr. 133:

> Let the very priest among the foremost, guiding the works of fire,
> Sprinkle [them] with the coagulated waves[14] of the deep-echoing sea.
>
> Αὐτὸς δ' ἐν πρώτοις ἱερεὺς πυρὸς ἔργα κυβερνῶν
> κύματι ῥαινέσθω παγερῷ βαρυηχέος ἄλμης.

and fr. 135:[15]

> It is essential that you do not regard these [dogs] before you are initiated in your body.
> For being earthly, difficult dogs, they are shameless,
> and charming souls they constantly lead them away from the initiations.
>
> Οὐ γὰρ χρὴ κείνους σε βλέπειν πρὶν σῶμα τελεσθῇς·
> ὄντες γὰρ χθόνιοι χαλεποὶ κύνες εἰσὶν ἀναιδεῖς
> καὶ ψυχὰς θέλγοντες ἀεὶ τελετῶν ἀπάγουσιν.

What is of note in these four fragments is the use of the terms "paean," "myste" and "initiations"/"initiate" (τελεταί/τελεῖσθαι), and also the description of sprinkling participants with sea water or salt. Together they indicate that rituals similar to those found in more traditional Graeco-Roman religion were used to accomplish at least some goals in the Chaldean system. They also indicate that the Chaldean system was "closed"--that is, one had to be initiated. It is unclear whether the initiations were intended solely as means of purifying the body (as fr. 135.1

---

[14]Exactly what "κύματι ῥαινέσθω παγερῷ βαρυηχέος ἄλμης" describes is uncertain. The fact that *sea* water is used is not the difficulty--sea water was the "most prized cathartic water" (Parker, *Miasma*, p. 226) and Proclus' remarks on this fragment at *In Alc.* 4, 2-3 (Westerink) confirm that the fragment describes a purification ritual. The problem lies in "κύματι ... παγερῷ." Des Places understands this to mean "icy" or "frozen" waves (*flot glacé*). But "παγερός" can mean "congealed," rather than frozen; the related noun, "πάγος," applies to a variety of congealed or stiffened substances: scum on milk, coagulated blood, and--most interestingly--the salt obtained by letting sea water evaporate. Salt, as well as sea water, commonly was used in purification rituals (Parker, p. 227); when the priest sprinkles the participants with the "coagulated waves of the deep-roaring sea" he probably is sprinkling them with salt.

[15]Fr. 131 = Kr. 54 = Olympiodor. *In Phaed.* 244, 21 N; fr. 132 = Kr. 55 = Proc. *In Cr.* 67.20P.; fr. 133 = Kr. 55 = Proc. *In Cr.* 101.6-7; for information on fr. 135, see p. 134 n. 2, below).

implies) before a greater, less ritualized purification of the soul that was based on spiritual contemplation, or as means of purifying the soul as well.

Other rituals described in the fragments are similar or identical to those in the magical papyri. The four most important (which will be discussed at length later in this and other chapters) are: the use of *symbola* to establish a sympathetic relationship with a god or daemon;[16] the invoking of a god's epiphany; the calling of a god into a statue or medium; and the use of the iynx or "top of Hekate."

There is plenty of evidence, then, for the general importance of religious or magical ritual in Chaldean theurgy. But several fragments indicate that something more was necessary as well. Fragment 112 (Kr. 51 = Psellus. *PG* 122, 1137 b 11-12),

> Open the immortal depth of the soul. Let all eyes
> vigorously open upwards.
>
> Οἰγνύσθω ψυχῆς βάθος ἄμβροτον· ὄμματα πάντα
> ἄρδην ἐκπέτασον ἄνω.

implies an intellectual or spiritual turning "upwards," that is, a turning of the soul towards the noetic realm. Fragment 116 (Kr. 52 = Proc. *In Cr.* 88.4-5 P.; cf. Des Places, *Delebecque,* pp. 327-28) supports this idea:

> For the divine is not easily accessible to those mortals who think
>   about the body,
> but those who are naked hasten upwards.
>
> οὐ γὰρ ἐφικτὰ τὰ θεῖα βροτοῖς τοῖς σῶμα νοοῦσιν,
> ἀλλ' ὅσσοι γυμνῆτες ἄνω σπεύδουσι πρὸς ὕψος.

The message, one commonly met with in mystic and soteriological literature of the second century, is that salvation of the soul requires control over, or even denial of, the body's needs. The dichotomy between the material and noetic worlds, and its importance to salvation, further is expressed by fr. 163 (Kr. 63 = Dam. II.317.3-7):

> Do not incline towards the sombre world
> under which is spread the formless, shapeless depth,
> wrapped in the darkness of filth, delighting in images, without
>   intellect,
> precipitous, eternally twisting around its own maimed depths,

---

[16]Fragment 224 describes the consecration of Hekate's statue by means of *symbola*. Fragment 149, "When you see a lunar daemon approaching, sacrifice the stone Mnizouris, invoking..." describes the use of a special stone as a *symbolon*. Fragment 210 gives two names of a bird, "χαλκίς" and "κύμινδις," the first of which, according to *Il* XIV. 291, was the gods' name and the second of which was men's name for the same creature; Proclus, *In Cr.* 35.2, tells us the Chaldeans used the divine name rather than the human--in other words, they used the secret *symbolon*.

always marrying a form invisible, inert, without *pneuma*.

Μηδὲ κάτω νεύσῃς εἰς τὸν μελαναυγέα κόσμον,
ᾧ βυθὸς αἰὲν ἄμορφος ὑπέστρωται καὶ ἀειδής,
ἀμφικνεφὴς ῥυπόων εἰδωλοχαρὴς ἀνόητος
κρημνώδης σκολιὸς πηρὸν βάθος αἰὲν ἑλίσσων,
αἰεὶ νυμφεύων ἀφανὲς δέμας ἀργὸν ἄπνευμον.

and fr. 172 (Kr. 63 = Proc. *In T*. III.326.1-2):

Many are swept away by the crooked streams of matter.

(ὕλης,) ἧς κατασύρονται πολλοὶ σκολιοῖσι ῥεέθροις.

In short, ritualized actions such as initiations were not sufficient; to some degree, or at least at certain times, the Chaldean theurgist needed to divorce himself from bodily concerns and turn his soul and intellect towards the noetic world, as a philosopher would. Doing this required knowledge of that noetic world and its workings: hence the Oracles' exposition of the universe's structure and of the relationships between various noetic entities, as well as such admonitions as those found in frs. 112, 116, 163 and 172.

What remains to be clarified is the interaction or interdependence between the ritualistic and spiritual aspects of Chaldean theurgy. Of great interest here is Oracle fr. 2 (Kr. 51 = Dam. I.155.11-14):

> Being dressed in the full-armoured force of the resounding light,
> and equipping the soul and the intellect with the weaponry of
>   three-barbed strength,
> you must cast into your mind the complete *synthema* of the Triad and
>   wander
> amongst the fiery rays not in a scattered manner but with
>   concentration.

Ἑσσάμενον πάντευχον ἀκμὴν φωτὸς κελάδοντος,
ἀλκῇ τριγλώχινι νόον ψυχήν θ'ὁπλίσαντα,
πᾶν τριάδος σύνθημα βαλεῖν φρενὶ μηδ' ἐπιφοιτᾶν
ἐμπυρίοις σποράδην ὀχετοῖς, ἀλλὰ στιβαρηδόν.

It will be shown below (pp. 127 ff.) that the "full-armoured force of resounding light," the "weaponry of three-barbed strength" and the *synthema* that the theurgist casts into his mind (i.e., secret words that he speaks silently), all refer to ritualistic preparations similar to those regularly found in traditional magic. When the theurgist desires to "wander amongst the rays with concentration"--that is, to send his soul upwards in a unified state--he must perform ritualistic acts. Fragment 110 (Kr. 51 = Psellus. *PG* 122, 1129 c 12-14, cf. Des Places, *Delebecque,* p. 327) similarly informs us that the ascent of the soul must be accompanied by an "action" (ἔργον) and "holy word" (ἱερὸς λόγος). Even the more spiritual or intellectual type of theurgy depends not only upon psychic or mental preparations, but upon the proper physical preparations, too. Indeed, the very nature of the Chaldean Oracles supports such an outlook. It was noted in the last chapter that the system behind the Oracles combined the cosmological and spiritual precepts of Middle-Platonism with certain aspects of traditional Graeco-Roman religion. The Cosmic Soul of the *Timaeus* became identified with Hekate, patroness of ritualistic magic. The Platonic daemon, as described in the *Symposium,* became identified with the iynx-wheel, a witch's and magician's tool, as the next chapter will show. The Oracles made philosophical and spiritual concepts more immediately practical by allying them with the tenets of popular religion and magic.

So far, then, Chaldean and Iamblichean theurgy would seem to be in agreement: ritual and spiritual contemplation were not mutually exclusive but mutually supportive, parts of a complex system embracing all aspects of human existence. The second question that was posed above--"is there evidence that a proper 'inner disposition,' rather than ritual action alone, was requisite for successful Chaldean theurgy?"--now is easy to answer. Several of the fragments just mentioned in answering the first question indicate how important it was to turn one's mind upward, away from earthly matters towards the "noetic" or "spiritual" realm (e.g., frs. 116, 163, 172). Other fragments speak to this point in even more detail. For example, fr. 1.1-6 (Kr. 11 = Dam. I.154.16-26; cf. Des Places, *Delebecque,* p. 321) tells us that:

> There is a certain Intelligence, whom it is necessary for you to perceive
>   with the flower of your mind.
> For if you incline your mind to it, perceiving it as you perceive
>   something [else], you shall not perceive it. For it is
> the power of the strength that is visible everywhere, flashing with noetic
>   divisions.
> And it is necessary not to perceive the Intelligence with vehemence,
> but with the outspread fire of an outspread mind....
>
> Ἔστιν γάρ τι νοητόν, ὃ χρή σε νοεῖν νόου ἄνθει·
> ἢν γὰρ ἐπεγκλίνῃς σὸν νοῦν κἀκεῖνο νοήσῃς
> ὥς τι νοῶν, οὐ κεῖνο νοήσεις· ἔστι γὰρ ἀλκῆς
> ἀμφιφαοῦς δύναμις νοεραῖς στράπτουσα τομαῖσιν.
> Οὐ δὴ χρὴ σφοδρότητι νοεῖν τὸ νοητὸν ἐκεῖνο
> ἀλλὰ νόου ταναοῦ ταναῇ φλογί...

In other words, one must approach perception of or unification with the Paternal Intelligence with the proper spiritual or mental attitude. Reconsider, too, fr. 112 (Kr. 51 = Psellus *PG* 122, 1137 b 11-12), which says:

> Open the immortal depth of the soul. Let all eyes

vigorously open upwards.

Οἰγνύσθω ψυχῆς βάθος ἄμβροτον· ὄμματα πάντα
ἄρδην ἐκπέτασον ἄνω.

This fragment indicates, again, that a certain spiritual outlook is necessary for success in theurgical operations. The soul, or its "eyes" must be completely receptive to what it is to receive from the divine. Fragment 127 (Kr. 53 = Psell. *PG* 122, 1133 c 9) instructs the theurgist to:

> Pull the reins of the fire with a completely unadulterated soul!

πάντοθεν ἀπλάστῳ ψυχῇ πυρὸς ἡνία τεῖνον.

The soul must be in a proper state before theurgical ascension (here described as interaction with the divine fire) can be attempted.

Who controlled these processes, both ritualistic and spiritual? Did the theurgist, as traditional witches and magicians were said to, coerce the divine into cooperation? According to Iamblichus, he very definitely did not. Theurgy and its goal--the unification of man's soul with the divine--were activated by the divine alone; the soul's role was strictly preparatory.[17] Established and sent down to man by God, the tools called *symbola,* which acted to help establish a link between man and god, worked almost automatically. The properly informed and pious theurgist could set them in motion, but never could comprehend them fully and thus hardly could be said to "manipulate" in the usual sense of that word.[18] And indeed, the uninformed or impious man could find himself in a lot of trouble, as Smith says (p. 88):

> The divine power is transmitted by certain cult actions, objects and words, all of which are actually dangerous to those not morally or intellectually prepared.

God chose to endow man, his "instrument and beneficiary,"[19] with whatever small knowledge of the *symbola* and other theurgic abilities he had.

Certainly, there is evidence of this outlook in the Oracles, too. The *symbola* (which, as the next chapter will show, were identified in the Chaldean system with both the iynx-daemones and with the Platonic Ideas) are said by frs. 37, 76, 87 and 108 to have been dispersed throughout the physical cosmos by the Supreme Father or

---

[17] See Smith, pp. 85 ff., and Shaw, pp. 7ff., for discussion. Their analyses are in sharp contrast to that of Dodds, *G&I,* who understood theurgy, like magic, to be an attempt to manipulate the gods.

[18] See, for example, *De Myst.* II.11; 96,13-97,9.

[19] Shaw, p. 13. Cf. Shaw's discussion in the pages that follow of how theurgical practices were held to fulfill the corporeal measures ordained by the Platonic Demiurge, and thus, to solve the Platonic problem of embodiment.

the Paternal Intellect. Similarly, in *fragmentum dubium* 222 (Eus. *PE* V.8, 193 d = Theodoretus *Gr. aff. san.* X.22 = Niceph. Greg. *In Syn. de Ins.*, *PG* 149, 540 a) Hekate says to the theurgist:

> I have come, hearing your eloquent prayer,
> which the nature of mortals discovered in the counsels of the gods.
>
> Ἤλυθον εἰσαΐουσα τεῆς πολυφράδμονος εὐχῆς,
> ἣν θνητῶν φύσις εὗρε θεῶν ὑποθημοσύνῃσι.

Thus, the theurgist's method of summoning the gods, like the *symbola*, was bestowed upon him by the gods themselves. The cooperativeness of the gods is evident, too, in the Oracle fragments in which Hekate tells the theurgist how to accomplish such theurgical tasks as the creation of her own statue or the invocation of her epiphany (frs. 146, 147, 148; *fragmentum dubium* 224).[20]

Finally we arrive at the last question: "what distinctions did Chaldean theurgy make between itself and traditional magic?" Two of the distinctions have been touched on already: the importance of having the proper "inner disposition" and the belief that the gods willingly endowed man with his theurgic abilities. Another distinction lies in the fact that some traditional Greek religious or magical practices were prohibited by Chaldean teachings. Most notably, the Oracles speak out against certain means of prophecy. Fragment 107 (Kr. 64-5 = Psellus. *PG* 122, 1128 b 8-c 7) is a list of natural phenomena on which the theurgist should not rely for prophetic information. Astrology, bird auspices and haruspicy are called "toys, the supports of a deceptive trade," and the theurgist is urged to "flee from all of them," if he intends "to enter the holy paradise of happiness, where virtue and wisdom and good laws meet together."[21] This indicates a distrust of artificial methods of divination (methods in which the god did not speak directly to the theurgist). The methods of

---

[20] Some of the *fragmenta dubia* included in Des Places' edition of the Oracles imply that the theurgist might coerce the gods: fr. 220 ("Listen to me, for I do not want to speak when I am bound by necessity"), fr. 221 ("Why do you call me, the goddess Hekate, here by means of god-compelling necessities?"), and fr. 223 ("Easily dragging some of these unwilling [gods] from the aether..."). This apparent element of coercion may argue against the selections being genuinely Chaldean. Alternatively, however, they may be Chaldean Oracles that indicate to the theurgist the *improper* manner of invoking deities; Hekate seems to deprecate the methods used, as if responding to an inappropriate request.

[21] Fragment 217 (listed by Des Places among the *fragmenta dubia*), similarly, describes the desire of all men to "dwell on Olympus as companions of the gods" after their bodies have dispersed. Such blessedness is not possible, however, for him who has "turned his mind towards σπλάγχνα," that is, him who has relied on haruspicy. Lewy, pp. 254 ff., explains the prohibition against traditional forms of prophecy as a prohibition against putting faith in the "workings of divine Necessity," that is, the operations of the hylic world. Like all hylic phenomena, the heavenly bodies, birds and entrails can be deceptive. Reliable divination depends on the gods themselves; the theurgist seeks information directly from the gods while they possess a medium, inhabit a statue or manifest themselves during epiphany. Cf. also Tardieu, p. 223.

divination that were employed in Chaldean theurgy, on the other hand--mediumistic prophecy, the use of *telestika* and direct speech during a god's epiphany--involve a much closer, more immediate relationship with the god, and less reliance on man's fallible interpretative skills. The Chaldean system also warned against reliance on the chthonic daemones--called by the Oracles "dogs"--that traditional magic made use of (see Chp. IX); the theurgist, instead, was to be aided by the celestial, Platonic iynx-daemones that had been dispersed throughout the cosmos by the Paternal Intellect. Again, the theurgist was advised to trust in what God gave, not on his own skills alone.

We are in a better position now to define Chaldean theurgy, which, as we have seen, had several important characteristics in common with Iamblichean theurgy.[22] Chaldean theurgy shared certain methodologies with γοητεία--e.g., the use of *symbola,* the invocation of gods and daemones, the animation of telestic statues--but warned against others, such as artificial means of divination. Its primary goal--the ascent of the soul and its unification with the divine--definitely differed from the carnal and greedy goals usually associated with the γόητες (attracting a beloved, winning a race, etc.), as did Chaldean theurgy's insistence on a spiritual or mental, as well as a ritual, component. Actions alone were insufficient for theurgical success: the soul or mind had to be "turned upwards." Finally, the gods or daemones cooperated with men. At least in the context of Iamblichus and the Chaldean Oracles, "theurgy" is not to be translated as "working *upon* the gods" but rather "being worked upon *by* the gods."

The final pages of this chapter will prepare for those to come by further clarifying some of the terms that will be used often to describe the *modus operandi* of the theurgist.

Three types of theurgical operations are mentioned frequently by ancient sources: 1) " τελεστικά," concerned with the consecration and animation of magical statues of the gods;[23] 2) "mediumistic," concerned with the induction of a trance state in an individual;[24] and 3) invocation of a god's epiphany. The primary purpose of all three acts was to obtain information from a god, such as how to perform further theurgical rites leading to the unification or purification of the soul. The invoked god

---

[22]There is one important point on which they seem to differ, however. As Shaw shows (pp. 15-16), Iamblichus regarded it as impossible for a theurgist to escape Fate; indeed, he had to submit his soul to Fate and to the fulfillment of the corporeal measures that the Demiurge established. The Oracles, on the other hand, indicate that theurgists "do not fall into the fated herd" (fr. 153) and can "flee the shameless wing of Fate" (fr. 130).

[23]For a thorough survey of τελεστικά and the theories that lay behind their use, see C. Faraone, "The Protection of Place: Talismans and Theurgy in Ancient Greece," in *Magika Hiera: Ancient Greek Magic and Religion,* ed. C. Faraone and D. Obbink (Oxford forthcoming 1990); also Dodds, *G&I* pp. 291 ff. and Lewy, Excursus X.

[24]See Dodds, *G&I* pp. 295 ff.

might also describe such aspects of the Cosmos' nature as would increase the theurgist's understanding of how it worked, which in turn would facilitate psychic ascension. Any contact between theurgist and god, including mediumistic possession or epiphany (as well as the unification of the theurgist's soul with the divine), could be called "σύστασις," a term found in the magical papyri as well as sources discussing theurgy.[25]

What made σύστασις and other theurgical goals possible, according to some ancient authors, was sympathy (συμπάθεια, *sympatheia*), the natural, underlying unity of the Cosmos that connected the noetic and the sensible worlds. Sympathy made it possible for the mortal theurgist or magician to establish a link with with a god or daemon, and even (in the case of traditional magic) to force them to do his bidding.[26] The tools that enabled him to partake of sympathy were the *symbola* or *synthemata*--the emblems of noetic or divine entities that God had placed within the hylic world. A *symbolon* could be anything--a rock, a plant, a type of incense, a "magic word" or even a sound. *Symbola* could be mixed into the material from which a telestic statue was made, inscribed on that statue, worn by the theurgist, spoken by him or otherwise handled by him. It was essential to use exactly the correct *symbola* when performing the spell; in an oracle from Porphyry's *Philosophy from Oracles* that may be Chaldean,[27] Hekate tells the theurgist precisely what he must use to make and consecrate her statue--wild rue, the sort of lizards that dwell around houses, myrrh, gum and frankincense.[28] Fragments 149 and 150 (Kr. 58 = Psellus *PG* 122, 1148 b 14-15 and 1132 c 1) also mention the use of certain *symbola,* a sacred stone and secret names such as are found in the magical papyri:

---

[25] See Lewy, pp. 228-38, and S. Eitrem, "Die σύστασις und der Lichtzauber in der Magie." *Symb. Oslo.* 8 (1929) 49-53.
[26] Psellus (*PG* 122, 1153 a) says that the Oracles affirmed the doctrine of organic sympathy between terrestrial and divine things, which is the basis of all magical acts.
[27] Ap. Eus. *PE* V.12, 200 b = *fragmentum dubium* 224 Des Places = 130 Wolff.
[28] Cf. a spell from the magical papyri in which two lists of *symbola* are included (*PGM* IV.2871-76). Should the magician wish to do good, he offers storax, myrrh, sage, frankincense and a fruit pit. But should the magician wish to do harm, he uses "the magical material of a dog and a dappled goat, as well as that of a virgin, untimely dead" (it is unclear what "magic material" is). The spell and the other procedures that accompany it are the same in either case--it is the variation in symbola that cause the variation in result. On the interpretation of this spell, see further Graf, *Prayer.*

When you see the lunar[29] daemon approaching,
offer the stone called Mnizouris, while you pray.

Ἡνίκα δαίμονα δ' ἐρχόμενον πρόσγειον ἀθρήσεις,
θῦε λίθον μνίζουριν ἐπαυδῶν.

Do not alter the foreign names!

ὀνόματα βάρβαρα μήποτ' ἀλλάξῃς.

The primary goal of the theurgist was ἀναγωγή, the temporary raising of his soul to the "intellectual fire" of the noetic realm while the body was still alive; repeated practice of ἀναγωγή purified the soul for its eventual release from Fate when the theurgist's body died.[30] Other theurgical operations such as initiations, invocation of gods and animation of their statues, as well as an ascetic life and contemplation, helped to prepare him for ἀναγωγή by purifying or unifying his soul.[31] The body was not forgotten completely, however: some fragments tell us that even man's corporeal portions were benefitted by theurgy.[32]

Platonism, popular religion and traditional magic all contributed to Chaldean theurgy. In the next three chapters, Hekate's involvement with the more practical side of these will be examined. The final chapter will discuss how this more practical side of her Chaldean personality was related to her cosmological duties as Soul. It also will evaluate Hekate's role as a magician's or witch's goddess throughout antiquity and attempt to elucidate the reasons that she assumed it.

---

[29] LSJ gives the superlative of "πρόσγειος" as used by Ti. Locr. 96d and *Stoic.* 2.196 to describe the Moon and by Porph. *Antr.* 21 to describe the zodiacal sign Cancer. The comparative is used by Arist. *Mu.* 392 a 16 to describe a planet. Although the word can also be used to describe sea creatures that dwell near the shore, it seems clear that in this fragment it describes a daemon who dwells in that portion of the universe closest to the earth, i.e., the portion extending from the Moon to the Earth.

[30] See discussion in Lewy, Chapter III, "Theurgical Elevation."

[31] See especially Eitrem, pp. 49-51.

[32] Frs. 98, 128, 129, 158. Cf. Lewy, p. 216.

Chapter VII
Hekate's Top and the Iynx-Wheel

When Psellus (*PG* 122, 1133 a) set out to explain a fragment of the Chaldean Oracles that reads "Work the top of Hekate" (ἐνέργει περὶ τὸν ἑκατικὸν στρόφαλον),[1] he described a piece of magical equipment

> Hekate's top is a golden ball, formed around a sapphire, whirled around by means of a rawhide thong, with characters [engraved] all over it. Whirling it, [the theurgists] used to make invocations. And they were accustomed to call these [tops] "iynges," whether they were spherical or triangular or of some other shape. Whirling them, [the whirlers] gave forth indiscriminate sounds, or sounds like a beast, laughing and whipping the air. [The Oracle] teaches that the movement of the top, having an ineffable power, works the rite. It is called "Hekate's top" because it is consecrated to Hekate.

> Ἑκατικὸς στρόφαλος σφαιρά ἐστι χρυσῆ, μέσον σάπφειρον περικλείουσα, διὰ ταυρείου στρεφομένη ἱμάντος, δι' ὅλης αὐτῆς ἔχουσα χαρακτῆρας· ἣν δὴ στρέφοντες ἐποιοῦντο τὰς ἐπικλήσεις. Καὶ τὰ τοιαῦτα καλεῖν εἰώθασιν ἴυγγας, εἴτε σφαιρικὸν ἔχοιεν εἴτε τρίγωνον εἴτε ἄλλο τι σχῆμα. Ἃ δὴ δονοῦντες τοὺς ἀσήμους ἢ κτηνώδεις ἐξεφώνουν ἤχους γελῶντες καὶ τὸν ἀέρα μαστίζοντες. Διδάσκει οὖν τὴν τελετὴν ἐνεργεῖν τὴν κίνησιν τοῦ τοιούτου στροφάλου, ὡς δύναμιν ἀπόρρητον ἔχουσαν. Ἑκατικὸς δὲ καλεῖται ὡς τῇ Ἑκάτῃ ἀνακείμενος.

According to Psellus, Hekate's top enabled the theurgist to invoke divinities. A passage of Damascius (II.95.15 = Kr. 56) supports this and gives details: "being whirled inwardly, this tool [the iynx] calls forth the gods; outwardly, it sends them away."[2]

---

[1] Discussed by Kroll, p. 41 n. 2. Des Places does not include the entire quotation as an Oracle fragment; as fr. 206 he gives the word "top," "στρόφαλος" alone, citing Psellus *PG* 122, 1133 a 4; Marinus *Procl.* 28, p. 165 l.3 Boissonade, and Nicephorus Gregoras, *In Synesii de insomniis PG* 149, 540 b 11. Cf. Bidez, *C.M.A.G.*, VI, p. 201, 20, where Psellus implies that the theurgist verbally invoked iynges as he whirled the top of Hekate.

[2] Cf. Marinus *Proc.* 28, who says that Proclus "moved" the divine, ineffable iynges of the Chaldeans in order to "move" rain and save Attica from a terrible drought. Marinus, as Psellus and Damascius, seems to be talking about a top or wheel. On the use of iynges to invoke divinities, cf. Josephus, *BJ* II.154.2, who, describing the descent of the soul into the body, says that it enters into the body just as if it were "pulled down into the prison of the body by some iynx from nature."

As Psellus reported, the Chaldean top of Hekate also is called the iynx.[3] This iynx-top brings to mind the iynx-wheel, an object mentioned by earlier authors such as Pindar and Theocritus that was whirled or spun in magic rites.[4] The implications of the information found in earlier texts for understanding the Chaldean rite will be discussed shortly below.

But "iynges" also was the name of daemon-like entities in the Chaldean system. Although we derive almost no direct information about this order from the extant fragments,[5] the Oracles' commentators give us a clear picture of their functions and nature.

Fragment 78 (Kr. 40 and 44 n. 1 = Dam. II.201.3-4) says that "they are established as ferrymen" (διαπόρθμιοι). Damascius, although citing the Oracles as his source, makes the subject of the phrase the "magical fathers," ("μαγειῶν πατέρες") who appear no where else in Chaldean lore. According to Proclus however, this title "ferrymen" applied to the Chaldean iynges; he says that the iynges have a "name that is appropriate to ferrymen" ("διαπόρθμιον") (*In Cr.* 33.14) and that they "have the ability of ferrymen," in that they transmit all things from the noetic sphere to the material sphere and back again (*In Prm.* 1199.36-38). Another ad-

---

[3] That Damascius also considers the iynx identical with the Chaldean "top of Hekate" is implied by the fact that the entire chapter (no. 213) deals with the magic symbols of the "theurgists," a term that in Damascius always refers to the Chaldeans. For further discussion of Hekate's top and the iynx see Th. Hopfner, *Griechisch-Aegyptischer Offenbarungszauber*, Studien zur Paläographie und Papyruskunde XXI (Leipzig 1921; rpt. Amsterdam 1974) (hereafter "Hopfner, *OZ*") § 602-4.

[4] E.g. Pi. *P.* IV.212-215 and *N.* IV.35; Xen. *Mem.* III.2.18; Theocr. *Id.* II passim; Laev. ap. App. *Apol.* 30; *A.P.* 5.205; Suid. s.v. "ἴυγξ." The fact that "iynx" was used metaphorically to mean "passion" or "desire" as early as Aeschylus (*Pers.* 989) and Sophocles (fr. 474.1 Radt) implies that the iynx-charm had existed for some time previously. Grace W. Nelson, "A Greek Votive Iynx-Wheel in Boston" *Am. Journ. Arch.* XLIV (1940) 443 ff., identifies an eighth- century Attic object as an iynx-wheel; it does not correspond very well to the supposed iynx-wheels that appear later in vase paintings, however, and Nelson's identification is not altogether convincing.

[5] The only fragment containing the word "iynx" (in the dative plural) is *fragmentum dubium* 223.1 (Eus. *PE* V.8, 193 d; Nicephorus Gregoras *In Synes.* 540; not cited by Kroll). The fragment is part of an oracle, attributed to Porphyry, that Eusebius quotes during his discussion of how mortals use compulsion, not persuasion, to invoke gods: (Hekate speaks) "Easily dragging some of these unwilling [gods] from the aether by means of ineffable iynges, you lead them earthward; but others, who are mounted on the middle winds apart from the divine fire, you send to mortals just like ominous dreams, treating these daemones outrageously" (the Greek text is quoted below, p. 132). Des Places' stated reason for including this passage under *fragmenta dubia* rather than the corpus of accepted fragments is the sense in which the word "iynx" is used, which, he says, is seen nowhere in the "authentic" Oracles; the sense he refers to is that of "magic charm." Because the extant fragments never actually use the word "iynx," however, and refer to iynges only four times, there is no strong evidence against this fragment and its use of "iynx." The fact that Psellus, Marinus and Damascius, all cited above, refer to Chaldean use of iynx-charms or iynx-tops supports the idea that the Chaldeans understood the iynx as both a magical charm and a daemon. The importance of this double meaning to understanding the Chaldean iynx and Hekate's connection with it will become clearer below. See also Lewy, p. 132, who assumes the double meaning.

Several other fragments, according to the ancient authors by whom they are cited, discuss the iynges, although the name itself does not occur in them: 75, 76, 77, 78. These fragments appear to be concerned primarily with the cosmological position and functions of the iynges.

jective used by Damascius in the passage cited above, "assimilative" (ἀφομοιωτικός), also was used by Proclus in an earlier part of the *In Prm.* passage to describe the iynges (1199.33). In short, it seems certain that fr. 78 originally referred to the Chaldean iynges and that Damascius' "magical fathers" are actually the iynges.[6]

The term "ferrymen" was borrowed by the Oracles from Diotima's speech at *Smp.* 202 e 3, where it describes Plato's mediating daemones, who travel between the divine and human worlds, transmitting messages, prayers, oracles and the like back and forth (cf. also *Epin.* 984 e 4). Examination of the contexts in which Damascius' and Proclus' statements appear will confirm that the terms "ferrymen" and "assimilative" were assigned to the iynges because, like Plato's daemones, they were concerned with transmitting messages and other things from the divine to the human sphere or vice versa, and with putting the noetic Ideas into effect in the material world.[7] Proclus *In Prm.* 1199.31-35 tells us that according to the Chaldeans, the duty of these "assimilative ferrymen" is to draw towards the noetic, demiurgical monad those things existing below it, and again to draw all things from the monad down to the material world; the *In Cr.* passage examined above (33.14) goes on to say that the Chaldeans credit the iynges with upholding or sustaining all the Sources, i.e., Ideas. The iynges' role as ferrymen is reflected also by Proclus' paraphrase of an Oracle (*In Cr.* 74.26 = Kr. 40; not in Des Places):[8] "these ineffable causes [the iynges] are called "swift" by the Oracles, and hastening away from the Father hasten again back towards him." Damascius explains that his "magical fathers," who, it was shown, really are to be understood as the iynges, are called ferrymen because they lead the invisible into visibility and the visible into invisibility, causing one to mimic the other. In other words, they effect transfers between the noetic and material spheres and help to implement the creation of the hylic portion of the universe. Elsewhere in Damascius (I.286.9), the iynges are described as "regulative" of the cosmos (διακοσμήσεις); the task of ordering the cosmos naturally falls to those middle entities who bring the physical world into creation.

A more exact idea of the iynges' nature as transmitters or mediators can be obtained from frs. 76 and 77. Fragment 76 (Kr. 40 = Damascius II.59.23-25 and 88.3-5) says:[9]

---

[6] It is not altogether incorrect for Damascius to replace "iynges" with "magical fathers;" the role of the iynges in Chaldean magic, as will be shown below, was significant.

[7] That the iynges were cosmologically mediating or transmitting entities in the Chaldean system is agreed upon by modern scholars of the Oracles. See Lewy, pp. 133 ff.; Des Places, p. 14; Cremer, pp. 69-76; and Geudtner, p. 42.

[8] Kroll, p. 40, Lewy, pp. 132-3, and Geudtner, p. 44, agree that the subject of Proclus' description is to be understood as the iynges; see especially Lewy for reasons.

[9] The completion of the third line was suggested by Lewy, pp. 132-33 n. 250), in conformity with Psellus *Hypotyposis* 3 p. 73, 7 K ff. = Kr. 39 and Proclus *In T.* II.57.9 = Kr. 31.

Many of these ride upon the gleaming cosmoi, having been thrust out;
among these the most exalted are
three [the fiery, the aery and the hylic].

Πολλαὶ μὲν δὴ αἵδε ἐπεμβαίνουσι φαεινοῖς
κόσμοις ἐνθρῴσκουσαι· ἐν αἷς ἀκρότητες ἔασιν
τρεῖς· [πυρίη γ' ἠδ' αἰθερίη καὶ ὑλώδης].

In both places that Damascius quotes the fragment, he indicates that the iynges are the subject of the oracle. His topic is the multiplicity of minor beings created by or emanating from the Father. Among them, the iynges are thrust away from the Father onto the cosmoi--the planets--upon which they "ride." Fragment 77 (Kr. 40 = Psellus *PG* 122, 1149 a 10-11) gives further information:

They are thought by the Father and also think themselves,
being moved by his ineffable will so as to think.

αἵ γε νοούμεναι [ἐκ] πατρόθεν νοέουσι καὶ αὐταί,
βουλαῖς ἀφθέγκτοις κινούμεναι ὥστε νοῆσαι.

The subject is again the iynges, according to Psellus (see also the arguments of Lewy, p. 132, whom Des Places follows). The similarity of the iynges' status and functions to those of the Ideas is readily apparent;[10] they are noetic entities conceived by the Father and sent forth into the cosmoi in order to transmit information or creative power to the material world (unlike the Ideas, however, the iynges apparently also are able to transmit information back from the material to the noetic sphere).

According to the commentators and Oracle fragments, then, Chaldean iynges are transmitters, assimilative links between the divine and human worlds. Interestingly, their activities often are described in terms of whirling or rushing movement.[11] This language reminds us that in Chaldean teachings, according to Psellus and Damascius, a "iynx" also is a magical device turned rapidly by the theurgist in order to invoke a god or daemon. As noted before, this use of the word recalls mentions by earlier authors of the more familiar iynx-wheel; it will be useful at this point to review what is known about the pre-Chaldean iynx.

The term "iynx" can refer to a bird, usually identified with a real Mediterranean bird called the wryneck;[12] to a wheel to which that bird has been bound; or to the wheel alone, without the bird. Most scholars equate the iynx-wheel

---

[10]This has been noted already by others; see discussion below, pp. 103 ff.
[11]Frs. 76, 77 and 87 (with notes at Lewy, pp. 133-4 and Cremer, pp. 73-4); Proc. *In Cr.* 74.26.
[12]On the iynx-bird, see Arist. *HA* 504 a 10 and *PA* 695 a 22. Ath. *Deipn.* 7.312 ff., quoting the first century B.C. naturalist Dorio, adds the information that the iynx's color was the same as that of the sea eel (μῦρος). Gow (see n. 15 below) includes a modern drawing of the wryneck in his article.

with a device frequently illustrated in vase paintings that resembles a child's toy still in use today.[13] A string or thong was passed first through one and then through the other of two holes pierced in the middle of a four-spoked disk.[14] Finally, the string was tied together so as to form a loop. By alternately increasing and relaxing the tension of the two sides of the loop, the operator caused the disk to spin. Sometimes vase paintings show the disk with serrated edges; the modern toy, too, often has serrations.

There exists confusion among the authors of late antiquity (which remains among modern scholars) as to how a iynx differs from a ῥόμβος (sometimes called by modern scholars a bull-roarer), and whether the Latin term *"turbo"* refers to one, the other, both or neither. In fact, by post-classical times the terms may have been interchangeable.[15] What is really important, and what caused the confusion between iynx-wheels, rhomboi and turbines in the first place, is that all are whirled or turned during magical operations; the very success of the magical operation seems to have

---

[13]Photographs of vase paintings showing iynx-wheels are included in Gow (below, n. 15) and Nelson (above, n. 4); M. Detienne, *The Gardens of Adonis: Spices in Greek Mythology*, trans. Janet Lloyd (1972; trans. Sussex 1977), reproduces Gow's photographs, pp. 72-98. Gow's article also includes a photograph of the author using a iynx-wheel of his own making. My son was given, several months ago, a "iynx-wheel" sold as a toy in the mountains of North Carolina.

[14]Although vase paintings most frequently show the iynx as a disk, Psellus' statement (given at the beginning of this chapter) that an iynx could be "spherical or triangular or of some other shape" should not be forgotten, as iynx-like objects of other shapes occasionally appear on vases. Susan Rotroff has brought to my attention an Athenian drinking cup of the first half of the third century B.C. on which appears a myrtle garland punctuated by small hollow squares. Each square is divided by four spokes; several have dots on their periphery resembling those that represent serrations on many round iynges shown in vase paintings. On the cup in question, the square iynges may be little more than decorations, as they are not shown in use, but the same can be said of many of the round iynges found on vase paintings. (The cup will be published in Rotroff's forthcoming work on Hellenistic pottery; its inventory number is P 7761 and it was taken from deposit E 3:1.)

[15]The definitive article on iynx-wheels, rhomboi, turbines and their distinction remains A.S.F. Gow, "Ἴυγξ, Ῥόμβος, Rhombos, Turbo," *JHS* 54 (1934) 1-13, although several scholars, rightly, have argued against his attempt to discriminate strictly between these various types of magical spinning objects. I would note that Gow's arguments to distinguish the iynx-wheel and the rhombos are weakened by the fact that, although we have vase paintings representing what he describes as a iynx-wheel, we have none of what he defines as the rhombos or "bull-roarer;" his recreation of this object (fig. 7) is based on knowledge of "bull-roarers" in other societies. See the article by Grace W. Nelson, above, n. 4, which argues against Gow's strict distinctions and rightly suggests that "rhombos" became a generic term including several types of objects that were whirled around, and the brief excursus at the end of Eitrem (above, Chp. VI, n. 1), which argues that the use of terms "iynx" and "rhombus" were fluid. See also E. Tavenner, "Iynx and Rhombos," *TAPA* LXIV (1933) 109-127 (not cited by Gow), which suggests that "rhombos" and "iynx" described a type of top; this argument, however, depends on his assertion, with which I do not agree, that the four-spoked, so-called iynx-wheels held by Eros in vase paintings are simply toys, having no erotic or magical significance. Tavenner, Gow and Nelson, being concerned primarily with the iynx in classical times, do not discuss the significance of the iynges in the Chaldean system and its relationship to the earlier "iynx."

depended on their motion.[16] Modern experiments, including some reported by Gow, have shown that the whirling of iynx-wheels--particularly those with serrations--produces a high-pitched, whistling sound; its sound was at least as important as its motion, as will be shown shortly below. Indeed, the very name of the tool signifies this: the word "iynx" is derived from the verb "ἰύζω," "shout, yell, cry out." Other cognates include "ἰυγμός"--a shout of joy or pain" and "ἰυκτής"--"a singer or piper".[17]

What the magician or theurgist imagined he was accomplishing by whirling the whistling iynx usually is stated. Especially in archaic, classical and Hellenistic sources, love was the goal--witness Theocritus' Simaetha and Pindar's Medea, who falls in love with Jason because he whirls a iynx. Later on, iynges were used for a wider variety of magical purposes, including rainmaking (Marinus, *Procl.* 28), and the invocation of divinities.[18]

To understand fully the use of the iynx in theurgy and late magic, however, we have to determine not only the goal of the operation but also the means by which the rotation and resultant sound were imagined to work. Archaic, classical and Hellenistic mentions of iynx-wheels do not offer much help, but some later passages from approximately the time of the Oracles' composition do; in any case, it is the understanding of these sources that are nearly contemporaneous with the Oracles that is of particular interest here.[19]

---

[16] Passages specifically describing iynges as being whirled or mounted on a wheel (implying that they are to be turned) include Pi. *P.* 4.214; *AP* 5.205; Marinus *Procl.* 28; Suid. s.v. "Ἴυγξ." Passages specifically describing rhomboi as being whirled or similarly reflecting the idea that rhomboi were turned include E. *Hel.* 1361; *AP* 6.165; Prop. 3.6.26, 2.28.35; Ov. *Am.* I.8.7; *PGM* IV.2296; *Etym. Magn.* 706.29; Schol. A. R. I.1139.

[17] The myths invented to explain the origin of the iynx-bird also reflect the importance of the iynx's ability to make a sound. According to the scholiast on Theocr. *Id.* II (= Call. fr. 685 P.), Callimachus said that Iynx was originally a nymph, who enchanted Zeus. Hera, as usual, changed her rival into something unattractive--in this case the iynx-bird, which seducers often used thereafter as a magic tool. The name of this nymph's mother was Echo. The lexicographer Photius (s.v. "Ἴυγξ") tells the same myth with a few variations; most importantly, he says that some called Iynx's mother Πειθώ (see below on the relationship between πειθώ and the magical tool called the iynx). Another myth explaining the origin of the iynx-bird is found in Antoninus Liberalis (*Meta.* IX), who attributes the myth to the 2nd-century B.C. poet Nicander. He says that, after a singing contest with the Muses, each of the Emathides was turned into a different bird, one of which was the iynx. The meaning of these myths is clear. In the first, iynx literally is born from sound--either from Persuasion, the personification of compellingly attractive sound, or Echo, whose sound has the reflective, almost magical effect of giving back to the speaker what he gave forth. In the second myth, the iynx is equated with a nymph whose singing rivals that of the Muses.

[18] Cf. Lewy, p. 235, who argues that the invocation of a daemon or iynx preceded virtually all theurgical operations; such a creature's aid was necessary for the accomplishment of any task.

[19] Much modern scholarship on this question has followed Tavenner (above, n. 15) p. 117, who notes "I am inclined to think that the bird [iynx] by writhing its head and the rhombus by its spinning set in motion exactly the same kind of magic force....The rhombus by its mere spinning could draw lovers...the bird...rotates its head as though pulling something towards itself." I cannot see a resemblance between the actions of spinning or turning and "dragging" or "drawing" (ἕλκω),

At Philostratus *VA* 1.25, Damis describes the palace of the Babylonian king. It includes a great judgment hall, the roof of which forms a dome intended to resemble the heavens. The roof tiles are gemstones of celestial blue. Attached to this roof are figures of the Babylonian gods, mounted as if they are shining forth from the aether. Inside, suspended from the ceiling of the judgment hall, are four golden iynges, which, Philostratus says, are intended to remind the king of *Adrasteia*-- "Necessity" or "Inescapable Fate"--and also to remind him not to exalt himself above men. The Magi, Philostratus continues, say that they themselves "attune" or "adjust" (ἁρμόττεσθαι) these iynges and call them the "tongues of the gods."

The Babylonian judgment hall replicates the universe; the vaulted, shining blue roof represents the heavens, home of the gods whose figures are displayed there. The stated purpose of the iynges' presence inside the hall is to remind the king of his place within that universe. The iynges also remind him of man's separation from and subordination to the gods by reminding him of *Adrasteia;* in later antiquity, this goddess--scarcely more than a personification--commonly represented the prerogative of the omnipotent gods to reward or punish men.[20] These golden iynges, then, suspended between the gods on the roof and the king on his throne, reminded the king of the basically bilateral division of the universe into human and divine portions and the corresponding division between man and god.[21]

The iynges were not merely symbolic ornaments, however. They also had a magical function, from which, indeed, the symbolic function probably arose. Their magical potential is indicated by Philostratus' statement that their maintenance was the responsibility of the Magi--well known in Graeco-Roman antiquity as magicians *par excellence*. The verb that Philostratus uses to describe this maintenance, "ἁρμόττεσθαι," was translated above as "harmonize" or "attune;" it indicates that the Magi carefully brought the iynges into the correct relationship with something

---

which is how the effect of the iynx on the enchanted is described with notable frequency (e.g., Pi. *P.* 4.218, *N.* 4.35; Xen. *Mem.* III.2.17; Theocr. *Id.* II *passim*; Luc. *De Domo* 13; *AP* 5.205; Plut. *Non Posse* 1093 d 2). Tavenner points to the fact that Simaetha in Theocritus *Id.* II 30, 31 prays that Delphis may be "whirled" to her (δινεῖθ', δινοῖτο), but Charles Segal, "Simaetha and the Iynx," *QUCC* 15 (1973) 32-43, convincingly argues (p. 36) that these words do not reflect any expectation of the way in which the beloved actually will approach the lover; they are metaphorical.

Of interest in the discussion of metaphorical descriptions of the iynx's power over the enchanted is the portrait of Medea's bewitched heart at A.R. III. 759-60: "[Her heart] shook, being driven hither and thither by a swift 'whirling' ('ὠκείῃ στροφάλιγγι'); just so was the heart of the maiden 'whirled' ('ἐλελίζετο') within her breast." Was Apollonius thinking of the iynx's motion and extending it to the heart of its victim?

[20]See the discussion of *Adrasteia* in R.L. Rike, *Apex Omnium: Religion in the Res Gestae of Ammianus* (Berkeley 1987) 11-17.

[21]Eitrem (above, Chp. VI, n. 1) in his discussion of the rhombus and the iynx-wheel, suggests that these Babylonian iynges are somehow apotropaic, although he adds that they have "une nuance qui nous échappe." I cannot find anything in the passage from Philostratus or in other discussions of iynges that supports an apotropaic role of this type.

else. Considering the rest of the passage, it seems likely that what they were brought into harmony with were the immortal and mortal elements of the universe, embodied on the one hand by the figures of the gods, poised above the iynges, and on the other hand by the Babylonian king, who sitting in judgment below represented his subjects as a whole. The possibility of the Magi bringing the iynges into simultaneous harmony with both immortal and mortal makes the iynges a potential link or connective element between the divine and human worlds, as well as a symbol of their separation.[22] Given the right knowledge, in other words, the Magi would be able to use the iynges to bridge the gulf between god and man. Philostratus' statement that the Magi called the iynges "tongues of the gods" supports this--the name suggests that they were transmitters of divine knowledge or oracles to men. Generally, the whole picture brings to mind the mediating duties of the Chaldean iynges and Platonic daemones.

Philostratus does not tell us whether these golden iynges were birds, daemones or wheels. It is probable that they are the last; it is difficult to imagine how the Magi could "attune" or "harmonize" figures of bird or daemones, whereas they could adjust the size of a iynx-wheel or its serrations, which in turn would alter the pitch of the noise it made when whirled.

Such adjustments could be important. Chapter VI mentioned that *sympatheia* (that is, the establishment of a bond between the practioner of magic and the powers he sought to manipulate) was crucial in theurgy and magic. There is evidence that the motion and tone of a carefully adjusted iynx-wheel created--or at least strengthened--such sympathy, placing the whirler in an advantageous, harmonious relationship to those powers. The fourth-century Neoplatonist Synesius, for example, indicates that the *"magoi"*--which is what he calls the Chaldean theurgists--believed that iynx-wheels created sympathy.[23] Marinus says that "by moving a iynx in the correct manner, Proclus moved rain and freed Attica from a dreadful drought" (*Procl.* 28). This statement, as Lewy notes, pp. 250-1, implies that the iynx's movement automatically or sympathetically elicited a corresponding movement in the heavens.

The sympathetic importance of the *sound* made by the whirling iynx-wheel fits in with the general importance of sounds in magical or theurgical acts. To take but two examples: magicians believed that the correct pronunciation of each of the seven Greek vowels affected one of the seven astral spheres and therefore aided in invoking and controlling the spheres' divinities; the twenty-four letters of the Greek

---

[22]As Rike points out (above, n. 20), pp. 12-13, the goddess Adrasteia's own role as a punisher or rewarder of men's deeds was understood to make her a mediator between the two worlds. In Ammianus she clearly is portrayed as being subordinate to a supreme *numen* yet superior to the *fata* and *elementa* that she is able to administer by virtue of her own somewhat physical or substantial character.

[23]*De insomn.* 132 c. See also discussion of this passage at Geudtner, p. 43 n. 180.

alphabet, similarly, each had its twin in the twenty-four elements of the cosmos.[24] Augustine remarks that the sympathetic tools of the theurgist included *"sonis certis quibusdam ac vocibus"*--"certain established sounds and voices" (*De Civ. Dei* X.11). Sounds helped the theurgist or magician to establish a sympathetic link with the divine in the same way that *symbola* such as herbs, stones, seashells and animals could.

Other mentions of iynges and iynx-wheels support this idea. For example, both Lucian and Philostratus compare the iynx to the Siren. Lucian, at *De Domo* 13, tells how the stunning beauty of a hall enables even the shy man entering it to rise to rhetorical heights. He sums up by saying:

> I, for my part, am persuaded of all this and was persuaded of it even as I entered the hall to speak, being attracted by its beauty just as if by a iynx or Siren.
>
> Ἐγὼ μὲν δὴ τούτοις πείθομαι καὶ ἤδη πέπεισμαι καὶ ἐς τὸν οἶκον ἐπὶ λόγοις παρελήλυθα ὥσπερ ὑπὸ ἴυγγος ἢ Σειρῆνος τῷ κάλλει ἑλκόμενος.

Philostratus mentions iynges again at *VA* 6.11, where Apollonius describes one of the temples of Apollo at Delphi: "it is said that golden iynges were hung up, having some of the persuasiveness (πειθώ) of the Sirens."[25] Here again, it is not certain what these iynges were--figures of birds, figures of daemones or iynx-wheels. The comparison of their abilities to those of the Sirens, who often are represented with avian bodies, at first glance encourages the assumption that they were figures of birds. But it is more likely that Philostratus' comparison arose from the fact that iynx-wheels--with or without the attached or engraved bird--like Sirens, produce a supernatural sound that has the uncanny effect of drawing the object of enchantment

---

[24] The invocation of deities by pronunciation of the seven vowels is akin to the use of "secret words" (*symbola, synthemata*), with which, as I shall discuss below, the iynges were connected or even identified. On the importance to magic of sounds in general and of letters of the alphabet more specifically see Patricia Cox Miller, "In Praise of Nonsense," in *Classical Mediterranean Spirituality*, ed. A.H. Armstrong, vol. 15 of *World Spirituality: An Encyclopedic History of the Religious Quest* (New York 1986) pp. 481-505. Note also that Psellus says the Chaldeans led forth their gods by means of θελκτηρίοις ᾠδαῖς and bind and release them (Script. Min. I.446.25 K-D).

[25] The passage is connected by A.B. Cook, *Zeus*, vol.I (1914; rpt. New York 1964) 258 ff., with Paus. IX.5.12, which describes the bronze temple of Apollo at Delphi. Pausanias mentions a quotation from Pindar about this temple (*Pa.* XI.8-9: "golden were the enchantresses (κηληδόνες) singing over the pediment"). Pausanias does not believe the enchantresses ever stood there and suggests that Pindar created them in imitation of Homer's Sirens. On the basis of the passages from Pausanias and Philostratus, Cook suggests that a solar wheel with iynx-birds or some other solar birds hung apotropaically from temple pediments at Delphi. He connects this practice with Apollo's solar associations (which surely, it seems, were not well established so early as Pindar). *Pa.* 11.8-9 also is alluded to by Athenaeus (290 e), who compares the Pindaric golden enchantresses to the Sirens, who make men wither with starvation by causing them to forget food, and by Galen, *In Hippocr. de Articulis* 3.23.

towards the enchanter. The persuasive ability of the Sirens traditionally depended on their voices, not their avian bodies (which indeed probably first were bestowed upon them in recognition of their voices).[26]

Philostratus described the sound emitted by the Sirens and iynges as having the power of "persuasion" ("πειθώ"). Lucian's passage makes a similar point. The speaker says he was persuaded of the hall's ability to inspire rhetoric just as if he were drawn by a iynx or Siren. A look at the way in which πειθώ is used in magical or theurgical contexts suggests that in the passage from Philostratus it describes the power of sound to establish a magical bond between attracter and attracted.

For example, "πειθώ" is used in this sense several times in the Oracles themselves. Fragment 14 (Kr. 15 = Psellus *PG* 122, 1141 d 6) says:

> The Father does not thrust in fear, but rather pours in Persuasion.
>
> Πατὴρ οὐ φόβον ἐνθρῴσκει, Πειθὼ δ' ἐπιχεύει.

Psellus primarily is interested in showing how this statement applies to the Christian god. He does remark, however, that the Chaldeans meant by this that God "enchants" or "attracts" (ἐφέλκω) the worshipper through persuasion and joy. Fragment 81 (Kr. 42 = Proc. *In Prm.* 941.27-8):

> But all yields to the noetic lightnings of the noetic fire,
> Enslaved by the persuasive will of the Father.
>
> Τοῖς δὲ πυρὸς νοεροῦ νοεροῖς πρηστῆρσιν ἅπαντα
> εἴκαθε δουλεύοντα πατρὸς πειθηνίδι βουλῇ.

similarly indicates that the attraction of the worshipper to the divine is caused by persuasion. In fr. 219 (not in Kroll; Eus. *PE* V.8, 193 c; Nice. Greg. *In Syn. de ins. PG* 149, 604 a-b)), Hekate says:

> After the dawn, limitless, filled with stars,
> I leave the undefiled, immense home of God and
>   come to
> the nourishing earth, at your orders and
> by the persuasion of your ineffable prayers,
> with which a mortal enjoys charming the spirits of
>   the immortals.
>
> Ἥριον μετὰ φέγγος ἀπείριτον ἀστεροπληθὲς
> ἄχραντον πολὺ δῶμα θεοῦ λίπον, ἠδ' ἐπιβαίνω

---

[26]The outstanding characteristic of the Pindaric κηληδόνες (above, n. 25), with whom Pausanias and Athenaeus connect the Sirens and with whom Cook identifies the iynges in Philostratus, also was an ability to produce a supernatural sound (the name itself is related to "κηλέω," "to charm by incantation or voice").

γαίης ζωοτρόφοιο τεῆς ὑποθημοσύνῃσι
πειθοῖ τ' ἀρρήτων ἐπέων, οἷς δὴ φρένα τέρπειν
ἀθανάτων ἕαδε θνητὸς βροτός.

This fragment gives the closest parallel to the "persuasive iynges" discussed above. The persuasive ability of ineffable prayers is used by a magician to draw Hekate down, to attract her and to bind her temporarily to himself.[27] Earlier passages in which in which πειθώ is used similarly include Aeschylus, *Pr.* 173-74, where Prometheus states his determination not to bend to Zeus' will:

not with the honey-tongued spells of Persuasion shall he charm me...

καί μ' οὔτι μελιγλώσσοις πειθοῦς
ἐπαοιδαῖσιν θέλξει...

Prometheus describes Persuasion as having an enchanting effect--note the words "ἐπαοιδαῖσιν" and "θέλξει." Another early example, from Pindar, *P.* 4.219, is especially interesting because persuasion, enchantment and iynges are combined: Pindar, describing the effect of Jason's iynx-wheel on Medea, says her heart was "agitated by the whip of Πειθώ."[28] As in the other examples just given above, the word "πειθώ" means "an ability to attract, to bind magically."

Philostratus *VA* 6.11 can be understood more fully now. The "persuasive iynges" that hung in Apollo's temple had the Sirenic power magically to bind or attract one thing to another through their sound. Given that these iynges hung inside a temple, it seems probable that what they bound together were men and gods, as did the iynges mentioned in the earlier passage from Philostratus. A passage from an oracle quoted by Eusebius--included in Des Places' edition of the Oracles as *fragmentum dubium* 223--supports this idea.[29] Lines 1 and 2 of the fragment, which Hekate speaks to the theurgist, read:

Easily drawing these unwilling [divinities] from the aether by means
of secret iynges, you lead them earthward...

Τοὺς μὲν ἀπορρήτοις ἐρύων ἴυγξιν ἀπ' αἴθρης
ῥηϊδίως ἀέκοντας ἐπὶ χθόνα τήνδε κατῆγες...

---

[27] As will be discussed below, "secret words" or *symbola,* in fact, are identical with the iynges in the Chaldean system.

[28] The image "agitated by the whip" alludes to the iynx-wheel itself, mentioned in the immediately preceding lines of the ode, for according to Psellus and other ancient sources, the iynx-wheel was caused to whirl with a thong or whip--μάστιξ. Pindar is using the whirling of the iynx-wheel metaphorically to describe its effect on its victim's heart.

[29] Eus. *PE* V.8.6, 193 d; also found in Niceph. Greg. *In Syn. de ins., PG* 149, 540 a.

By the use of iynges, the theurgist or magician could invoke and temporarily bind a god.

An important element in consideration of this aspect of the iynx's magic is the great interest among Middle and Neoplatonists in the Pythagorean and Platonic concept of the music or harmonious movement of the spheres.[30] Lewy suggested briefly, p. 250, that the spinning motion of the iynx-top was imagined to affect *per analogiam* the revolution of the heavenly spheres, and thus to attract the celestial iynges who "leap into" them (fr. 76; fr. 87 with Lewy's notes). I would suggest in addition that, as the iynx-wheel was able to be "attuned" or "harmonized" (that is, the pitch of the sound could be altered by changing the size of the wheel or its serrations), individual iynx-wheels were intended to affect--and thus control--individual celestial spheres by imitating not only the spheres' motion but also the specific tones that they contributed to the music of the spheres.[31] Such sympathetic control of the celestial spheres, in theurgy and other forms of magic, was crucial to the completion of many tasks.

It is significant that the Sirens, who, as was noted, sometimes were compared to iynges because they shared with them an ability to attract or form a bond between invoker and invoked through sound, were credited by the Pythagoreans[32] and Plato with producing the music of the spheres. The passage from Plato (*Rep.* 617 b) describes the Sirens as riding upon eight cosmic spheres, which rotated at different speeds around an axis called the Spindle of Necessity. The cumulative singing of these Sirens produced cosmic harmony. This connection between Sirens and cosmic

---

[30] A good general discussion of this theory in Pythagoreanism can be found in W. Burkert, *Lore and Science in Ancient Pythagoreanism* (Cambridge 1972) Ch. IV, sect. 4.

[31] Nelson (above, n. 4), p. 449, in fact, suggests that the iynges in *VA* 1.25, examined above, represent the spheres and their attunement represents the music of the spheres; she arrives at this conclusion by a road somewhat different from that I have used, however, presuming that Philostratus really describes Babylonian sun, moon and star disks. Even if she is correct, Philostratus' attachment to them of the name "iynges" itself signifies his understanding of iynges as cosmically intermediate powers; sun, moon and stars in late times commonly were understood to exist between heaven and earth. It should be remembered that at least from the time of the *Timaeus,* this music or harmony of the spheres was connected closely with the creation and function of the Cosmic Soul, who later became identified with Hekate.

It may be significant that some of the terms used for rotating magic tools also were used in astronomy; "στροφάλιγξ" can mean "planetary orbit" in late writings, and *"rota"* (used in Latin poetry in connection with the rhombus) can mean the circular course of the moon (Val. Fl. 5.414) or year (Sen. *HF* 182). Des Places, in his edition of Iamblichus' *De Myst.*, p. 18, notes that the verb "ῥοιζέω," "whirl or spin with a whistling noise," often is used to describe the harmony of the spheres; this verb also is used to describe the activity of the iynges/Ideas (see below, pp. 104 ff.). On the significance of whirring noises in the Oracles in general, see below, pp. 108 ff.

[32] The Pythagorean acusmata include the question "What is the Oracle of Delphi?" and the answer "The Tetractys; that is, the harmony under which the Sirens sing" (Iamb. *VP* 85). Considering the significance of the Tetractys in cosmic proportion, harmony and structure in late mystic writings, this acusma gives the Sirens and their songs a very important cosmological role. Burkert (above, n. 30) p. 187, understands the statement to mean that the Sirens produced the music of the spheres.

harmony was taken up eagerly by later Platonists, especially those who, like the authors of the Chaldean Oracles, considered the ideas found in Plato's *Republic* and *Timaeus* to express absolute cosmological truths.[33] If the hypothesis that a iynx-wheel's tone strengthened sympatheia by mimicking the tone emitted by a cosmic sphere is correct, then it is likely that this idea was influenced by the *Republic'*s portrayal of the Sirens riding on cosmic spheres and helping to produce their music.

During this general examination of iynges and iynx-wheels, the specific question of their functions in Chaldean teachings has been left aside temporarily. It has been suggested that iynx-wheels and the closely related rhomboi or turbines were understood to aid in magic because their spinning and the resultant noises imitated cosmic movements and music--specifically those of the spheres. This created or strengthened the sympathetic bond upon which the theurgist relied. Early in the discussion, it was noted that the mediating and transitional activities of the Chaldean "ferrymen" iynges (as opposed to iynx-wheels as objects) also often were described in terms of rushing movement; this language surely reflects the importance of the iynx-wheel's movements in magically bridging the gap between human and divine worlds. The whirling tool that the Chaldean theurgist used in his practical operations to exploit cosmic sympathy was awarded an appropriate place in his cosmological structure; the mediating iynx-daemon personified the iynx-wheel.[34] As happened so often in the Chaldean system, traditional magic and Platonic philosophy were wed.[35]

---

[33] See, for example, Plut. *QC* IV-VI (744 f-746 b).

[34] There is perhaps some evidence that the Chaldeans also incorporated the traditional avian aspects of the iynx into their hybrid portrait. John Mansfield has brought to my attention a passage in Damascius' *Vita Isidori*. (fr. 200, p. 173.15 Zintzen), which he translates in his forthcoming edition as:

> At any rate, though Proklus used to raise difficulties concerning Isidoros' imitations of the cries of birds and of discordances, sometimes in their Chaldaian pursuits he himself used to demonstrate for him the method of the imitation of the flight both of other birds and of these little house sparrows, the noise that they made with their wings when they are rousing themselves to take flight.

> διαπορουμένῳ γοῦν τῷ Πρόκλῳ περὶ τῶν Ἰσιδώρου μιμήσεων τῶν ὀρνέων [καὶ] τῶν φωνῶν [καὶ] τῶν ἀπηχημάτων ἐνίοτε ἐν τοῖς Χαλδαϊκοῖς ἐπιτηδεύμασιν αὐτὸς ὑπεδείκνυε τὴν ὁδὸν τῆς μιμήσεως ἄλλων τε καὶ στρουθῶν τῶν μικρῶν τούτων καὶ κατοικιδίων τῆς πτήσεως, οἷα ψοφοῦσι ταῖς πτέρυξιν ἐγειρόμενοι πρὸς τὸ πετᾶσθαι.

Mansfield suggests that "ἐν τοῖς Χαλδαϊκοῖς ἐπιτηδεύμασιν" should be understood to mean that Isidorus and his students studied certain Chaldean Oracles that referred to house sparrows. The passage seems to indicate a Chaldean interest in the sounds and motions of sparrows and other various types of birds that went beyond simply *studying* them, however; the competitive interest shown by Isidorus and Proclus in precisely *imitating* the birds' motions and sounds implies their practical--i.e., theurgical--interest in such matters. Perhaps the manipulation of the iynx as a *symbolon* was accomplished not only by the whirling of the iynx-wheel or invocation of the iynx-daemon but also by the imitation of the iynx-bird's cries and motions. This would agree with Psel-

It remains to examine further the way in which the Chaldean iynx-daemones and their assimilative or transmissive duties are described and to establish Hekate's relationship to them more precisely. This, in turn, will reveal Hekate's role in the Chaldean system in more depth.

The iynges generally are identified by modern scholars with two other groups of entities important to Chaldean cosmology and theurgy: 1) the Paternal Ideas, dispersed throughout the cosmos by the Paternal Intellect,[36] and 2) the spoken *symbola* or *synthemata* (the "secret words" of magical rites).[37]

The basis for the first identification largely rests on fr. 77, already mentioned above briefly:

> They are thought by the Father and also think themselves,
> being moved by his ineffable will so as to think.
>
> αἵ γε νοούμεναι [ἐκ] πατρόθεν νοέουσι καὶ αὐταί,
> βουλαῖς ἀφθέγκτοις κινούμεναι ὥστε νοῆσαι.

Lewy notes in support, p. 136, that the "lightnings," identified with the Ideas, and the iynges both are described as "leaping" (ἐνθρῴσκω) into the world or Hekate's womb (lightning--fr. 34.3, iynges--fr.76.2). Further support is found in the fact that the descriptions of the iynges offered by commentators, discussed at the beginning of this section, show a close connection between the iynges and the Ideas. For example, Proclus (*In. Prm.* 1199.33 ff.) makes it the iynges' duty to "draw" things down from the Monad to the material world. At *In Cr.* 33.15 he makes iynges sustain the Sources or Ideas, which seems a metaphorical way of equating the two; the personalized entity upholds the philosophical concept. Damascius' ferrymen lead the "invisible" into the "visible" (II.201.3-6), in other words, bring the noetic to

---

lus' statement (see the first paragraph of this chapter) that the theurgists made sounds like beasts when using the iynx.

[35]Cremer, pp. 69-76, has studied in detail the question of what sort of creatures iynges were. He suggests, too, that the iynges are the Chaldean version of the daemones portrayed in Plato's *Symposium*, whose primary role was to bridge the gap between divine and human worlds, carrying prayers to gods and oracles to men, for example; they were mediators, transmitters.

Cremer goes on to argue convincingly that Iamblichus then "translated" the Chaldean iynges into his "good daemones," and that we can obtain information about the Chaldean iynges from study of Iamblichus' "good daemones." The bad daemones of the Chaldean system, too, were connected with *symbola* or *synthemata*, but false ones (fr. 90). The question of Hekate's relationship to bad daemones will be discussed in Chapter IX "The Chaldean Daemon-dogs."

[36]Lewy, pp. 132-7; Cremer, p. 74 and n. 305; Geudtner, pp. 43-5; Des Places, p. 14.

[37]Lewy, pp. 132-4, 249, 438; Cremer, pp. 75-77; Geudtner, pp. 44-7. The Ideas and the *symbola* also were equated (e.g., Psellus *PG* 122, 1149 a); the *symbola* were regarded as manifestations, available to the earthbound man, of the Ideas that existed only in the noetic realm (cf. Lewy, p. 438; Cremer, pp. 44-45).

materialization.³⁸ All three duties are shared by the Ideas in Middle-Platonism and Neoplatonism.³⁹

Another fragment describes the journey of the Ideas from the Noetic to the Sensible World in terms that echo the iynges' activities. Fragment 37 (Kr. 23 = Proc. *In Prm.* 800.20-801.5; given in its entirety on p. 57 n. 28, above) discusses the descent of the Ideas from the Paternal Intellect into the Cosmic Womb (Hekate's womb) and thence into the Sensible World. Lines 1-2 say:

> The Paternal Intellect, thinking with a vigorous will,
> sends the multi-formed Ideas whirring through the air...

> Νοῦς πατρὸς ἐρροίζησε νοήσας ἀκμάδι βουλῇ
> παμμόρφους ἰδέας, πηγῆς δὲ μιᾶς ἄπο πᾶσαι...

and ll. 8-9, also describing the Ideas emergence from the Paternal Intellect, say:

> ...From one source
> whir forth other, divided, mighty [Ideas]...

> ...ὧν μία πηγή,
> ἐξ ἧς ῥοιζοῦνται μεμερισμέναι ἄλλαι ἄπλατοι...

"'Ροιζέω" is used in each case--once transitively and once intransitively. Either way, this verb refers to a whirring, whistling, noise-producing motion; such a motion, as was noted above, is the iynges' *modus operandi.* ⁴⁰

The second identification--that of the iynges with *symbola* or *synthemata*--first was suggested by Lewy, pp. 132-4. He emphasized the fact that iynges often are described as "ineffable" or "unspoken," ("ἀφθέγκτος") as are *symbola* or *synthemata,* the secrecy of which, like that of other elements of magical ritual, naturally would be guarded.⁴¹ "The iynges are, essentially, magical names sent forth by the Supreme Father into the spheres," says Lewy. The Father has sown these

---

³⁸These magical tools also become organizing elements within the cosmos. Lewy comments, p. 439, "...the spiritual organism which guarantees the order of the universe becomes the medium of magical action..." The regulative iynges can aid in magic, especially sympathetic magic, because they understand and uphold the proportions and relationships within the cosmos that magic manipulates.

³⁹It should be remembered that these commentators allow the iynges, like the daemones of the *Symposium* from whom they are descended, to effect transferrals in the opposite direction, too, leading the visible into the invisible and the material into the noetic sphere. Communication from the human to the divine sphere is reflected in the identification of the iynges with the *symbola,* which were used by men attempting to invoke the gods.

⁴⁰The next chapter will argue that the other use of the verb "ῥοιζέω" in the Oracle fragments (fr. 146.4) is used to refer to an iynx itself. See p. 122.

⁴¹E.g., fr. 223; Psellus *Hypotasis* 3 (73, 7 ff.); *PG* 1133 a 14; Marinus *Procl.* 28; Procl. *In Cr.* 67.19 and 74.26 (= Kr. 40; not in Des Places); Michael Italicus Letter XVII, 181.26 ff.

names throughout the cosmos in order to aid theurgists who succeed in discovering them (fr. 108 = Kr. 50 = Procl. *In Cr.* 21.1-2):

> For the Paternal Intellect has sown the *symbola* throughout the cosmos,
> The Paternal Intellect who thinks the Ideas; and [the *symbola*] are called "ineffable beauties."
>
> Σύμβολα γὰρ πατρικὸς νόος ἔσπειρεν κατὰ κόσμον,
> ὅς τὰ νοητὰ νοεῖ· καὶ κάλλη ἄφραστα καλεῖται.

By pronouncing them, the theurgist communicates with the divine. The *symbola* or *synthemata*, like the iynges, mediate and transmit, partaking of cosmic sympathy. As numerous fragments attest, they are important to the completion of various magical acts, including invocation of gods and the ascension of the soul.[42]

One of clearest proofs for the identity of the *symbola* and the iynges comes from *fragmentum dubium* 223.1-2, the text of which was given above, p. 100. *Symbola* were used in magical rites intended to command the presence of a god or daemon; in fr. 223, Hekate complains that men use ineffable iynges to draw daemones from the sky. Further proof is found in fr. 87 (Kr. 43 = Proc. *In Cr.* 20.29-30, cf. 33.15-17 and *In Alc.* 68, 13 Westerink):

> The holy name leaps with eternal circular motion
> Into the cosmoi at the mighty order of the Father.
>
> ἀλλ' ὄνομα σεμνὸν καὶ ἀκοιμήτῳ στροφάλιγγι
> κόσμοις ἐνθρῴσκον κραιπνὴν διὰ πατρὸς ἐνιπήν.

The phrase "eternal circular motion" (ἀκοίμητος στροφάλιγξ) inevitably brings to mind the traditional behavior of iynges and iynx-wheels; in fact, the word for "circular motion," "στροφάλιγξ," is almost identical with that used for the top of Hekate, "στρόφαλος," and can itself refer to a spinning object as well as a movement. The passage at *In Cr.* 20.29-30 discusses the assimilative energy of the demiurgical order, one duty of which is to assign proper names or symbols to all in the cosmos; "holy name" is synonymous with these specially significant symbols. The passage at *In Alc.* 68,13 indicates that "holy name" in this case refers specifically to that of the ferrymen, i.e., the iynges.[43] The fragment and Proclus' comments on it together indicate that iynges were concerned especially with the *symbola* or names--

---

[42]Fragments 2, 109 and 110 discuss the role of *symbola/synthemata* in the ascension of the soul; fr. 219 indicates such words were used in invoking gods. Fragment 90, "For indeed, from the womb of the earth spring forth earthly dogs, who reveal to mortals a sign (σῆμα) that is never true," indicates that some signs (i.e., *symbola*) were provided by bad, earthly daemones--the negative counterpart of the iynges. The theurgist must beware of such deceptions.

[43]See further Lewy, p. 134 n. 256.

probably were identical to them. The functions of the iynges and those of the *symbola/synthemata* are virtually identical; both are sent by the Paternal Intellect into the hylic world in order to aid the theurgist in various magical acts, particularly those leading to the ascension of the soul.

The iynges themselves, as daemones or tops, provide ways to cross the boundary between man and god; they become associated and ultimately identified with the Ideas and *symbola* because these entities, too, bridge the gap, delivering, in one case, noetic information from god to man and, in the other, theurgical requests from man to god. The identifications of the iynges with the Ideas and with the *symbola* expresses diverse aspects of a single concept. They were theurgical tools, of practical use in magic, and cosmological entities, necessary to the operation of the universe. In either case, the iynx-daemones' function emerges as being connective and transmissive--no surprise in view of what already has been concluded about them above. They participate in the enforming of the physical world, and they aid in the establishment of a sympathetic link between theurgist and god, therefore aiding in ascension of the soul and transmission of divine information to men.

Before leaving discussion of the iynges' identification with or similarity to the Ideas and *symbola,* fr. 49 (Kr. 27 n.1 = Proc. *In T.* III.14.3-10) should be considered:[44]

> [Aion is] the Father-born Light. For he alone, having
> Plucked the abundant flower of Intellect from the Paternal Strength,
>   is able to know the Paternal Intellect
> And to bring [Intellect] to all the Sources and Principles
> And to whirl them and keep them eternally in endless circular motion.
>
> πατρογενὲς φάος· πολὺ γὰρ μόνος ἐκ πατρὸς ἀλκῆς
> δρεψάμενος νόου ἄνθος ἔχει τὸ νοεῖν πατρικὸν νοῦν
> [καὶ νόον] ἐνδιδόναι πάσαις πηγαῖς τε καὶ ἀρχαῖς
> καὶ δινεῖν αἰεί τε μένειν ἀόκνῳ στροφάλιγγι.

The words used in l. 4, "whirl" (δινέω) and "circular motion" (στροφάλιγξ), as was noted above in discussion of fr. 87 where they describe the *symbola*, echo many descriptions of the iynges' motions. It was suggested already that the iynges were equated with the Sources, which in turn represented the Ideas; the second group of entities described here in terms recalling the iynges, the Principals, also can be

---

[44]That Aion is the subject of this fragment is agreed upon by Lewy, pp. 99-100 and notes, and Des Places, notes to fr. 49, who cites previous work on the question (Proclus makes the subject "the order of aions"). Damascius II.29.15 ff. quotes part of the fragment, making the subject Aion.

The object of l. 3, for which I have used "Intellect," following Des Places and Kroll, must be supplied; Lewy suggested "Light," p. 100 n. 138. "Intellect" seems more consistent with the rest of the fragment: Aion plucks the flower of Intellect and is able to know the Paternal Intellect. Furthermore, if "Sources" and "Principles" are to be understood as the Ideas, as they often are, then it is logical for Aion to endow them with Intellect.

identified with the Ideas.⁴⁵ The language of l. 4, therefore, supports the equation of the iynges and the Ideas, and the fragment confirms the hypothesis that the cosmological role of the ferrymen-iynges was understood by the Chaldeans as virtually identical to that of the Ideas and the *symbola*.⁴⁶

At the beginning of this chapter, Psellus' description of Hekate's top, which he identified with the iynx, was considered. Psellus reports that the top is called "Hekate's" because it is consecrated (ἀνάκειμαι) to her." Ultimately, she is responsible for the success or failure of the theurgist's attempted invocation, she controls the iynges who carry it out and therefore, in a sense, she is their mistress. If, as has been shown previously in this chapter, the iynges are theurgically important elements in the establishment or strengthening of *sympatheia* between man and god, and are cosmologically the link between the sensible and noetic worlds, then Hekate's reign over them indicates her control over these functions.⁴⁷

Such a relationship between Hekate and the iynges is supported by other evidence that indicates connections, both theurgical and cosmological, between Hekate and the iynges. The iynges are the mediating or transmissive daemones of the Chaldean system. Chapter III discussed Hekate's control of and close connection to daemones of several types throughout late antiquity, suggesting that the connection in part was due to their common status as intermediary and transmissive entities. In view of this, it was logical for the Chaldean Hekate/Soul to reign over the intermediary, transmissive Chaldean iynx-daemones, as well. More specific conclusions reached in Part I about Chaldean cosmology also support the idea of Hekate/Soul's cosmological superiority over and control of the iynges. Chapter IV showed that Hekate/Soul receives into her womb the Thoughts or Ideas of the Paternal Intellect,

---

⁴⁵See Lewy, pp. 114-5 and Cremer, p. 73 for discussion; cf. Damascius II.200.23.

⁴⁶Although the subject of Aion's role in the Chaldean and related systems is too complex to examine thoroughly here, I would note Lewy's observation, p. 403 and n. 12, that the Cosmic Soul and Aion are very similar in function. In fact, as Lewy comments, Hermetic doctrine sometimes identifies the two. Lewy suggests that the Chaldeans imported Aion from Iranian religion, forcing him into their otherwise Platonic scheme and allowing him to keep roles and attributes already possessed by the Platonic Cosmic Soul (e.g., he exists just above the globe of the Cosmos). In view of the relationship between Aion and the Soul, it is interesting that Aion here controls the iynges; as will be shown shortly below, the Chaldean system regularly assigns this task to Hekate.

⁴⁷Geudtner, pp. 34-43, esp. pp. 39-43, suggests that the iynges are under the control not of Hekate but of Eros, who is also a mediating entity in the Chaldean system, having derived this role from the *Symposium*. Geudtner argues that iynges are individual ἔρωτες; in support of this he points out that iynx-charms originally were used primarily for love. Eros certainly is a mediating deity in the Chaldean system, and as such might be involved with the iynges' operations to some degree. Geudtner's argument concerning the reason for the relationship between Eros and the iynges is unconvincing, however. First, by the time of the Oracles' composition, iynx-charms no longer were used exclusively for love (indeed, iynges appear in none of the love spells found in *PGM*). Second, the love that iynx-charms were imagined to secure, judging from the citations, was very much of a corporeal, passionate nature (see Segal, above, n. 19, who strongly connects the iynx with "sensuality and debauchery" and Detienne, above, n. 13); the Platonic/Chaldean Eros is not concerned with such love.

which are represented as "lightnings." She then proceeds to transmit these Ideas to the Demiurge, who embodies them in the Sensible World. If, as shown above, the iynges are to be equated with the Ideas or Thoughts of the Father, then they, too, are transmitted by Hekate/Soul. She receives them from the Paternal Intellect and then disperses them.

A broad analysis of the Chaldean system and Hekate's place within it, then, logically indicates her control of the iynx-daemones. Supportive evidence can be found in the Oracles' commentators. Damascius (II.59.9 ff.) discusses the number of iynges and similar entities and their places within the cosmos. The sphere of the visible and divided, he says, stems from the sources of Hekate; the innumerable iynges are representatives of this sphere.[48] His remarks reflect the idea that Hekate/Soul represented the limit between the divided and the undivided; all things emerging from her, such as sublunar iynges or daemones, are increasingly hylic.

Fragment 37, discussed above on p. 57 n. 28 and p. 104, describes the Ideas as "whirring forth," "ῥοιζέω," from the Paternal Intellect into the womb of Hekate; it was argued that the use of "ῥοιζέω," which indicates a rapid, noise-producing motion, strengthens the conviction that the Ideas and the iynges are one and the same. Damascius twice uses cognates of "ῥοιζέω" to describe Hekate's duties. At II.154.18 (Kr. 29), discussing Hekate's position between the Father and the demiurge, he says, "The Great Hekate sends forth a lifegiving whir" ("ἥ τε μεγάλη Ἑκάτη...ζωογόνον ῥοίζημα προίησι"); this "whirring" that she receives and then transmits would seem to be the iynges/Ideas. At II.156.15-16, Damascius says that "the life-giving goddess [i.e., Hekate] possesses and reveals the divided 'whirring forth' of the life-giving light that wanders over all things" ("[ἡ ζωογόνος]...διακεκριμένην ἔχει καὶ ἐκφανῆ...τὴν ἐπὶ πάντα φοιτῶσαν ἐκροίζησιν τοῦ ζωογόνου φωτός."). That is, Hekate controls the dispersal of the divided Ideas/iynges that descend, whirring and whistling, over the entire physical Cosmos.[49]

It was shown that the iynges represent the "secret words" (*symbola*) or names by which the theurgist can manipulate cosmic sympathy. Proclus indicates that the Chaldean system situated the *symbola* or the iynges within the Cosmic Soul,

---

[48] It is here that Damascius introduces fr. 76.

[49] One more fragment bears on the subject of Hekate's role as the disperser of whirring Ideas/iynges. Fragment 56 (Kr. 30 = Proc. *In Cr.* 81, 6-8) reads: "Rhea truly is the font of stream of the blessed noetic [substances], for she is first of all in power and receiving into her marvelous womb she pours forth a whirling (τροχάουσαν) generation upon All" (the Greek for this fragment is quoted above, p. 66). The previous chapter (pp. 66-68) discussed the Chaldean equation of Rhea and Hekate. Here, she is presented as the transmitter of "spinning generation." "Generation" refers generally to Hekate's role as the lifegiving and ensouling goddess. But here, more specifically, "generation" also refers to the Ideas themselves, which are generative in the sense that they enform and thus create the physical world.

alias Hekate. His comments on *Rep.* 616 c ff., which describes the Spindle of Necessity and the spheres revolving around it (*In R.* II.212.20 ff.), portray the visible world as a statue (ἄγαλμα) representing divine eternity; the Demiurge is a telestic priest who breathes into this statue life, intelligence and certain movements that serve as oracles to men who understand. The entire analogy echoes the actions undertaken by Chaldean theurgists and other magicians in attempting to animate telestic statues. Proclus goes on to say that the Demiurge enveloped his statue (i.e., the visible cosmos) in the "χαρακτήρ" (or visual symbol) of the Soul and its revolutions (περιφοραί). Within the Soul's revolutions he placed names (ὀνόματα). He surrounded the Soul with phylacteries and in the middle of her womb inserted noetic entities that Proclus calls the *symbola* of the iynges. Proclus suggests that those who find the name "iynges" a little strange may think of them instead as divine causes.

According to this passage, the Soul is permeated and surrounded by *symbola*, χαρακτῆρες, secret names and iynges. The metaphor that Proclus chose to represent this condition, as well as what we otherwise know about the use of names, *symbola* and phylacteries in magic and theurgy, suggest that Proclus is describing not only a cosmological relationship but a theurgical one; the theurgist derived practical knowledge and tools--including iynges--from the Cosmic Soul, alias Hekate.

At *In T.* II.255.24 ff., Proclus briefly mentions this relationship between *symbola* and the Soul once more. One of the most ineffable mysteries of Platonic theory, he says, is the Demiurge's transmission of the names, which are to be understood in the context of this discussion as secret words or iynges, knowledge of which aids the theurgist in establishing sympathy. The Demiurge, in his capacity as "namemaker," placed the names or iynges within the revolutions of the Soul. The Soul, again, is the repository of secret knowledge; she is presented as being able to send this knowledge forth to men, in the form of iynges or otherwise.

Before leaving discussion of these two passages from Proclus, it should be noted that they describe the Soul's *revolutions,* in particular, as being filled with iynges or with the secret names, words and characters identified with iynges in the Chaldean system. *Timaeus* 36 b ff., from which so many Chaldean and Neoplatonic beliefs about the Soul were derived, indicates that these revolutions are the spheres of the planets. This brings discussion back to the earlier observation that iynges, or their close relatives the Sirens, were understood to represent or produce the music of the spheres. The picture we derive is one of the Soul surrounded by harmoniously revolving circuits. In or on these circuits ride the iynges; from these circuits they can be called down by men. The music enwrapping the Soul--essential to the coherence and harmony of the universe and thus to cosmic sympathy--comprises separate "notes" played by the iynges.

What does analysis of Hekate's top and the iynges reveal about Chaldean theurgy and Hekate/Soul's importance to it? Like many other entities and practices that can be glimpsed behind the fragments of the Oracles, the iynx-daemon was born from the characteristically Chaldean combination of reverence for Plato's exposition of the universal order and reliance on magic. The daemones of the *Symposium* still travelled in and out of man's world, but now, as iynges, their passage could be set in motion by knowledgeable men whirling the proper tool, the iynx-top, and thus making the proper sounds. Philosophical theory was given mystical justification and practical application; sympathetic magic was validated by Platonic cosmology.

The Chaldean system placed the iynges under the control of Hekate/Soul, who is herself a combination of philosophical concept and traditional goddess. Cosmologically, the iynx-daemones spring forth from her or her revolutions; the Soul, herself a mediator, is the source of these ferrymen who mediate between noetic and sensible worlds. Theurgically, the iynx-wheel, whose whirling and sounds both symbolize and strengthen the cosmic sympathy upon which the theurgist relies, depends on Hekate; it works by her grace. These relationships are logical, considering the cosmological position and duties of the Cosmic Soul and Hekate in late antiquity. Establishment or utilization of cosmic sympathy depends on replicating appropriate elements of the larger divine world within the smaller human one. Such replication involves crossing the cosmic boundary represented by Soul in two ways: 1) the Ideas/*symbola* or iynges first must be sent by the Paternal Intellect from the noetic sphere into man's world via Soul, who disperses them; 2) once received, the *symbola* must be manipulated correctly to erect a bridge joining the theurgist to the divine. As mistress of the iynges, Hekate can help men utilize cosmic sympathy and thus take their first steps towards the theurgical ascension of the soul. The next chapter will examine the procedure by which she shared such theurgical information and tools with men.

Chapter VIII
The Epiphany of Hekate

Three fragments (146, 147, 148) describe what the theurgist will experience after speaking certain magical words or phrases:[1]

> Having spoken these things, you will behold a fire leaping skittishly
> like a child over the aery waves;
> or a fire without form, from which a voice emerges;
> or a rich light, whirring around the field in a spiral.
> But [it is also possible] that you will see a horse flashing more
>   brightly than light,
> or a child mounted on the swift back of a horse,
> a fiery child or a child covered with gold, or yet again a naked child;
> or even a child shooting arrows, standing upon a horse's back.

> ...ταῦτ' ἐπιφωνήσας ἢ παιδὶ κατόψῃ
> πῦρ ἴκελον σκιρτηδὸν ἐπ' ἠέρος οἶδμα τιταῖνον·
> ἢ καὶ πῦρ ἀτύπωτον, ὅθεν φωνὴν προθέουσαν·
> ἢ φῶς πλούσιον ἀμφὶ γύην ῥοιζαῖον ἑλιχθέν·
> ἀλλὰ καὶ ἵππον ἰδεῖν φωτὸς πλέον ἀστράπτοντα
> ἢ καὶ παῖδα θοοῖς νώτοις ἐποχούμενον ἵππου,
> ἔμπυρον ἢ χρυσῷ πεπυκασμένον ἢ πάλι γυμνόν,
> ἢ καὶ τοξεύοντα καὶ ἑστηῶτ' ἐπὶ νώτοις.

> If you say this to me many times, you will observe all things
>   growing dark,[2]
> For the curved bulk of the heavens disappears
> and the stars do not shine; the light of the Moon is hidden
> and the Earth does not stand steady. All things are revealed in
>   lightning.

> Πολλάκις ἢν λέξῃς μοι, ἀθρήσεις πάντ' ἀχλύοντα.
> Οὔτε γὰρ οὐράνιος κυρτὸς τότε φαίνεται ὄγκος,
> ἀστέρες οὐ λάμπουσι, τὸ μήνης φῶς κεκάλυπται,
> χθὼν οὐχ ἕστηκεν· βλέπεται δέ [τε] πάντα κεραυνοῖς.

> But when you see the sacred fire without form,
> Shining skittishly throughout the depths of the Cosmos,
> Listen to the voice of the fire.

> Ἡνίκα [δὲ] βλέψῃς μορφῆς ἄτερ εὐίερον πῦρ

---

[1] Fragment 146 = Kr. 57 = Proc. *In R*. I.111.3-11; fr. 147 = Kr. 57 = Psellus *PG* 122, 1133 b 5-8; fr. 148 = Kr. 58 = Psellus *PG* 122, 1136 b 11-c 1.
[2] Accepting the reading of Lobeck. See pp. 112 ff., below.

λαμπόμενον σκιρτηδὸν ὅλου κατὰ βένθεα κόσμου,
κλῦθι πυρὸς φωνήν.

It is Hekate who speaks these lines, describing her epiphany and the phenomena that accompany it.[3] Examination of these fragments will help to clarify Hekate's nature and duties in the Chaldean system by revealing the manner in which she appeared to the theurgist and the purposes for which she did so.

Before considering the fragments or their lines individually, however, a textual problem in l. 1 of fr. 147 must be resolved. The second half of the line has been translated here as, "you will observe all things growing dark," following the textual emendation of Lobeck (*Aglaophamus*, I 104, n. rr), with which Kroll, p. 57, and Lewy, p. 242, agree.[4] The fragment as transmitted by Psellus, however, reads "you will observe all things [to be] a lion," "πάντα λέοντα," or, as Des Places translates in his editions of the Oracles, "*en forme de lion.*" Psellus himself had difficulty explaining the text, apparently, for his commentary is somewhat forced.[5] He attempts to tie the lion to the zodiac sign Leo, which, he says, is the source of a lion-like assembly of stars called "λεοντοῦχος" by the Chaldeans. In the Chaldean rites, he continues, if one calls on the name of this source, he will see nothing other than a phantasm of a lion in the sky, hiding all the rest of the heavenly bodies.

To begin with, however Psellus attempts to explain it or Des Places attempts to translate it, the Oracle's first line does not make sense. What does "you will observe all things [to be] a lion" mean? Secondly, even if Psellus' manipulation of the words were to be accepted, and the fragment translated, with Des Places, "all things in the form of a lion," it must be admitted that nothing in the extant Oracle fragments or their other commentators indicates that the Chaldeans conceptualized the zodiac signs and their effect on men in the way Psellus describes (indeed, fr. 107, examined above, pp. 86-87, implies a Chaldean aversion to traditional astrology in

---

[3] That Hekate speaks these lines is assumed by Lewy, pp. 240-6, Des Places (notes to the fragments), and Cremer, pp. 99-100, although most of Lewy's reasons for this supposition (which largely are followed by Cremer and Des Places) are misguided, as will be shown below. The best reasons for presuming that these Oracles are spoken by Hekate (not mentioned by Lewy or Des Places) are 1) Michael Italicus (Letter XVII 182.26), discussing the symbols of Chaldean Hekate's statue, applies to Hekate an uncommon adjective used in Psellus' exegesis of fr. 147 (see n. 6, below) 2) Iamblichus, repeating fr. 147 almost verbatim, claims it describes the epiphanies of gods; the only gods that communicated with men, according to Chaldean doctrine, were Hekate and, occasionally, Apollo, and 3) Iamblichus describes the epiphany of the "Soul of the Whole" (i.e., the Cosmic Soul) as a "formless, speaking fire," a characterization that agrees with the descriptions of epiphanies in frs. 146 and 148 (see further below pp. 113 ff).

[4] Lewy, however, seems to accept Psellus' version at p. 94 n. 114, where he discusses evidence for a connection between Hekate and lions.

[5] Des Places, p. 171 n. 4, points out that Psellus' clumsiness in discussing the "lion" indicates he had read no other, more explicable text. This, however, indicates only that the text included the word "lion" when Psellus received it, not that the original form of the Oracle included the word.

THE EPIPHANY OF HEKATE

general). Nor does the word "λεοντοῦχος" appear elsewhere in Chaldean lore.[6] In fact, there is no mention of lions in any form in the extant fragments.[7]

There is, on the other hand, good support for accepting Lobeck's emendation. First, the overall darkening of the cosmos in l. 1 accords with the disappearance of the sky's vault and the extinguishment of the stars and Moon described in ll. 2 and 3--it sums up the two subsequent lines. More generally, all these phenomena fit in with the final one described in l. 4, the shaking of the earth; all are effects of the deity's epiphany on the natural world, not apparitions or phantasms such as a lion would be, or such as the children and horses of fr. 146 are. *Comparanda* from the magical papyri and traditional literature, to be examined below (pp. 115-18), keep the two types of phenomena separate; anthropomorphic or theriomorphic visions do not occur at the same time as the cosmic or natural disturbances.[8]

Second, Iamblichus' remarks on epiphanies, many of which are derived from Chaldean doctrine,[9] include no remarks on lions. Most importantly, a passage that is considered to paraphrase fr. 147,[10] *De Myst.* II.4; 75,11 ff., makes no mention of lions: [11]

> The magnitude of the epiphanies that accompany the gods is manifested in such a way that, as [the gods] descend, the whole sky, the sun and the moon are hidden, and the earth no longer is able to stand steady.

---

[6] The exception to this is Michael Italicus, Letter XVII 182.26 (dated to the thirteenth century). Discussing the various attributes of Chaldean Hekate and her statue, he states shortly that she is called λεοντοῦχος. However, Italicus depends almost completely on Psellus for his information about Chaldean matters and undoubtedly derived his comment on λεοντοῦχος from Psellus' exposition of fr. 147. Italicus' connection of the Chaldean Hekate with λεοντοῦχος, an uncommon word, does, however, support the contention that fr. 147 discusses the epiphany of Hekate.

[7] Despite Lewy's statement, p. 94, little evidence can be brought forth proving that the lion was a special symbol for or an attribute of Hekate herself, either, although, like other deities originating in Asia Minor, she occasionally is portrayed as flanked by lions or standing on one (such is the conclusion of Kraus, who discusses the question in detail at pp. 30 ff.). Porph. *Abst.* III.18 calls her "bull, dog, lioness;" but, as Kraus states, p. 33 n. 133, further evidence for Hekate as a lion is not available.

[8] The last part this fragment, which does not describe cosmic phenomena as the earlier parts do, is discussed on p. 119, below; it looks ahead to fr. 146.

[9] The close relationship between Chaldean doctrines and Iamblichus' *De Myst.* has been examined by Cremer. The reliance of Iamblichus' descriptions of divine epiphanies on those of the Chaldeans is discussed in Ch. IV, "Die göttliche Epiphanie (*de myst.* II 3-9)," esp. pp. 45-7.

[10] T. Gale, in his edition of Iamblichus (Oxford 1678) p. 209, was the first to suggest Chaldean influence on the Iamblichean passage. See also Cremer, p. 47; Lewy, p. 242-3 n. 57. Des Places, in his edition of Iamblichus, p. 88-9 n. 2, alludes to the similarity between the two passages, but does not offer an opinion on whether the Oracle influenced Iamblichus.

[11] The passage continues: "When the archangels appear, certain portions of the cosmos are stirred up and a divided light, running ahead, comes forth; they themselves manifest a proportional magnitude of light that accords with the magnitude of their supremacy." This may refer to the varied forms of light ("lightnings") mentioned at the end of fr. 147 and described in fr. 146, which accompany or precede the unformed fire that represents Hekate herself.

Πρὸς δὲ τούτοις τὸ μέγεθος τῶν ἐπιφανειῶν παρὰ μὲν τοῖς θεοῖς τοσοῦτον ἐπιδείκνυται ὡς καὶ τὸν οὐρανὸν ὅλον ἐνίοτε ἀποκρύπτειν καὶ τὸν ἥλιον καὶ τὴν σελήνην, τήν τε γῆν μηκέτι δύνασθαι ἑστάναι αὐτῶν κατιόντων.

According to Iamblichus, godly epiphanies cause the entire sky, sun and moon to be hidden, and prevent the earth from standing steady. Admittedly, Iamblichus' prose omits specific reference to the first line of the Oracles, "If you say this to me many times, you will observe all things growing dark;" Iamblichus' more general statement, that epiphanies cause the whole sky to hide, seems to refer to both l. 1 and l. 2 of fr. 147. Also, Iamblichus or his source describes the disappearance of the *Sun* and Moon, rather than of the *stars* and Moon as the Oracle does in l. 3. These differences between Iamblichus and the Oracle fragment are relatively minor, however; both passages describe the darkening of the sky, the disappearance of celestial features and earthquakes. Given this generally close reliance of Iamblichus on the Oracle fragment, it seems unlikely that so impressive a manifestation as a lion could have been ignored by him if it were included in the Oracle verse as he knew it. And the version that Iamblichus knew, writing only one century after the commonly accepted date of the Oracles' composition, is more likely to reflect the original Chaldean verse than is a version seen by Psellus, who followed Iamblichus by eight centuries. Clearly, Lobeck's emendation makes sense.

To analyze the individual fragments, the relationship between them--and thus the relationship between the phenomena they describe--must be established. Lewy's suggestion, pp. 243-4, that the fragments are excerpts of a single Oracle rightly has been accepted by subsequent scholars. But is Lewy's schematic arrangement of them, which Des Places follows in his numbering, correct? Do the phenomena of fr. 146 precede those of frs. 147 and 148?

The following sequence of events emerges from Lewy's suggested arrangement: first, various fiery apparitions enter the earthly sphere to reveal themselves to the theurgist; second, meteorological or cosmic disturbances occur, darkening the heavens and shaking the earth; and third, a formless fire begins to speak. Lewy argues that fr. 146 describes the phenomena manifested after the theurgist has spoken certain words only once, and that the phrase "if you say this to me many times" in l.1 of fr. 147 refers to a subsequent chanting of these same words, which secondarily produces the cosmic phenomena--darkened skies and earthquakes. Finally, Lewy suggests that the formless, speaking fire in fr. 148 is

Hekate, who manifests herself after the preliminary phenomena described in frs. 146 and 147.[12]

These fragments should be read in the order 147, 146, 148, instead. To begin with, the progression of the phenomena described makes more sense when the fragments are arranged in this way. First (fr. 147), everything grows supernaturally dark, as the "curved bulk" of the sky, its stars and its moon are blotted out. Against this darkness, fiery apparitions, including a formless fire, dramatically appear (fr. 146). Lastly, (fr. 148), the theurgist is told what to do after the various apparitions have arrived; he will see a wide variety of them, but must listen to the voice of only one--the formless fire whose appearance was described in fr. 146.

Moreover, the verbs in the first lines of frs. 146 and 147 make more sense this way. By using the aorist subjunctive and future indicative as she does in fr. 147, Hekate describes an action that the theurgist has yet to undertake: "*if you say* (λέξης) this to me many times, you *will observe* (ἀθρήσεις) all things growing dark," she says. In fr. 146, Hekate uses an aorist participle and a future indicative, which normally would be translated as: "*having spoken* (ἐπιφωνήσας) these things, you *will see* (κατόψῃ) a fire leaping like a child...etc."[13]

In other words, the two sentences describe the same action at different points in time. Fragment 147 describes what the theurgist will see as he speaks a certain formula several times--as he speaks it, all things grow dark, the curved bulk of the heavens disappears, the stars quit shining, the Moon is hidden and the Earth refuses to stand still. Fragment 146 describes what the theurgist will see after he has spoken the formula several times and the cosmic disturbances have begun--the various fiery apparitions will begin to appear.

Comparanda also support this arrangement of the fragments, under which the cosmic or meteorological phenomena of fr. 147 precede or accompany, rather than follow, the individual, fiery phenomena of frs. 146 and 148, which (as will be shown below) represent angels, daemones and a god.

---

[12] Fragment 148, which orders the theurgist to listen the voice of a formless fire, necessarily would seem to follow fr. 146, which describes the initial appearance of an identical fire. Lewy, however, apparently does not understand the two fires to be one and the same; although he nowhere states an opinion on the matter either way, his interpretation of the apparitions in fr. 146 (see below pp. 120 ff.) implies that he makes no connection between them. By inserting fr. 147 between fr. 146 and 148, which as will be shown below describe a different type of manifestation than those described in fr. 147, he separates further than is necessary the initial description of the formless fire from the lines instructing the theurgist to listen to it.

[13] The "πολλάκις," "many times," of fr. 147 does not indicate that the words alluded to in l. 1 of fr. 146 were repeated later, after the manifestation of the fiery apparitions described in ll. 2-8 of fr. 146, as Lewy suggests, but rather refers to an initial, ritualistic repetition of magical fomulae, such as is found regularly in magical texts. The plural "these things" (ταῦτα) in l. 1 of fr. 146, which refers to words already spoken when fr. 146 commences, describes the same ritual repetition of words referred to in l. 1 of fr. 147 as a group.

Manifestations of gods and goddesses in traditional Greek and Latin literature regularly are preceded immediately or accompanied simultaneously by such cosmological or meteorological disruptions. One of the earliest examples is *Il.* XIII.18: the mountains and forests tremble under Poseidon's stride. The *Homeric Hymn to Artemis* (no. XXVII) describes what happens when the goddess wanders the mountains, hunting: the peaks tremble (ll. 6-7), the whole earth and the sea shake (ll. 8-9). At Euripides *Ba.* 1084 ff., the revelation of Dionysus' divinity is accompanied by a flash of lightning and an abnormal stillness in the forest. Apollonius Rhodius describes two divine epiphanies: at II.679, Apollo's arrival on the island of Thynias brings with it earthquakes and an abnormally high tide; at III.1218, Hekate's advent is accompanied by an earthquake. Hekate's epiphany similarly is said to be immediately preceded by "bellowings of the ground" at *Aeneid* VI.256. Lucian (*Philops.* 22) describes the arrival of Hekate as preceded by earthquakes and thunder.

The magical papyri also offer examples in which cosmic or meteorological phenomena precede or accompany--not follow--divine epiphanies. *PGM* XIII.734-1077, a lengthy spell telling the magician how to invoke a god, includes one. Lines 871 ff. say that if the magician completely pronounces the name of the god (that is, invokes him correctly),

> there will an earthquake, the sun will stop and the moon will be afraid and the rocks and the mountains and the sea and the rivers and every liquid will be petrified; the whole cosmos will be thrown into confusion (Morton Smith's translation in Betz's edition of the magical papyri).

PGM IV.475-829 (the "Mithras Liturgy") describes two series of phenomena that precede separate epiphanies of Helios and Mithras. In the earlier part of the text, after the magician has uttered a formula, the sun's disk expands (l. 576), stars leap forth from the disk and fill the air (l. 580). He recites further formulae, and thunder and earthquakes rumble (l. 624). Then occurs the epiphany of the god (ll. 635-637). In the latter portion of the text, after the magician recites certain formulae, lightning bolts fall, lights flash and the earth quakes (l. 695) as the god descends (l. 697). In both cases, the cosmic phenomena precede or accompany, rather than follow, the appearance of the god or gods.[14]

---

[14]Portions of *PGM* IV.475-829 have been cited already by Kroll, p. 57, and Lewy, p. 243 n. 58, as a source of general comparison for Oracle fr. 147, but were not analyzed closely by either. This spell makes an especially good *comparandum* for the Oracles because it is not a spell for accomplishing mundane things--attracting a lover, curing an illness--but rather, like Chaldean theurgy, seeks the ascension of the soul and unification with the divine. It also includes names of deities familiar from the Oracles, such as Aion and Psyche, and practices associated with Chaldean theurgy, such as "drawing in breath from the rays" (l. 539). Moreover, the divine repeatedly is described as fiery and full of light (ll. 591 ff.), which accords with Chaldean doctrines concerning the nature of noetic entities. The purpose for which the latter of the two manifested gods is said to descend further makes this text an excellent *comparandum* for the Oracles; ll. 724-731 states that the god responds to the

THE EPIPHANY OF HEKATE 117

A final example of the motif can be found in Iamblichus *De Myst.* II.4; 75,11 ff., which, as was already mentioned above, is understood by most scholars to allude to fr. 147:

> The magnitude of the epiphanies that accompany the gods is manifested in such a way that, as [the gods] descend, the whole sky, the sun and the moon are hidden, and the earth no longer is able to stand steady.
>
> Πρὸς δὲ τούτοις τὸ μέγεθος τῶν ἐπιφανειῶν παρὰ μὲν τοῖς θεοῖς τοσοῦτον ἐπιδείκνυται ὡς καὶ τὸν οὐρανὸν ὅλον ἐνίοτε ἀποκρύπτειν καὶ τὸν ἥλιον καὶ τὴν σελήνην, τήν τε γῆν μηκέτι δύνασθαι ἑστάναι αὐτῶν κατιόντων.

Iamblichus, by using the present participle, indicates that the cosmic disturbances occurred *as* the gods descended. Lewy, by understanding the cosmic disturbances to begin only *after* the appearance of the apparitions described in fr. 146, confuses the true sequence as illustrated in Iamblichus and in examples from Graeco-Roman literature. Cosmic disturbances precede or accompany epiphanies.

What is the meaning of the cosmic disturbances in fr. 147? Certainly Lewy, p. 242, is correct in saying that the signs serve as assurances that the magical or theurgical operation is proceeding correctly: "the absence of [these signs] points to the operation having been disturbed by some hostile influence." But this is only a secondary effect; some of the examples Lewy adduces (n. 56) indicate that he misunderstands the ultimate cause and thereby the basic significance of the phenomena. Lewy compares the cosmic phenomena in fr. 147 to such signs as those found in *PGM* IV.2940-41:

> if you see a star shining steadily, it is a sign that she [the object of the love charm] has been smitten, and if it is lengthened like the flame of a lamp, she has already come." (E.N. O'Neill's translation in Betz's edition)

Several other examples like this one are found in the magical papyri.[15] In each case, however, the "sign" that the magician is told to expect either 1) turns out to have a practical purpose (e.g., the falcon "sign" of I.65 descends bringing a stone to wear as

---

theurgist with a oracle in verse, which the magician will be able to remember later regardless of its length or complexity.
On the nature of the system behind "The Mithras Liturgy," see A. Dieterich, *Eine Mithrasliturgie* (Heidelberg 1903; rpt. Leipzig 1923) and M.W. Meyer, *The "Mithras Liturgy,"* (Missoula, Mont. 1976). The most recent translation and commentary is Meyer's revision of his earlier work, which is printed in *The Greek Magical Papyri in Translation,* ed. Hans Dieter Betz (Chicago 1986) I 48-54. The papyrus on which this spell is found is dated to the fourth century A.D.; the date of the spell itself is difficult to determine. Dieterich suggested the second century A.D., which would place it close to the time of the Oracles' composition.

[15] *PGM* I.65, 74, 154; III.272; IV.209 ff., 1903; VII.614, 890; LVII.1-37.

an amulet), 2) itself turns into the divinity whose epiphany is sought (I.74), or 3) is clearly a contrived sign, sent by the god specifically for the purpose of expressing the spell's success (e.g., IV.1903, a dog hisses to indicate the success of a love spell). The alteration of the star's light in the example cited above belongs to the third category.

In contrast, the phenomena of fr. 147 have no such practical purpose. And, although their appearance certainly would reassure the theurgist that he was on the right track, they were not contrived solely as signals; such signals in the magical papyri are of a more minor nature (hissing dogs, flickering lamps), are found in isolation rather than in groups, and are artificial in the sense that they are not connected directly to the purpose of the spell (for example, a flickering lamp is the pre-established sign, not the natural result, of a daemon seizing the "unmanageable woman" of *PGM* VII.614).

The phenomena of fr. 147 can be illuminated better by re-examining the similar cosmological disturbances occurring in literary epiphanies such as those cited above. Two points must be considered. First, as was stressed above, the disturbances immediately precede or simultaneously accompany the arrival of the god. Second, none of the sources describing such phenomena imply that the god or goddess intentionally acts to bring them about; rather, nature's normal course spontaneously is confounded by the very presence of divinity. In short, far from being wonders that the god or goddess may choose to produce at any given stage of his or her contact with the theurgist, cosmic or meteorological disturbances are to be understood as the automatic--indeed, inevitable--accompaniments of a god or goddess' descent into the earthly realm. Epiphanies represent the overstepping of a boundary; something foreign intrudes into the mortal, earthly sphere, which cannot contain a god easily. The very presence of a god immediately causes the ground to shake, the tides to exceed their normal limits, the atmosphere to bristle with lightning and thunder.

The idea behind this point was important to Greek religious thought in general, and in particular to the Chaldean system, to later Platonism and to magic.[16] The Universe was divided into distinct physical and hierarchical zones, each with its appropriate inhabitants--the gods were divine and belonged on Olympus (or in later times, above the moon); men were mortal and belonged on earth (or below the moon). Crossing these zones' boundaries was in some cases desirable (e.g., the theurgist strove to send his soul out of the Sensible realm) but in all such cases a

---

[16]See Chapter X.

hierarchy was overturned, resulting in a temporary disturbance of the Universe's normal workings.[17]

Most of fr. 147, then, describes this disruptive effect of the goddess' descent from her proper, celestial sphere into the earthly sphere of the invoking theurgist. The final phrase of fr. 147, "all things are revealed in lightning," remains to be explained. Although in the Oracles "lightning" can symbolize the Ideas, iynges or *symbola/synthemata*, here the word means simply heavenly fire. The phrase looks forward to fr. 146, in which a variety of fiery apparitions descend to manifest themselves against the backdrop of darkened sky provided in fr. 147; they all are "revealed" by means of their lightning-like brightness.[18]

Lewy, pp. 241-2, divides the lightning-like apparitions of fr. 146 into two groups: a) visions of formless fire or light and b) horses and boys:

> The luminous or igneous character of the phenomena of the first group indicates that the approaching deity was none other than Hecate, who was habitually preceded by fiery phantoms. The shapes of the second group may also be identified with the apparitions, which according to a widespread belief accompanied this goddess. The boys are those who have come to an untimely end (ἄωροι); disincarnate souls who, having been deprived of burial and of the proper funeral rites, are doomed to escort Hecate on her rovings. The archer represents those who have suffered violent death in fight (ἥρωες) and have not been buried; condemned for similar reasons to perpetual unrest, they also join Hecate's band. As for the horse, it is one of the typical symbols of Hecate--one of the heads of her four-headed image being equine.

There are several problems with Lewy's analysis, which lead to his misinterpretation of the apparitions.[19] First, his division of the phenomena into two groups--fiery apparitions and boys and horses--is incorrect; with the possible exception of the naked boy in l. 7 (see pp. 123-24, below), the group as a whole is fiery or luminous. A better division would be between fire in recognizable shapes and unformed fires.

Second, he is mistaken in assuming that the apparitions' fieriness is due to the fact that they accompany Hekate.[20] The Chaldean system associated fire with

---

[17] Pfister, "Epiphanie," *RE* suppl. IV 319, instructively compares the cosmic disturbances surrounding the birth of godlike men, e.g., Apollonius of Tyana (Philostr. *VA* I.5). The same boundary is overturned as a "superman" enters the world of man.

[18] In particular, the verb of fr. 146.5, "ἀστράπτω," "flash as if with lightning," suggests this conclusion.

[19] Other scholars of the Oracles--including Kroll, Des Places, Cremer and Geudtner--offer no detailed analysis of this fragment.

[20] Lewy uses as evidence for fiery visions of Hekate *PGM* IV.2727; Hipp. *Ref.* IV.35.4; Eus. *PE* IV.23, 175 c-d (151 Wolff). The problem with these is that they all are later than, or at best contemporary with, the Oracles and may in fact draw on them. Moreover, even Lewy's most convincing citation, Marinus *Procl.* 28, ("[Proclus] after having performed the purificatory rites of the

divinity in general; all noetic entities were characterized as fiery or luminous.[21] Iamblichus' discussion of epiphanies, which draws on Chaldean doctrine, confirms this; even the lowest entity --a disembodied soul--has a small amount of luminosity (*De Myst.* II.4; 77,10-18).

Third, although he attempts to explain the significance of the boys and horses, he offers no explanation of the apparitions that are not anthropomorphic or theriomorphic. Until all the apparitions are explained, both as a group and individually, the meaning of fr. 146 will not be clear.

Of all the apparitions in fr. 146, the easiest to identify is the formless fire from which a voice emerges (l. 3), which, I argue, is the same fire as that one mentioned in fr. 148, also described as formless and having a voice. Lewy, pp. 243-4, correctly suggested that the fire in fr. 148 represented Soul/Hekate; for evidence he adduces *De Myst.* II.7; 84,6:[22]

> The fire of the Soul of the Whole...appears formless throughout the Cosmos.
>
> Ψυχῆς δὲ τῆς μὲν ὅλης...πῦρ ὁρᾶται ἀνείδεον περὶ ὅλον τὸν κόσμον.

Strangely, Lewy does not apply his conclusion about the identification of Hekate and the formless, speaking fire of fr. 148 to the formless, speaking fire of fr. 146. The identity of the two fires scarcely can be doubted, however. It is clear that in fr. 146, Soul/Hekate manifests herself.

The remaining apparitions are a mixed lot. Some are of no particular shape, others are recognizable. They all partake of movement and activity, but to varying extents; their most obvious common quality is some degree of luminosity or fire.

Chaldeans, spoke with luminous apparitions of Hekate that he saw with his own eyes") does not exclude the possibility that other Chaldean gods appeared in fiery forms. See also the following note.

[21] This is shown not only by the numerous fragments describing divine entities as fiery or luminous, but by the commentators' remarks. For example, Simplicius *Phys.* 613.7: "The gods reveal through this [light] the sight of their epiphanies to those who are worthy; and in this [light], according to the Oracles, the formless is endowed with form." (see discussion at Kroll, p. 57 and Lewy, p. 244). Similarly, Iamb. *De Myst.* II.4; 77,10 says that the images (ἀγάλματα) of the gods flash forth (ἀστράπτει; cf. fr. 146.5) with light; clearly, he perceives all the gods, not merely Hekate/Soul, to be fiery. His discussion of mediumship, which probably draws on Chaldean doctrine, (III.6; 112,10 ff.) describes various fiery or luminous entities as entering and exiting the medium's body; sometimes, as in epiphanies, these are visible to all in attendance. On fiery phenomena in theurgy in general, see also Dodds, *G&I* p. 299.

[22] The similarity between the Iamblichean passage and fr. 148 also has been noted by Des Places in his edition of Iamblichus, pp. 88-9, n. 2, and by Cremer, pp. 99-100, who argues that Iamblichus specifically refers to the fragment.

THE EPIPHANY OF HEKATE

The Oracles' successors can help to identify them. In the second book of *De Myst.*, which as Cremer showed was influenced heavily by Chaldean doctrine,[23] Iamblichus is concerned with how the epiphanies of various entities can be distinguished from one another. He discusses the differing degrees to which these epiphanies possess certain traits--brightness, size, degrees of mobility and immutability, for example.

His system is not strictly Chaldean. For instance, Chaldean doctrine, unlike Iamblichus, includes no mention of archangels.[24] It also is doubtful that the Chaldean system stratified its entities' traits as enthusiastically and incrementally as did Iamblichus. But Iamblichus' discussion generally reflects the fact that the Chaldean system included a variety of divine entities, all capable of epiphany but differing from one another in such things as size, brightness, level of activity and the form in which they appeared. It is just such a mixture of entities that is portrayed in fr. 146.

Other ancient sources help to identify the apparitions in fr. 146 more precisely. According to them, the Chaldean system taught that during epiphany the gods often were accompanied by "angels."[25] The term "ἄγγελος," as used by the Chaldeans, seems to have been a general one for entities purer and more exalted than daemones, who aided in the transmission of the Father's will; there were several types of angels.[26] Daemonic entities also could accompany the gods. Both angels and daemones, but particularly daemones, sometimes attempted to convince the theurgist that they were gods themselves.[27] If the formless fire is Hekate--a goddess--then it is likely that the other apparitions in fr. 146 are either angels or daemones or a mixture of both.

Two of the other apparitions in fr. 146 do not have recognizable shapes; they are "a fire, leaping skittishly like a child over the aery waves" (l. 2), and "a rich light, whirling around the field in a spiral" (l. 4). These are grouped, by means of parallel sentence structure, with the formless, speaking fire identified as Hekate (l. 3). The description of these three epiphanies makes up the first half of the fragment. The second half of the fragment is separated from the first by "ἀλλὰ καί," "but also," and like the first half is unified within itself by parallel sentence structures. It describes anthropomorphic or theriomorphic apparitions: "a horse flashing more

---

[23]See Chapter IV, "Die göttliche Epiphanie (*de myst.* II 3-9)," esp. pp. 45 ff.

[24] On the absence of archangels in the Oracles see Cremer, pp. 63-4.

[25]E.g., Psellus, *Hypostasis* 75, 14-20; Iamb. *De Myst.* II.7; 83,10-14 and II.4; 76,16; Proc. *In R.* I.91.19, II. 255.20; *In Alc.* 377.35 ff.; *In T.* III.262.14; Porph. *ap.* Aug. *De Civ. Dei* X.26 may reflect Chaldean doctrine as well. See also Lewy, p. 245 and Cremer, pp. 57, 63-7.

[26]See Lewy, p. 162.

[27]E.g., Proc. *In R.* I.91.19 ff.; Aug. *De Civ. Dei* X *passim* (drawing on Porphyry); Iamb. *De Myst.* II.3; 70,9 and III.31; 177,7 ff.; Eunap. *V. Soph.* 473; Synes. *De Insom.* 142 a; Niceph. Greg. *PG* 149, 540 a. See also Lewy, p. 245 n. 65; Cremer, pp. 52, 57 and 63-85; Dodds, *G&I* pp. 297-8.

brightly than light," "a child mounted on the swift back of a horse," who is either "fiery or covered with gold or naked," and "a child shooting a bow, standing upon a horse's back."

Platonic doctrine taught that the incorporeal was closer to divinity than the corporeal; embodiment was the mark of the hylic world. This concept is glimpsed in the Oracles themselves, which often warn the theurgist against placing undue importance on the material. Similarly, Iamblichus uses the increasing complexity of shape as one of the means of distinguishing the epiphanies of entities; those of angels, archangels and gods are all simple in form or formless, whereas daemones, heroes and souls take on more complex, specific shapes. If this concept is used to interpret fr. 146, the first group of apparitions is seen to be a god and two higher entities, which can be called by the general Chaldean term of angels. The other group is made up of lower, more hylic entities.

The first of the angelic apparitions, the fire that "leaps skittishly like a child over the aery waves," evades more detailed identification, given our present knowledge of the Chaldean system. The other angelic apparition, however, seems to be a iynx. The language of l. 4, "...a rich light, whirring around the field in a spiral," strongly recalls the language used in the Oracles and elsewhere to describe the noises and circular motions of the iynges and their alter egos, the Ideas and the *symbola/synthemata* (see previous chapter). In fact, the verb "whir," "ῥοιζέω" (used in l. 4), is twice used of the Ideas' motion in the Oracles (frs. 37, ll. 1 and 9).[28] The iynges' duties as messengers, and their positive, helpful character places them among the higher "angelic" entities in the Chaldean system; Lewy, p. 438, in fact, suggests that the iynges actually comprised a sub-class of angels.[29]

To identify the lesser apparitions, it is necessary to reconsider Lewy's interpretation of fr. 146, which was quoted at length on p. 200. At first glance, Lewy's suggestion that the youths and the archer are members of Hekate's traditional "swarm" makes sense; those who died as παῖδες certainly were eligible for membership in this swarm, as were unburied warriors. But the wanderings of both ἄωροι and the unburied dead traditionally were limited to the earth, and sometimes even to the immediate vicinity of their graves or places of death. It is difficult to see why these creatures would accompany a celestial goddess--such as Hekate is in the Chaldean system--or how they could shine with the fire that the Chaldeans associated with heavenly, noetic entities. Moreover, the anthropomorphic apparitions of fr. 146 have awe-inspiring but splendid appearances, rather than the threatening, terrifying

---

[28] See pp. 104, 108.

[29] In the last section, the term "iynx-daemones," was used to distinguish the entities from the magical objects, "iynx-wheels." By "daemon" was meant, in that case, a superhuman but not divine creature; no implication concerning their status as daemones as opposed to angels, for example, was intended.

appearances expected of the restless dead.[30] For example, the archer on the horse has a warrior's appearance but nothing to indicate that he was specifically an ἄταφος warrior. And a dead child would scarcely be imagined as "covered in gold."[31] Fragment 146 does not portray Hekate's swarm.

Lewy's interpretation of the equine apparitions must be rejected as well. First, there are in reality few associations of Hekate with the horse, and all of those that do exist are later than the traditional date for the Oracles.[32] Second, it must be asked why the horse would be singled out as a symbol for Hekate when it is but one of the heads of her three- or four-headed image; why aren't the bull, boar, puppy, hydra, lion or any animal whose head is attributed to Hekate used as a symbol as well? Moreover, the horse as an animal, such as is portrayed in fr. 146, is not the same thing as a horse-headed deity. Finally, even if the horse were meant to symbolize one of Hekate's heads or even Hekate herself, it is unlikely that it would appear carrying riders on its back.[33]

These apparitions are not ἄωροι, ἄταφοι or symbols for Hekate, as Lewy suggested, but rather sublunar daemones, entities that existed just above disembodied souls in the Chaldean hierarchy and were capable of epiphany. According to Iamblichus, the epiphanies of daemones were varied and constantly changing, tum-

---

[30] Lewy bases his discussion of the "swarm" of Hekate on Rohde, *Psyche* II 83 ff., 411 ff. (= 297 ff., 593 ff. of the eighth edition in English); Cumont, *Afterlife in Roman Paganism*, pp. 128 ff.; and Bidez-Cumont, *Mages Hellen.* I 180 ff. But these scholars themselves note, as I have here, that ἄωροι and ἄταφοι traditionally were bound to earth or to their place of death, unable to rise to heaven (e.g., Rohde, pp. 594-5; Cumont, pp. 129, 134), and that they were vengeful and violent, showing themselves sometimes in the form of terrifying monsters (Rohde, pp. 594-5; Cumont, p. 130). The ancient citations can be found in these discussions. Other discussions of ἄωροι and ἄταφοι can be found in M. Golden, "Did the Ancients Care When their Children Died?" *G&R* 35 (1988) 152-63; R. Garland, *The Greek Way of Death* (Ithaca 1985) pp. 77 ff. and 101 ff. (Garland, however, is not concerned as much with the imagined fate of their souls as with the ceremonies surrounding their burials); Jan Bremmer, *The Early Greek Concept of the Soul* (Princeton 1983) pp. 100-103; J.H. Waszink "Biothanati" in Klauser (ed.) *Reallexicon für Antike und Christentum* II (1954) 391-94; Nilsson, *GGR* II.2 548-49; A.D. Nock, "Tertullian and the Ahori," *VigChr.* 4 (1950) 129-41; F. Cumont *Lux Perpetua* (Paris 1949) 303-342 and *Afterlife in Roman Paganism* (New Haven 1922) 128-47; Th. Hopfner, *OZ passim* (see index), and "Nekromantie'" *RE* XVI.2 Halbband XXXII 2218-2233; K. Preisendanz, "Nekydaimon" *RE* XVI.2 Halbband XXXII 2240 ff.; S. Reinach "'Αωροι βιαιοθάνατοι," *ArchRW* 9 (1906) 312-20.

[31] The gold sheets that covered a baby's body in a Mycenean tomb (see Garland, above, n. 30, pp. 77-8 and fig. 16) provide an enticing *comparandum* for this line. But as Garland argues, this was by far the exception to the normal rule of carelessly burying childen. The adjective in fr. 146 refers to the luminosity of the apparition.

[32] Lewy cites Porph. *Abst.* IV.16, p. 254, 21; Lydus *Mens.* III.8, p. 41, l. 20; *PGM* IV.2549 and 2614. To this I can add only Orph. *Argon.* 977 ff.

[33] Cremer suggests, p. 45, n. 57, that the horse alludes to the *Seelenross* of Pl. *Phdr.* 253 d 3, which is described as a "good white horse." The major obstacle to this suggestion is the same as that to Lewy's suggestions; it accounts for only some of the apparitions and leaves the others unexplained. Moreover, if the horses represent the theurgist's soul (or any other soul), it must be asked what the children on the horses' backs represent.

ultuous and confused. Although they did not have the intense brightness of the gods or angels, they appeared luminous or fiery to some degree, depending on how polluted they were by hylic influences. Most importantly, Iamblichus says that the epiphanies of daemones were "bounded in form;" that is, recognizable, in contrast to the formless or barely formed epiphanies of higher entities. The lesser epiphanies of fr. 146 share all these characteristics and clearly represent daemones of differing rank;[34] the naked boy, who has little or no luminosity, is perhaps a daemon of the lowest rank.

The presently limited knowledge of Chaldean beliefs makes it impossible to pinpoint the reasons these daemones manifested themselves in the forms of boys, horses and archers with any certainty. Although these forms must have held some significance for the theurgist, here it can be said only that their well defined, familiar shapes and their general activity indicate that they are daemonic.[35] Fragment 146 as a whole brings to mind Porphyry's statement that those who engage in purificatory rites have marvellously beautiful visions of angels or gods--and Augustine's rebuttal that those visions are, rather, demonic.[36] Fragment 146 describes the epiphany of Hekate, but also the epiphanies of such entities, according to Iamblichus, as a theurgist would expect to accompany any god, including Hekate--angels, iynges and daemones.

---

[34]Iamblichus' system also included heroes, a class just below daemones but sharing most of their characteristics. Although heroes do not appear in the extant Oracle fragments, Psellus (*Hypostasis* 75, 12 ff.; *Ekthesis* 123, 5 ff. Bassi; *De Aur. Cat.* 216, 24) says that the Chaldean system comprised angels, daemones, heroes and souls. Proclus mentions them repeatedly (e.g., *In Prm.* 617.13-23; *In T.* III.229.21-8), although Cremer, p. 38, argues that Proclus draws on original Platonic influences as much as Chaldean. Olympiodorus (*Alc.* 22.3) and Synesius (*Hymn* I [3] 289-97), who also mention the series "angels, daemones, heroes and souls," may draw on Chaldean sources. The general ubiquity of the series gods-daemones-heroes-souls in antiquity also argues for the inclusion of heroes in the Chaldean hierarchy. For a brief review of the series' development in late antiquity, and discussion of whether Iamblichus' heroes in *De Myst.* are based on a Chaldean source, see Cremer, pp. 38-9. Kroll, p. 44, cites only Olympiodorus, whom he distrusts, as evidence for heroes in the Chaldean system. If the Chaldean system did include heroes, it is possible that at least one of these daemonic apparitions was a hero. The archer mounted on a horse fits Iamblichus' description of the heroes' apparitions as "courageous;" the frequent connection between horses and heroes in the iconography of grave stelai tends to confirm this possibility.

[35]There are several possible ways of interpreting the shapes, although none of them can be confirmed. The importance of παῖδες in magic ritual, especially mediumistic trance, suggests one explanation for daemones' appearance as boys (see Th. Hopfner, "Die Kindermedien in den griechisch-ägyptischen Zauberpapyri" in *Recueil N.P. Kondakov* [Prague 1926] 65-74). Alternatively, the boys may represent ἔρωτες, which were portrayed in art of the first and second century as youths, sometimes even as youths with bow and arrows; see Carl C. Schlam, *Cupid and Psyche; Apuleius and the Monuments* (University Park, PA, 1976). The prominence of Eros in the Chaldean system supports this possibility. The possibilty that the youths on horseback might be heroes was examined in the preceding note.

[36]*Ap.* Aug. *De Civ. Dei* X.10. Cf. X.9, where Augustine quotes Porphyry as saying that the theurgic *teletai* enable a soul to welcome spirits and angels and see the gods.

Iamblichus' precise and careful delineation of the different types of epiphanies indicates a concern with being able to distinguish lesser entities from gods. Other ancient sources mention that angels delighted in being called by the name of the god they served, and that daemones purposely confused the theurgist by masquerading as gods.[37]

Similarly, the instructions in fr. 148 imply that when confronted with the apparitions of fr. 146, the theurgist had to know which of the many would give him correct information. Fragment 148 gives some help with this problem, instructing the theurgist to listen only to the voice of the sacred, formless fire, alias Hekate (apparently excluding voices that might emerge from the other fiery apparitions that appear in fr. 146). Psellus, commenting on fr. 148, confirms this interpretation of the fragment, saying that the unenformed light (or fire) is the only reliable source of information and that enformed lights are deceptive (*PG* 122, 1136 b 11 ff.). Platonism's general preference for the incorporeal over the corporeal, mentioned above in connection with the apparitions of fr. 146,[38] also would support this: the formless fire logically would be the epiphany of a higher, thus more trustworthy, entity.

The formless fire "shines skittishly throughout the depths of the Cosmos."[39] Lewy, p. 244, n. 63, suggests that "depths of the Cosmos" refers to the "terrestrial zone." It is not clear exactly what Lewy means by this term, but it is fair to say that the fire's presence in the "depths" describes the descent of the goddess from her natural home in the heavens to a lower sphere, closer to earth.[40] The first line of fr. 146 describes the angelic apparition as leaping skittishly[41] over the aery waves;

---

[37] Citations at n. 27, above. Iamblichus himself suggests (*De Myst*. III.31; 176,3 ff.) that the less purified the theurgist is, the more likely he is to be taken in by bad daemones masquerading as gods. Of particular interest with regard to deceptive angels are Aug. *De Civ. Dei* X.16, 19, and with regard to deceptive daemones X.10, 11, in all of which Augustine draws on or responds to Porphyry's remarks in *Letter to Anebo*. Augustine discusses the attempts of daemones to pretend not only that they are gods, but also that they are angels, througout books IX and X of *De Civ. Dei*.

[38] The notable absence of formless fires (or formless apparitions of any kind) in the magical papyri and literary sources supports the idea that the Chaldean portrayal of Hekate as a formless fire, and the exegetes' subsequent comments on that fire have their basis in Platonic theory rather than traditional magic. Cf. Pfister "Epiphanie" *RE* suppl. IV 277-323, who at no point in his lengthy article cites an example of gods or daemones appearing other than anthropomorphically or theriomorphically.

[39] This line is echoed by Iamblichus in a passage distinguishing the types of fire emitted by different entities (*De Myst*. II.4; 77,19) "the undivided, ineffable fire of the gods shine forth, and fills the whole depths of the Cosmos in a fiery manner, not mundanely."

[40] See discussion at Cremer, pp. 48-9.

[41] The adverb "σκιρτηδόν," which arises twice in descriptions of the fiery apparitions (l. 1 of fr. 146 and l. 2 of fr. 148), is derived from the verb "σκιρτάω," "to leap or spring playfully," which is used of young horses, goats, Bacchae and the wind (see entry in LSJ). Des Places, in the comments on fr. 146, notes that Plutarch uses the adjective "σκιρτητικός" to describe the restive impestuosity of youth (*De Liber. Educ*. 12 c). Des Places further suggests that this fire is a "will-o'-the-wisp" (*feu follet*); Psellus (*loc. cit.*) elucidates the adverb by explaining that the fire "jumps for joy." The adverb can be accounted for more simply, however; "σκιρτηδόν" is a natural word to apply to fires, referring to the skittish, dancing quality of flames.

traditionally, the aery sphere was the lowest sphere, positioned between the Earth and the Moon. The third apparition in fr. 146, the "rich light," whirs around a field; that is, just above the ground, also in the aery sphere. Together, fr. 146 and 148 reflect the idea that a series of different entities manifest themselves in the air just above the earth. The theurgist waits until Hekate herself enters this zone, described in fr. 148 as the depths of the Cosmos.[42]

In conclusion, the scene that emerges from a study of frs. 147, 146 and 148 is as follows. After repeating a magical formula several times, the theurgist sees the sky grow dark and feels the earth begin to shake; nature's course is disrupted as Hekate leaves her realm and enters the earthly sphere. Against the darkened sky "lightnings," noetic apparitions shining with heavenly fire, begin to appear in the aery sphere. These are the epiphanies of Hekate and of lesser celestial entities--angels, iynges, and daemones--who accompany her. The theurgist must ignore most of this confusion, however, and listen only to the voice of Hekate, which emerges from the

Study of these fragments has clarified the sequence of events leading to Hekate's epiphany and the identity of the entities who accompany her. This clarification, in turn, illuminates further the nature of Chaldean Hekate. First, she manifested herself not anthropomorphically[43] or theriomorphically but as a formless, speaking fire, an apparition that combines the Platonic concept of perfection--incorporeality--and the Chaldean divinization of fire. This portrayal of Hekate differs from that of the magical papyri and many other late sources; she is not terrifying or repulsive but rather awe-inspiringly beautiful.

Second, she is a celestial goddess, appearing in the darkened sky, rather than a chthonic one, emerging from the depths of the earth. The "swarm" that accompanies her is not the usual band of threatening, restless souls but a varied troop of noetic entities, glowing with heavenly light.

Hekate descends to speak--to give the theurgist information, which, unfortunately, is not included in frs. 147, 146 and 148. Several of the other extant Oracle fragments were delivered by Hekate, however, and give some idea of the sort of information she might have provided during epiphany.[44] Some of it is

---

[42]Two of the *fragmenta dubia* to be examined shortly below support the idea that Hekate descended into the aery sphere from a higher zone, i.e., the aether. In fr. 221, Hekate asks why the theurgist calls her down from the aether; in fr. 223, she describes the gods as being drawn down from the aether by the theurgist's use of iynges.

[43]Hekate's description of herself as carrying weapons and dressed in armour (fr. 72) is symbolic and should not be understood to imply an anthropomorphic manifestation; see discussion immediately below. Fragment 142 (Kr. 56 = Proc. *In R*. II.242.11-12) says "because of you [mortals], bodies are attached to our epiphanies." "Σῶμα," however, need not refer to an anthropomorphic or theriomorphic body, but simply to a form perceptible by the human senses. Cf. discussion and notes at Lewy, pp. 246-7.

[44]In most cases, the ancient sources for the Oracles do not indicate which god delivered the Oracle, and often the content of the Oracle gives no clues, either. Because Hekate was known generally in

cosmological, concerning in particular Soul/Hekate's position and roles in the Cosmos. For example, frs. 38 and 53:[45]

> These are the Thoughts of the Father, below which is my winding fire.
>
> Ἔννοιαι πατρὸς αἵδε, μεθ' ἃς ἐμὸν εἰλυμένον πῦρ.
>
> I, Psyche, dwell below the Thoughts of the Father, ensouling all with my warmth.
>
> ...μετὰ δὴ πατρικὰς διανοίας
> ψυχὴ ἐγὼ ναίω θέρμῃ ψυχοῦσα τὰ πάντα.

Such information helped the theurgist understand the workings and structure of the Cosmos, which was the first step towards controlling it or overcoming its obstacles.

Some of Hekate's declarations were more immediately practical. The previous chapter, which discussed Hekate's relationship to the iynges and the *symbola,* showed that Soul/Hekate cosmologically was the source and disperser of these theurgical tools, and also suggested that she taught the theurgist the practical side of his trade by revealing to him, during epiphany or through other means, the specific *symbola* or other information he needed to accomplish σύστασις and ἀναγωγή. Examination of two fragments will support this hypothesis. In fr. 72 (Kr. 36 = Proc. *Theol. Plat.* 324, 8) Hekate[46] says:

> For I have come, a goddess in full armour and with weapons.
>
> Καὶ γὰρ δὴ πάντευχος ἐνόπλιος ἧκα θεείη.

The verb "ἧκα," "I have come," indicates that these words were spoken during an epiphany.

Lewy suggested that this fragment referred to statues of Hekate that had six arms, each bearing a shield, a sheath, a sword or another weapon; he saw the Hekate of this Oracle as quite literally carrying weaponry. He also suggested that the Oracle alluded to the goddess' fearsome aspects, familiar from late literary sources.

Lewy's suggestion that the fragment alludes to Hekate's fearsomeness in late literature is unconvincing in view of the fact that this side of Hekate's nature appears nowhere in Chaldean sources, and also because the tone of fr. 72 is not terrifying or

---

late antiquity as an oracular goddess, it is probable that Hekate delivered a far greater number of them than can be assigned to her with certainty.

[45]Fragment 38 = 24 Kr. = Proc. *In Parm.* 895, 12 Co.^{2}; fragment 53 = 28 Kr. = Proc. *In T.* I.408.16-17; II.61.24-5

[46]See Des Places' notes and Lewy, p. 95.

horrible, but rather military. Moreover, so far as I can discover, there are no examples of statues such as Lewy mentioned.[47] The fragment need not be explained in terms of actual weaponry that Hekate carried at all; the fragment's language is symbolic and describes the theurgical "weapons" that Hekate provides to those who invoke her. This is suggested by fr. 2 (Kr. 51 = Dam. I.155.11-14; cf. Des Places, *Delebecque,* p. 322):

> Being dressed in the full-armoured force of the resounding light,
> and equipping the soul and the intellect with the weaponry of
>   three-barbed strength,
> you must cast into your mind the complete *synthema* of the Triad and
>   wander
> amongst the fiery rays not in a scattered manner but with
>   concentration.
>
> Ἐσσάμενον πάντευχον ἀκμὴν φωτὸς κελάδοντος,
> ἀλκῇ τριγλώχινι νόον ψυχήν θ' ὁπλίσαντα,
> πᾶν τριάδος σύνθημα βαλεῖν φρενὶ μηδ' ἐπιφοιτᾶν
> ἐμπυρίοις σποράδην ὀχετοῖς, ἀλλὰ στιβαρηδόν.

The word "πάντευχος" ("in full armour") of fr. 72 is also found in fr. 2.1; a close cognate of the word "ἐνόπλιος" in fr. 72 is found in fr.2.2--"ὁπλίσαντα."

Lewy, pp. 192 ff., has suggested that fr.2 describes the preparations a theurgist must make before attempting to enter the "fiery rays," that is, to ascend. He rightly understands "sounding light" (l. 1) to refer to the music or harmony of the spheres, but is incorrect in interpreting its "force" to be the aether in which these spheres revolve. The last section discussed the close relationship between the music of the spheres and the iynges/*symbola* ; the theurgist who dresses himself in the "force of the sounding light" is protected by these *symbola* as he ascends through the rays. Perhaps he even has arrayed himself in them literally.[48]

---

[47] Lewy cites Roscher's article on Hekate, p. 1909, but the only example Roscher offers of an image of Hekate whose six arms all bear weaponry is that one appearing in the gigantomachy shown on the Pergamum frieze. There, her weaponry is justified by the fact that she is engaged in war; all the gods that are portrayed hold weapons. Roscher does, however, describe coins on which she is shown holding two torches, two whips and two swords. This may be the example of which Lewy is thinking.

[48] Dodds, *G&I* p. 296, discusses the use of special garments covered with *symbola* in the mediumistic trances used by theurgists. The purpose of the symbolic garments was to strengthen the sympathetic link between theurgist and god. As the establishment of a sympathetic link was of equal importance during epiphany, it is possible that the invoking theurgist also wore such garments, wreathes or amulets as Dodds discusses; see Lewy, pp. 290-1, for a discussion of remarks in ancient commentators that imply this.

The "weaponry of three-barbed strength" (l. 2),[49] with which he equips his soul and intellect, refers to the soul-saving theurgical skills provided by Hekate, from whom ἀλκή flows.[50] When the theurgist "casts the *synthema* of the Triad into his mind" (l. 2), he pronounces (apparently silently to himself) the magic words or phrases necessary for completion of the act.[51]

Fragment 2 as a whole describes the knowledge and preparations required by a magical act in terms of weaponry that a theurgist must put on or wield. This weaponry--iynges, *symbola*, ἀλκή--is derived from Hekate/Soul. When fr. 72 portrays Hekate as appearing to the theurgist identically equipped with weaponry and armour, it symbolizes the fact that she has come to provide him with these "weapons" (know-

---

[49] It is difficult to evaluate Lewy's suggestion that "τριγλώχις" means that the strength was composed of three substances, for he does not specify what those substances are. However, it seems likely that it is simply an adjective typically applied to weapons, following Homeric usage (Lewy also cites its use in Homer).

[50] For Hekate's connection with ἀλκή, see Chapter IV, n. 30. That ἀλκή specifically represents skills necessary for σύστασις or ἀναγωγή is suggested not only by fr. 2, but also by fr. 117 ("saved by [Soul's] ἀλκή"), fr. 119 ("ἀλκή that unites one with God") and 118.2 (God gives ἀλκή, in other words soul-saving skills, to some theurgists during sleep).

[51] On silence in prayer in general see H.S. Versnel "Religious Mentality in Ancient Prayer," in *Faith, Hope and Worship: Aspects of Religious Mentality in the Ancient World* II. Studies in Greek and Roman Religion, ed. H.S. Versnel (Leiden 1981) 25-37. Versnel suggests that the two main situations in which worshippers prayed silently were when they prayed for help in love or for help in destroying the object of their hatred. Both of these prayers, for obvious reasons, preferably would be kept secret from the worshipper's neighbors, hence the silence. Versnel also notes that silent prayer might alternatively express an unusual intimacy with the deity.

But see also Lewy, p. 194, n. 71, who in discussing fr. 2 cites the remark of Martianus Capella (II.203) that "secret words" ("ἄρρητα ὀνόματα") are to be spoken *voce mentis*. The fact that the identity of the *synthemata* must be kept hidden from the uninitiated certainly would prompt silent prayer (cf. Oracle fr. 132: "Keep silent, myste!" and Des Places' accompanying notes, which compares this admonition for secrecy to those given to the Eleusinian initiates).

Finally, one other explanation for the admonition in fr. 2 to mentally pronounce the *synthema* must be taken into consideration. Several Oracles fragments indicate that the Chaldean system emphasized turning the *mind* towards God and accomplishing theurgical goals through mental effort. E.g., fr. 1.1:

> For there exists a certain Intelligible [entity], which you must perceive with the
> "flower of your mind" (that is, the summit of your mental concentration)...

Ἔστιν γάρ τι νοητόν, ὃ χρή σε νοεῖν νόου ἄνθει...

and fr. 128:

> ...if you extend your mind, illuminated by the fire,
> to the work of piety, you will also save the flowing body.

...ἐκτείνας πύριον νοῦν
ἔργον ἐπ' εὐσεβίης ῥευστὸν καὶ σῶμα σαώσεις.

The theurgist is told in fr. 2 to cast the *synthema* of the Triad into his mind because it is through mental manipulation of the *synthema* (i.e., concentration) that he succeeds in his task.

ledge of the *symbola*) and "armour" (theurgical skill).[52] The suggestion that Hekate endowed the theurgist with practical knowledge during epiphany as well as with cosmological information thus is confirmed.

Before leaving the subject of Hekate's epiphany, a series of oracles that Eusebius quotes from Porphyry's work *Philosophy of Oracles* (included in Des Places' edition under the category of *fragmenta dubia*) should be considered. Several of these are delivered by Hekate herself, apparently during her epiphany. The question of whether some or all of them are genuine fragments of the Chaldean Oracles is difficult to resolve;[53] if they are not genuine, however, some of them can nonetheless serve as comparanda for the Oracles, having been collected by Porphyry only a little later than the time of the Oracles' composition.

One of the Oracles from Eusebius gives information that a theurgist would find practical (fr. 224 = Eus. *PE* V.12, 200 b = Nic. Greg. *In Synes.* 539 b-c = 130 Wolff). Hekate says:[54]

> But make me a statue, purified as I shall teach you.
> Make the form from savage rue, and then add little creatures--
> domestic lizards--as adornments. And kneading with these animals a mixture of myrrh and gum and incense,
> and going outside under the crescent moon,
> finish this imprecation, praying it yourself.

> Ἀλλὰ τέλει ξόανον, κεκαθαρμένον ὥς σε διδάξω·
> πηγάνου ἐξ ἀγρίοιο δέμας ποίει, ἠδ' ἐπικόσμει
> ζῴοισιν λεπτοῖσι, κατοικιδίοις σκαλαβώταις,
> σμύρνης καὶ στύρακος λιβανοῖό τε μίγματα τρίψας
> σὺν κείνοις ζώοισι, καὶ αἰθριάσας ὑπὸ μήνην

---

[52] The objection might be made that Hekate is called down to provide a theurgist with the "weapons" that he needed in order to call her down in the first place. But as is shown by *fragmentum dubium* 224, in which Hekate appears to the theurgist in order to tell him how to make and consecrate her *xoanon*, the goddess could be invoked to give information about theurgical practices that the invoker had not yet attempted. Fragment 2 describes the preparations a theurgist must make before attempting to "wander amongst the fiery rays," not the preparations he must make simply to invoke Hekate. When she is appears to him in fr. 72 she provides him with the means to make the preparations for wandering amongst the rays.

[53] On this question, see Des Places' remarks on fr. 219. Their Chaldean origin first was suggested by N. Terzaghi, "Sul Commento di Niceforo Gregorio al ΠΕΡΙ ΕΝΥΠΝΙΩΝ di Synesio." *Studi italiani di filologia classica* XII (1904) pp. 181-217. See also discussions of Porphyry's relationship to the Oracles in the Introduction, pp. 4-5.

[54] Eusebius continues the oracle:

> Take as many lizards as are my forms,
> and do all things that I command you with care.
> Make a spacious house for me with plaited laurel branches.
> Then offer many prayers to my image, and in your sleep you will see me near.

Terzaghi and Des Places do not include these lines as part of the Chaldean fragment.

αὔξουσαν, τέλει αὐτὸς ἐπευχόμενος τήνδ' εὐχήν.

This fragment describes the construction and consecration of a statue of Hekate, probably for telestic purposes.[55] Telestic statues (statues of gods that were animated by the magician in order to obtain oracles) regularly were made from and adorned with physical *symbola;* that is, plants, stones, animals and other objects that aided in the establishment of συμπάθεια and communication with the god. The rue, lizards, myrrh and incense of fr. 224 are typical examples of *symbola.*[56]

Although none of the other extant Oracle fragments give direct evidence for Chaldean τελεστικά, secondary sources indicate that it existed;[57] the scholiast on Lucian's *Philops.* 12 tells us, in fact, that Julian the Theurgist wrote a work called *Τελεστικά,* for which, Marinus tells us, Proclus wrote a lost commentary (*Procl.* 26). It is likely, then, that Terzaghi is correct in calling the oracle found in Eusebius (*fragmentum dubium* 224) Chaldean. Oracle frs. 51 and 52, which describe soul pouring forth from the right side of Hekate's abdomen and virtue remaining within the left side, also refer to a statue of the goddess, although it is unclear whether the statue was telestic or simply a cult statue.[58]

In fr. 224, Hekate teaches the theurgist his craft. It was argued above (pp. 127-28) that fr. 72 also portrays her as having descended in order to teach the theurgist. One of Hekate's roles, then, was to instruct the theurgist, so that he could progress further.

Two other Porphyrian oracles spoken by Hekate describe the circumstances under which she and other gods were invoked. Both are included by Des Places as *fragmenta dubia* :[59]

---

[55] On telestic statues and their animation by means of *symbola,* see C. Faraone, "The Protection of Place: Telestics and Theurgy in Ancient Greece," in *Magika Hiera: Greek Magic and Religion,* ed. C. Faraone and D. Obbink (Oxford forthcoming 1990). See also Dodds, *G&I* pp. 291 ff.; Hopfner *OZ passim* (v. indices "Statuen"); Lewy, pp. 495-6; and Wolff, *De philosophia ex oraculis haurienda librorum reliquae* (Berlin 1856; rpt. Hildesheim 1962) pp. 206 ff.

[56] Some of the other oracles recorded by Eusebius (but not considered to be Chaldean) offer further examples of *symbola* used for the consecration of statues: *PE* V.13, 201 c-d; V.15, 203 d; V.14, 202 d. See also Psellus, *Epist.* 87 (Sathas), who lists animals, leaves, stones, plants, roots, gemstones, scents and engraved incantations as *symbola* used in telestic operations; Proclus, *C.M.A.G.* VI.151.148 ff., who lists such objects and their uses; Iamblichus, *De Myst.* 233; 10 ff.; Porph. *ap.* Aug. *De Civ. Dei* X.11; and many examples in *PGM*. Discussion at Wolff, pp. 195 ff.

[57] For citation and discussion of the sources, see Lewy, pp. 495-6.

[58] See also Lewy pp. 88 ff. Fragment 186 *bis* (Olympiod. *In Alc.* 125, 23-4 Westerink = *In Phaedon.* 23,3; 68,23 N.) "...multiformed image (of the Soul)," ("...ψυχῆς πάμμορφον ἄγαλμα") may also refer to a statue of Hekate/Soul. The animating of Hekate's statue apparently was a favorite pursuit of theurgists and magicians in late antiquity; see Lewy, pp. 247 ff.; Wolff, pp. 130-7.

[59] Fr. 221 (Eus. *PE* V.8, 193 d) fr. 223 (Eus. *PE* V.8, 194 a-b).

132   CHAPTER VIII

> Why do you call me, the goddess Hekate, here from the swift aether
> by means of god-compelling necessity?

> Τίπτε μ' ἀεὶ θείοντος ἀπ' αἰθέρος ὧδε χατίζων
> θειοδάμοις Ἑκάτην με θεὴν ἐκάλεσσας ἀνάγκαις;

> Easily dragging some of these unwilling [divinites] from the aether by
>   means of ineffable iynges,
> you lead them earthwards;
> but others, who are mounted on the middle winds,
> apart from the divine fire, you send to mortals
> just like ominous dreams, treating these daemones outrageously.

> Τοὺς μὲν ἀπορρήτοις ἐρύων ἴυγξιν ἀπ' αἴθρης
> ῥηϊδίως ἀέκοντας ἐπὶ χθόνα τήνδε κατῆγες,
> τοὺς δὲ μέσους μεσάτοισιν ἐπεμβεβαῶτας ἀήταις
> ωόσφι πυρὸς θείοιο πανομφέας ὥσπερ ὀνείρους
> εἰσκρίνεις μερόπεσσιν, ἀεικέα δαίμονας ἔρδων.

The first fragment is too short to provide much information, but the use of the words "θειοδάμοις ἀνάγκαις" does imply that Hekate did not always come willingly when she was invoked. The second fragment also implies this by its description of the gods as "unwilling" to come.[60] It was noted briefly above (p. 86, n. 20) that it is difficult to determine whether these fragments are "Chaldean." As Chapter VI showed, the best evidence available to us indicates that Chaldean theurgists were supposed to work with the consent and cooperation of the gods; this would seem to argue against the inclusion of frs. 221 and 223 in the Chaldean corpus. But the deprecatory tone used by Hekate in both fragments may be understood as admonishing a theurgist who has dared to use unsanctioned means to accomplish his task, a theurgist who has not been content to await the voluntary help of the gods.[61]

---

[60] Another *fragmentum dubium* (fr. 220 = Eus. *PE* V.8, 194 b) also implies the unwilling descent of a god (neither the oracle nor its context tell us which one):

> Listen to me, although I do not wish [to speak], as you have bound me by
> necessity.

> Κλῦθί μευ οὐκ ἐθέλοντος, ἐπεί μ' ἐπέδησας ἀνάγκῃ.

[61] The problem presented by the two Porphyrian oracles is interesting in view of recent arguments discounting the long-held opinion about the distinction between magic and religion. Scholars used to follow Frazer's distinction: in religion, one prayed for the gods' help; in magic, one coerced the gods. More recently, others, including Graf, "Prayer," have shown that this strict dichotomy cannot be upheld; the magician prayed and used rituals in much the same way as the religious worshipper did. Graf himself notes that coercion could be used, but stresses that its use was infrequent and usually occurred when the deity addressed failed to respond to prayers. There is no mention in the

This section has discussed Hekate's personal relationship with the theurgist--how he called her, in what form she appeared, what he could expect from her. The earlier portion of the section showed that she was pictured as a celestial deity, rather than a chthonic, daemonic goddess as the magical papyri or contemporary literature often portrayed her. Her cohort was celestial, too, composed of fiery angels, iynges and daemones, rather than the restless, terrifying dead. The latter portion of the section discussed her purpose in appearing to the theurgist. Fragment 221, "Why do you call me from the aether?" implies that she could be invoked by the theurgist for a variety of purposes. Fragments 224, 2 and 72 indicate that one of those purposes was the conveying of *symbola* and theurgically significant information from the Intelligible to the Sensible realm--another facet of her nature as a mediator. The conveyance of this information, because it aids in the establishment of sympathy and thus in σύστασις and ἀναγωγή, is an important part of the Chaldean soteriological process. Thus, to the theurgist, Hekate's mediating role as Cosmic Soul and her position between the divine and human was significant not only cosmologically, but personally. Her activities as a transmissive goddess helped to make her a savior goddess.

Porphyrian oracles quoted above of whether the magician first tried to obtain Hekate's aid through less coercive means.

Chapter IX
The Chaldean Daemon-dogs

Several Oracle fragments mention daemones[1] called "dogs" (frs. 90, 91, 135, 156, quoted in order):[2]

.....For indeed, from the womb
of the earth rush forth earthly dogs that never
reveal a true sign to mortal man.

...................ἐκ δ' ἄρα κόλπων
γαίης θρῴσκουσιν χθόνιοι κύνες οὔποτ' ἀληθὲς
σῆμα βροτῷ δεικνύντες.

Chariotress of the aery, earthly and watery dogs.

ἠερίων ἐλάτειρα κυνῶν χθονίων τε καὶ ὑγρῶν.

For it is essential that you do not regard these [dogs] before you initiate your body.
For being earthly, difficult dogs, they are shameless,
and charming souls they constantly drag them away from the rites.

Οὐ γὰρ χρὴ κείνους σε βλέπειν πρὶν σῶμα τελεσθῇς·
ὄντες γὰρ χθόνιοι χαλεποὶ κύνες εἰσὶν ἀναιδεῖς
καὶ ψυχὰς θέλγοντες ἀεὶ τελετῶν ἀπάγουσιν.

[Those living a wretched life] do not stay far away from the unreasoning dogs.

Οἵδε γὰρ οὐκ ἀπέχουσι κυνῶν ἀλόγων πολὺ μέτρον.

According to the fragments, these dogs plague the theurgists in various ways, deceiving them with false signs or *symbola* (fr. 90), shamelessly charming their souls

---

[1] Proclus informs us that the Oracles were accustomed to call the daemones dogs or to compare them to dogs (scholion to Hes. *WD* 155; *In R.* II.337.18). Other ancient commentators confirm this: Olympiodorus *Phaed.* 230.32 (Kroll) says that the dogs are irrational daemones; Psellus *PG* 122, 1140 b 12-14 interprets the dogs as daemones of matter, existing far from divine Zoë. Synesius, who drew on the Oracles, several times compares daemones to dogs; see *Hymn* 2 (4) 245: "a shameless chthonic dog, a daemon of the earth."

[2] 90 = Kr. 45 = Psellus *PG* 122, 1140 b 12-14; 91 = Kr. 45 = Olympiodorus, *Phaed.* 230.32 N; 156 = Kr. 60 = Proclus, *In R.* II.309.10-11. Fragment 135 was composed of three lines derived from separate sources by H.D. Saffrey, *Revue de Philologie*, 1969, pp. 64-5: l. 1 = Kr. 55 = Proclus *In Alc.* 18, 5 Westerink; l. 2 = Paris. gr. 1853, fol. 68 r., ed. Saffrey, *ibid.*; l. 3 = Kr. 55 = Proclus *In Alc.* 7 Westerink.

away from rites that would save them (fr. 135), and presenting an inescapable attraction for those too weak to live the proper life (fr. 156). Fragment 157 (Kr. 60 = Psellus *PG* 122, 1140 a 3) "Earthly beasts shall dwell in your vessel," ("Σὸν [δὲ γὰρ] αγγεῖον θῆρες χθονὸς οἰκήσουσιν") probably also refers to these daemonic dogs.[3] The nature of the Chaldean dogs is expressed succinctly by Synesius' description of them as "soul-devouring."[4]

A reader of these fragments who is familiar with Greek religion will be reminded of Hekate's close and virtually exclusive connection with the dog; given the prominence of Hekate in the Chaldean system, it is a natural assumption that any dogs mentioned in the Oracle fragments must be involved with her in some way.[5] The assumption is encouraged by the fact that "chariotress," the feminine version of the noun "charioteer," is used in fr. 91, indicating that a goddess, or at least the personification of feminine noun, controls these dogs.[6]

But the dogs' behavior does not conform to the nature of Chaldean Hekate as it has been revealed thus far; Hekate/Soul nurtures and helps the theurgist, sending him iynges and *symbola* to aid in his theurgic endeavors or manifesting herself to answer his questions. She is both the source and the temporary Elysium of his soul, and also the source of such desirable commodities as "virtue" and "life."[7] How can she be the mistress of these daemonic dogs?

From early times, Hekate was associated with phantasms and apparitions, marginal creatures who wandered with her, usually at night. Some merely frightened men. Others were imagined to bring bad dreams, illness or madness.[8] Although it is difficult to discern the exact identity of these creatures, it can be said that they are of a

---

[3] Psellus interprets these beasts to be hylic daemones, or human passions, and "vessel" to be the human body. On the activities of these daemones, see also discussion at Lewy, pp. 263 ff.; Geudtner, pp. 27-9.

[4] Hymn 1 (3) 96-7. Synesius drew both inspiration and material from the Chaldean Oracles; see Theiler. On this line in particular, see Des Places' edition of the Oracle fragments, p. 39.

[5] Des Places (commentary to fr. 91) and Lewy, pp. 269-71, both assume that Hekate is the chariotress of the dogs and the leader of the bad daemones.

[6] This fragment, which describes the dogs as "aery, earthly and watery," may bring to mind Hekate's domination over the three realms "heaven, earth and water" (Hes. *Th.* 413-14; Orph. *H.* 1.2), and thus seem to imply her connection with the dogs. But "heaven" in these descriptions of her domination is "οὐρανός," not "ἀήρ." In Chaldean doctrine and in antiquity in general there was a distinction between the two: "ἀήρ" was the region below the Moon, and thus a comparatively "polluted" realm; "οὐρανός" refers to the home of gods (fr. 216, which lists a variety of minor Chaldean entities, distinguishes between spirits of the ἀήρ and those of the οὐρανός). The description of the dogs in fr. 91 as "aery, earthly and watery indicates their hylic, sublunar nature, not their allegiance to Hekate, as Lewy, p. 271, and Des Places, commentary on fr. 91, assume.

[7] On Hekate as source of souls, see the Appendix; as source of virtue and life see Chapter IV, "Hekate as Ensouler and Enlivener." On Hekate as the final Elysium of souls, see Lewy, p. 213.

[8] E.g., E. *Ion* 1048, *Hel.* 569-70; Trag. Incert. fr. 375; Hipp. *Morb. Sacr.* 6.362; Plut. *De Super.* 166 a. See also Chapter III, "The Mistress of the Moon; Rohde, *Psyche* pp. 593-4.

generally daemonic nature, for like daemones they are liminal--neither man nor god--and like daemones they interact with man. At least by the time of the magical papyri and probably earlier, Hekate's "swarm" of daemonic creatures clearly is identified with the restless dead (ἄωροι and βιαιοθάνατοι), disembodied souls who are trapped between the upper world and Hades, who carry out the magicians' curses or desires.[9]

After philosophy became interested in daemones as mediating creatures, Hekate sometimes was portrayed as their mistress and as the mistress of disembodied souls, in great part by virtue of her own mediating nature (see Chapter III, "The Mistress of the Moon," *passim*). These daemones could be bad or good, intent either on carrying out the gods' wishes or on deceiving men. Later, some systems began to call the "good" daemones angels or iynges and retained the name "daemon" only for the bad.[10]

At the time that the Chaldean Oracles were composed, then, Hekate generally was associated with daemones, who were mediators, but who could be good or bad. These were imagined to dwell between heaven and earth in the sublunar region. But she also continued to be associated with bad, chthonic daemones or apparitions, who emerged from the infernal regions to terrify and harm men. In fact, in other contexts, such as the magical papyri and Graeco-Roman poetry, this side of her personality had grown ever more prominent.

In adopting Hekate as its Cosmic Soul, a celestial entity removed from the turmoil and pollution of Earth, the Chaldean system had to rid her of undesirable, threatening traits, including her role as mistress of the bad daemones. As it happened, Middle Platonic philosophy conveniently provided the means to do this. Some Platonists posited a double Soul, the upper half of which remained secluded from the Sensible World and the lower half of which came into contact with men and the hylic sphere;[11] justification for this could be found in certain remarks in Plato.[12] Through the efforts of this irrational Soul, the sublunar physical world operated. At

---

[9]E.g., *PGM* IV.2708-84, a love spell of attraction, calls on Hekate, her fire-breathing phantoms and the ἄωροι, particularly the heroes who have passed away without wives and children "yearning in their hearts."

[10]It is a matter of debate whether the Chaldean system included "good" as well as "bad" daemones. See, most recently, Geudtner, pp. 56 ff., for a summary of the evidence and arguments.

[11]Discussions of the concept of the irrational, disorderly or lower Soul in specific Platonists can be found in Dillon and Wallis: Plutarch, pp. 204-5, Dillon; Albinus, pp. 206, 284, Dillon; Gnosticism, p. 387, Dillon; Atticus, p. 254, Dillon; Numenius p. 375, Dillon; Plotinus, pp. 51-2, Wallis.

[12]*Lg.* X, 896 d-898 d (potential for disorderly of "evil" Soul); *Tim.* 34 c 5 (The Soul as the mistress and mover of the Cosmic Body).

least as early as Plotinus, possibly earlier, this lower part of Soul was identified with Aristotle's Physis.[13]

The Chaldean system had a Physis, too; her character agrees with that of the Platonic irrational Soul. Fragment 70 (Kr. 36 = Damascius II.157.18-20) says:

> Tireless Physis rules the cosmoi and the works,
> so that the sky might run, dragging out its eternal course,
> and the rapid sun might go, as usual, around its center.

> Ἄρχει γὰρ φύσις ἀκαμάτη κόσμων τε καὶ ἔργων,
> οὐρανὸς ὄφρα θέῃ δρόμον ἀΐδιον κατασύρων,
> καὶ ταχὺς ἥλιος περὶ κέντρον ὅπως ἐθὰς ἔλθῃ.

Like the Platonic Irrational Soul, the Chaldean Physis rules the "cosmoi," (the planets) and the "works," (the operations of the physical universe).

Specific admonitions against becoming involved with Physis are directed towards the theurgist. Fragments 101 (Kr. 49 = Psellus *PG* 122, 1136 c 12) and 102 (Kr. 49 = Proc. *Theol. Plat.* 317.29) say:

> Do not invoke the self-manifesting image of Physis!

> ...μὴ φύσεως καλέσῃς αὐτοπτον ἄγαλμα.

> Do not look at Physis! For her name is like Fate.

> Μὴ φύσιν ἐμβλέψῃς· εἱμαρμένον οὔνομα τῆσδε.

The first fragment instructs him not to solicit an epiphany of Physis; the second tells him not to look at Physis should she appear anyway.[14] The remark "her name is like Fate (εἱμαρμένον)" refers to the Chaldean belief that to escape the common Fate of man and raise his soul towards the Father the theurgist must subjugate the passions and appetites that Physis excites.

If the Platonic Irrational Soul is the lower half of the Cosmic Soul, then is not Chaldean Physis really Hekate/Soul? Lewy, who first proposed an equation of the

---

[13] On Plotinus' Physis and its antecedents, see Wallis' discussion of Plotinus, esp. pp. 51-2. See also the discussion of Physis in Lewy, pp. 355-7; he also suggests a connection between the Chaldean Hekate and Εἱμαρμένη, "Fate."

[14] Proclus (*In R.* II.133.15-17) says that the ἄγαλμα of Physis is the Moon itself; Lewy, pp. 271 ff., suggests that both these Oracles reflect the old precaution of turning away while sacrificing to Hekate. Such an explanation is not necessary; the prohibition against invoking Physis is based on her own character; she, and the daemones who accompany her, will give deceptive, unreliable information. Lewy also suggests that the admonition against looking at or invoking Physis refers to a fear of looking at the face on Moon. This suggestion can be rejected for the same reason as the first.

two, regards "Hekate" and "Physis" as little more than alternative names for a single divinity (pp. 95-7; 357 ff.).[15]

But the relationship between the two is more subtle than one of outright equation. Lewy uses fr. 54 to prove that Hekate and Physis are identical (Kr. 29; see ancient citations in n. 19):

Boundless Physis is suspended from[16] the back of the goddess.

Νώτοις δ' ἀμφὶ θεᾶς φύσις ἄπλετος ἠώρηται.

Lewy correctly assumes that "the goddess" refers to Hekate.[17] The fragment does not equate her with Physis, however; it makes them separate entities, one of whom hangs from--that is, is dependent upon--the other.[18] According to the ancient commentators who discussed fr. 54,[19] Physis was closely related to yet distinct from Hekate/Soul, who was her "source." She performed such tasks as guiding the heavenly bodies, which would have polluted Soul by bringing her directly into association with the movements and physical operations of the Sensible World.

The Chaldean system had taken Platonism's idea of a divided Soul one step further: it detached the irrational portion of the Soul from Soul itself and gave it an existence and duties of its own. This is proven not only by the descriptions of Physis emerging from or hanging from Hekate, but also by the indication that she could be invoked in her own right, under her own name, as any other god could (fr. 101). Moreover, Physis' epiphany is distinguished from that of Hekate by the fact that the theurgist is advised to avoid it (frs. 101, 102); as the last section showed, Hekate's epiphany was sought by the theurgist.[20]

---

[15]Geudtner, pp. 56-63, also equates Hekate and Physis.

[16]The fragment as it appears in Proc. *In Prm.* 821.7 would be translated "*around* the back of the goddess..." But the "ἀμφί" seems to have been understood as "from" rather than "around," for the other ancient commentators of the Oracle omit the "ἀμφί" and use the verb "ἀπαιωρεῖσθαι" rather than "αἰωρεῖσθαι."

[17]The ancient commentators' remarks on this fragment clearly show that Hekate was meant (see n. 19). Kroll and Des Places also understand "the goddess" to refer to Hekate.

[18]Des Places, p. 81 n. 2, and Lewy, p. 90, suggest that Physis here is to be imagined as the Moon, "Le séjour d'Hécate considérée comme 'nature'." This is possible--the Moon itself, as a portion of the physical world could represent Physis--Hekate's more hylic subordinate.

[19]Proclus (*In R.* II.150.21; *In T.* I.11.19 ff.) interprets the fragment to mean that "the life-giving goddess" (i.e. Hekate) was the source of Physis. At *In T.* III.271.2 ff., referring to the fragment, he explains that a noetic form of Physis exists within the "life-giving goddess," emerges from her and is suspended to guide the hylic world, assimilating it as far as possible to the noetic one. Damascius (II.157.15) says that Physis, who hangs from "the Great Hekate," is the implementer of all motion within the hylic sphere. In addition to these passages, the fragment, or allusions to it, can be found at Psellus *Hypostasis* 74, 13; Proc. *In T.* I.11.19, III.271.11 and *In R.* II.93.28-9; and Dam. II.235.15.

[20]It has been noted previously that the Oracles' Neoplatonic commentators often endowed the characteristics or roles of an entity, particularly Hekate, with separate existences of their own.

This Physis was not so much evil as she was simply hylic, involved with the functioning of the material world. But any system such as the Chaldean that preached the denial of the material as a means to salvation[21] could not help but find her a dangerously disruptive goddess. The world that Physis ruled, and everything in it, were obstacles that the soul must overcome; temptations were everywhere.

It was characteristic of the Chaldean system to personify concepts or intangible qualities, making them into independent entities;[22] it has been shown that Physis--previously the lower half of the Cosmic Soul--became a goddess, a sort of chthonic Hekate. The temptations presented by Physis and the hylic world in general deceived and harmed the souls of the theurgists in the same way as the bad, chthonic daemones or apparitions that traditionally were said to be under Hekate's control tortured the ordinary man. These hylic temptations were personified, too, and identified with the chthonic daemones who formerly followed Hekate. Ancient commentators of the Oracles state that Physis was imagined to be the mother and leader of deceptive, earthly daemones,[23] and fr. 88 (Kr. 44 = Psellus *PG* 122, 1137 a 1-2) says:

> Physis persuades us to believe that the daemones are pure,
> and that the products of evil matter are propitious and good.

Instead of being Soul itself for example, Hekate sometimes was described as the source of Soul. But whereas Soul and Hekate genuinely are one and the same in the Chaldean system, Physis seems to have had a separate existence from the start: 1) Whereas there are direct statements of Hekate's and Soul's equation (e.g., Porph *ap*. Aug. *Serm*. 241.6-7), there are none for Hekate and Physis--Physis always is presented as a lesser entity dependent upon or emerging from Hekate. 2) In the Oracle fragments, Soul speaks in the first person (e.g., fr. 53), which implies her identity with Hekate, who often delivers Oracles in the first person and regularly is the oracular goddess in the Chaldean system; Physis never speaks and always is referred to in the third person (this accords with the fact that the theurgist is told not to invoke Physis). 3) The Middle Platonic concept of Physis, from which the Chaldean concept developed, purposely makes Physis an entity separate from Soul and any deity identified with Soul; if Hekate is Soul, then Physis must be understood as subordinate to her as well as to Soul.

[21]E.g., "Do not hasten towards the Cosmos that hates light," says fr. 134, "the torrent of matter, where there is murder, insurrection, harsh winds, parching sickness, putrifications and works in a state of flux, for it is necessary for him who seeks the love of the Father to flee these things." Cf. frs. 163, 172, 180, 213, 217 for further examples of the Chaldean belief in the evil of the hylic world. See also discussion at Lewy, pp. 304 ff., Geudtner, pp. 11-12.

[22]For example, the Father's Intellect and Power are represented as existing separately from him.

[23]Psellus *PG* 122, 1137 a 1-10 says that the epiphany of Physis is preceded by daemones; *Hypostasis* 75, 25 says that the evil daemones "turn themselves towards Physis;" Synesius *Hymn* 5 (2) 52-3 says Physis gives birth to the race of daemones. See also Cremer's discussion, pp. 78 ff., of the hylic sphere as the natural home of bad daemones.

[ἡ φύσις] πείθει πιστεύειν εἶναι τοὺς δαίμονας ἁγνούς,
καὶ τὰ κακῆς ὕλης βλαστήματα χρηστὰ καὶ ἐσθλά.

It was noted above that the "soul-devouring" Chaldean dogs represented daemones. Their description and the methods by which they destroy the theurgist make it likely that they are to be equated with these daemones that Physis controlled. The dogs are earthly, that is, of the hylic world, like Physis. Like her, they lead the theurgist astray; through the hylic temptations that Physis produces they draw his soul away from the purifications and rites that would save it. Moreover, "Physis," the personification of a feminine noun, could be the "chariotress" of fr. 91, who controls the daemonic dogs; the three realms in which these dogs dwell--the aer, the water and the earth--all fall in Physis' sublunar sphere.

That Physis' daemones were called "dogs" should not be surprising. The Chaldean system regularly validated its philosophical or theurgical entities by equating with them creatures familiar from traditional religion and magic. The iynx, a cosmic messenger and philosophical concept, received its name from a magical tool commonly used from the archaic period onwards; the Cosmic Soul's equation with Hekate is itself due in part to this practice. Dogs usually were associated with the darker, more frightening side of Hekate, particularly in post-classical antiquity--Apollonius of Rhodes (III.1211 ff.) describes them barking shrilly as a horrifying, snakey-haired Hekate emerges from the Earth; Lycophron's Cassandra tells how her mother, Hecuba, will terrify mortals with her nocturnal baying once she joins Hekate's dogs (l. 1175 ff.); Horace describes the goddess' *infernae canes* as roaming abroad when Canidia performs her ghoulish magic (*Sat.* I.8.33) and in Vergil (*A.* VI.257; cf. IV.609) shadowy, howling hounds precede Hekate's arrival. Even when not connected with Hekate, in Greek and Roman thought dogs generally are viewed as disreputable,[24] shameless--even daemonic[25]--creatures. Identifying the hylic daemones with Hekate's dogs vividly expresses their "soul-devouring" nature and also validates them through the use of traditional religious beliefs.

In the Chaldean system, Physis was the leader and the source of daemones and daemonic dogs--nowhere in the Oracles or their commentators are these entities connected with Hekate. The Chaldean system divided the traditional Hekate;

---

[24] Glances at the LSJ entry "κυνώδης" and the entry for "*canis* " in Lewis and Short suffice to show this; the Greek word is used to mean despicable, shameless, currish and ravenous, for example; the Latin to mean a vile or shameless person. And of course, Diogenes "The Cynic" earned his title "'Ο κύων" through his shamelessness. Lewy notes, p. 271 n. 41, that the adjective "ἀναιδής," used in fr. 135, regularly is used to describe dogs (he does not, however, cite examples). See also Plut. *Quaest. Rom.* 111, 290 a, and N.J. Zaganiaris, "Sacrifices de chiens dans l'antiquite classique," *Platon* XXVII (1975) 322-329.

[25] Cf. Clytemnestra's description to Orestes of the Erinyes ("your mother's protectors") as "malignant dogs" at A. *Ch.* 924 and the manifestation of a plague-demon as a rabid dog at Philostr. *VA* 4.10.

everything within her that was beneficial to man became Hekate/Soul; all that threatened him or retained his soul in the hylic world became Physis and her dogs.

The Chaldean division of the traditional goddess into "Hekate" and "Physis" was reflected in other contemporary or subsequent religious thought. This subject cannot be studied in depth here, but one example can be examined briefly: a fragment from Porphyry's *Philosophy from Oracles* (*ap.* Eus. *PE* IV.23, 175, c-d = 151 Wolff).

Porphyry cites this oracle during his discussion of the bad daemones and their rulers, who he says are Sarapis and Hekate. Hekate herself delivers it:

> I come, a virgin of varied forms, wandering through the heavens,
> bull-faced, three-headed, ruthless, with golden arrows;
> chaste Phoebe bringing light to mortals, Eileithyia;
> bearing the three *synthemata* of a triple nature.
> In the aether I appear in fiery forms
> and in the aer I sit in a silver chariot;
> Earth reins in my black brood of puppies.

> Ἥδ' ἐγώ εἰμι κόρη πολυφάσματος, οὐρανόφοιτος,
> ταυρῶπις, τρικάρηνος, ἀπηνής, χρυσοβέλεμνος,
> Φοίβη ἀπειρολεχής, φαεσίμβροτος Εἰλείθυια,
> τριστοίχου φύσεως συνθήματα τρισσὰ φέρουσα·26
> αἰθέρι μὲν πυρόεσσιν ἐειδομένη εἰδώλοις,
> ἠέρα δ' ἀργεννοῖσι τροχάσμασιν ἀμφικάθημαι·
> γαῖα δ' ἐμῶν σκυλάκων δνοφερὸν γένος ἡνιοχεύει.

The oracle portrays a Hekate who has been syncretized with several other deities--Phoebe (Selene), Eileithyia and perhaps Artemis.[27] But it also separates celestial Hekate from the darker side of her traditional nature. Hekate says that she herself wanders through the heavens, appearing in fiery, aetherial forms, or flies through the aer in a silvery chariot (the Moon); it is the Earth, on the other hand, who restrains and guides the dogs normally associated with her.

Wolff, p. 152, suggested that Porphyry artificially created this oracle out of Greek philosophical doctrines. If this is correct, then Porphyry reflects some system very much like that of the Chaldeans, in which an effort was made to dichotomize Hekate's character, freeing the celestial, helpful goddess from the maleficent, earthly dog-daemones.

---

[26] It is grammatically possible that this line means "bearing the *synthemata* of triple Physis," referring to the goddess. In view of the fact that the previous lines name three different goddesses, and the fact that Physis herself is nowhere called "triple," it seems more likely that "physis" is to be understood here as it is translated above.

[27] "With golden arrows," "χρυσοβέλεμνος," would seem to describe Artemis, as would "chaste," "ἀπειρολεχής," which is used to describe her at Ar. *Thesm.* 119.

It is also possible, however, that Porphyry did not compose this oracle himself. The stated goal of his *Philosophy from Oracles* was to collect and discuss *older* oracles; if this oracle is in fact genuine, then it reflects a system, established at some time prior to Porphyry, in which Hekate's nature had been divided just as it was by the Chaldean system. Whatever the oracle's source, it attests to an attempt by someone to free Hekate from her less desirable traits by at least the late third century.

The concept of Physis--an irrational Cosmic Soul--that the Chaldean system had borrowed from Platonism turned out to be a very convenient one to have on hand. Having adopted Hekate as its saviour goddess and emphasized the positive and transmissive or mediating aspects of her traditional personality, the Chaldean system was left to account for her less desirable qualities. One of these, ironically, had grown from the very role of mediator that made Hekate attractive in the first place. Hekate long had been the queen of daemones--mediating entities--but some of these daemones had become increasingly dangerous. Physis stood ready; as the lower half of the Soul and thus closely tied to Hekate, she could take charge of the deceitful, destructive daemones whose power, in any case, was imagined to stem from the hylic world that Physis permeated. Hekate herself retained control of the "good" daemones or mediators--the angels, the iynges and the *symbola/synthemata* that aided men seeking salvation. In effect, the traditional Hekate became two goddesses in the Chaldean system--the celestial Hekate/Soul and the earthly Physis.

Chapter X
Hekate and Magic

The preceding chapters have examined how Hekate interacted with the Chaldean theurgist. Two points can be made: 1) Chaldean Hekate was willing to aid men. She was celestial and beneficent rather than chthonic and threatening, exhibiting none of the horrific aspects that she sometimes presented in the magical papyri and late literature. 2) Her ability to aid men found its basis in the mediating or transmissive aspect of her personality. The cosmological side of this aspect was examined in Part I; it resurfaced in Part II in more practical guises: Hekate received and then sent forth the iynges, who were equated with the Ideas and the *symbola*. These iynges were themselves theurgically mediating entities, enabling men's prayers or requests to cross the cosmic boundary and thus enabling men to form bonds with the divine world. As an oracular goddess, appearing to men in order to transmit information, Hekate taught theurgists how to make use of the *symbola* and other magical tools or skills through which they could reach beyond the limits of the physical world.

Chaldean Hekate helped the theurgist by means of her mediating or transmissive nature. In the context of theurgy, this better is expressed by saying that Hekate represented cosmic sympathy and controlled sympathetic processes, for sympathy was the theurgist's practical means of overcoming the gulf separating man and god.[1] The *symbola* that Hekate revealed to men worked by means of sympathy; they were the hylic emblems of the celestial powers the theurgist sought to reach. The closely related iynges, which sprang from and depended on Hekate, helped the theurgist to "attune" himself sympathetically to the celestial realm; the sounds and movements that they gave forth represented the cosmic harmony or music of the spheres.

Hekate/Soul's control of cosmic sympathy and its representative entities makes sense. Sympathetic magic in general is based on the premise that by manipulating one object, another, distant object or person will be affected; those that are divided are affected as one, those that are separated become linked. In reference to theurgy and Neoplatonic philosophy,[2] the term "sympathetic magic" more specifically applies to the belief that even the divine powers could be affected sympathetically by manipulation of the proper hylic objects. Everything in the divine realm had its *symbolon* in the earthly realm; the hylic world was a material echo of

---

[1]Psellus, *PG* 122, 1153 a, specifically attributes a belief in sympathy to the Chaldeans. Cf. also Syn. *de Insom.* 132 a.

[2]On sympathy in Neoplatonism, see Wallis, p. 107.

the noetic world.[3] One of the things that made this cosmic sympathy possible was Soul, who stood between yet connected macrocosm and microcosm, holding together the diverse parts of the Cosmos.[4] Soul's control of sympathy agreed with Soul's other traits; for example, she received and then transmitted the Ideas, a process that replicated noetic material in the hylic sphere.

If Soul's cooperation was necessary for the success of sympathetic magic, then logically, Chaldean Hekate's role as a theurgist's goddess, controlling cosmic sympathy, could have arisen from her identity with Soul. Any hypothesis that attempts to account for Hekate's role as a theurgist's goddess, however, must take into consideration the earlier aspects of her role as the patroness of magicians and witches. What is the nature of her classical and Hellenistic connections with magic, and how does it fit in with what now is known of her duties in Chaldean theurgy?

Hekate's role as a witch's goddess must be approached through study of her role as the mistress of daemones, about which something already has been said.[5] It was argued that she became associated with daemones and daemonic creatures because they were liminal entities, wandering between worlds or between states of existence. Rohde[6] long ago noted that

> Whenever a soul is entering into partnership with a body--at birth or in childbed--[Hekate] is at hand; where a soul is separating from a body, in burials of the dead, she is there.

She was a birth goddess[7] and she was a death goddess,[8] accompanying souls on their two greatest journeys. Those souls who did not succeed in making the trans-

---

[3]For the philosophical development of this theory, see Wallis, pp. 123 ff., who notes Iamblichus' doctrine that "everything was in everything, but in each thing appropriately to its nature."

[4]For discussion of Soul and sympathy, see also Smith, p. 123; Lewy, pp. 437 and 157. In the latter passage, Lewy discusses the Chaldean interest in the governance and cohesion of the world; he rightly argues that this preoccupation "is not due to love of knowledge for its own sake, but to the exigencies of magical world orientation. In the Chaldean system, the basic belief in the sympathy of all the powers of the world is bound up with the conception of a rational organization of the cosmos." Soul, of course, was largely responsible for that rational organization.

[5]See the section of Chapter III entitled "The Mistress of the Moon," and Chapter IX, "The Chaldean Daemon-dogs."

[6]*Psyche*, p. 297.

[7]For discussion of Hekate's role as a birth goddess, see Kraus, pp. 25 ff. and 86. Cf. her role as *kourotrophos* (e.g., Hes. *Th.* 450 and the Herodotean*Vit. Hom.* 410-420, where women are said to sacrifice to *"Kourotrophos"* at the crossroads) and Plut. *Super.* 170 B (= Sophr. fr. 2 in *Suppl. comic.* ed. J. Demiańczuk), which describes her as being present during childbirth.

[8]The same fragment of Sophron listed above as portraying her as a goddess concerned with birth connects her with death: she rushes towards those who carry the corpse towards burial--perhaps to receive the soul as it passes from the body?

ition into or out of a body, however, were eternally under her control, forced to wander with her.[9]

Many magical acts depended on these wandering souls or daemones. For example, from the fifth century onwards (but especially in the Hellenistic age), curse tablets were placed in graves and other places where souls would be expected to linger.[10] In particular, they were placed in the graves of children, whose souls, as ἄωροι, would be expected to linger between life and death longer than normal. The soul was expected to carry the curse to the chthonic daemones or deities who would enforce it.[11] In later times, the magical papyri give examples of love spells, as well as curses, that the ἄωροι or βιαιοθάνατοι were expected either to fulfill or to carry to others for fulfillment (the distinction is not clear).[12] The papyri also indicate that the first action of the magician in any operation was to obtain the help of a daemon or soul; apparently they aided in the fulfillment of almost all magical acts.[13]

Disembodied souls or daemones were the magician's tools; their ability to travel between worlds enabled them to make good his requests, their unsettled status put them at his mercy.[14] But ultimately they were still under the control of Hekate. To obtain a soul or daemon's help--to make magic work--required her cooperation. The frequent presence on the curse tablets of her name, with that of Hermes Psychopompos, reflects her role as escorter of the soul that the magician commandeered.[15]

---

[9] On the idea that those who died early were condemned to wander eternally with Hekate, see Rohde's discussion of the host of Hekate (Appendix VII) and Cumont's discussion in *The Afterlife in Roman Paganism*, Chapter V ("Untimely Death"). See also Johnston, "Crossroads."

[10] The most complete collection of these curse tablets remains A. Audollent, *Defixionum Tabellae* (Frankfurt 1904). See also the important article by David Jordan supplementing Audollent's collection, "A Survey of Greek Defixiones Not Included in the Special Corpora," *GRBS* 26 (1985) 151-197. Further discussion in Jordan, "Defixiones from a Well Near the Southwest Corner of the Athenian Agora," *Hesperia* 54 no. 3 (1985) 205-255; Jordan, "Two Inscribed Lead tablets from a Well in the Athenian Kerameikos," *AThMitt* 95 (1980) 225-39; Jordan, "CIL VIII 19525(B).2QPVVLVA = q(uem) p(eperit) vulva" *Philologus* 120 (1976) 127-32; K. Preisendanz "Fluchtafel (Defixio)" *RAC* 8 (1969) 1-24; and the sources listed in n. 30 of Chapter VIII.

[11] On this topic see the works listed in the previous note and the older discussions at Cumont, pp. 134 ff.; Rohde, p. 594. Garland, pp. 6 ff., suggests "The practice of placing in cemetaries, graves, pits or rivers the small folded lead plaques known as *katadesmoi* (curse tablets) is not an indication that the dead themselves possessed awful powers, but rather that they were useful deliverers to chthonic powers."

[12] E.g., *PGM* IV.1872-1927; 1930-2005; 2006-2125; 2708-84 (Hekate also is invoked in this last one).

[13] E.g., *PGM* I.1-42; 42-195; 247-62; XII.14-95 (the last tells the magician how to obtain Eros himself as an assistant daemon).

[14] Betz (p. xlvii) has described the magician as, among other things, a "power and communications expert" and an "agent of worried, troubled and worrisome souls;" these phrases describe accurately the interactions between magician and daemon or soul. Garland, pp. 7 ff., discusses the defenselessness of the dead against manipulation.

[15] See also Johnston, "Crossroads."

It was Hekate's role as leader of the daemones and disembodied souls that led to her connection with witchcraft.[16] Later, the image of Hekate leading bands of exiled souls was joined by the portrait of her opening the gates of the Underworld to let forth the souls trapped within it; this portrait became increasingly popular in Hellenistic and Roman literature, in part, undoubtedly, because of its potential sensationalism. Although these souls from Hades were not marginal creatures as the exiled souls of ἄωροι or βιαιοθάνατοι were, Hekate's role as their leader nonetheless was an expression of her control over the entrances and exits to death, as a few examples will show. At Ovid *Met.* VII.234, it is by Hekate and Youth that Medea calls forth from Hades chthonic *numina* to aid in Aeson's rejuvenation; the imprecation of Youth can be explained in this case by the nature of Medea's task; Hekate is called on because she is the goddess who releases the required *numina*. The seer in Seneca's *Oedipus* (ll. 568 ff.), intent on calling up shades, declares that he has succeeded as soon as he hears Hekate's dogs bark: "Blind Chaos is opening, Dis' inhabitants are given a path to the upper world!" he cries. The advent of the goddess herself opens the desired passageway--she leads the way. Conversely, Hekate can prevent the emergence of Hades' inhabitants or draw them back: Apuleius (*Meta.* XI.2) remarks that "three-faced Proserpina," i.e., Hekate, has the power to keep apparitions under the closures of the Earth and Lucian (*Philops.* 15) describes apparitions plunging back into the Earth behind Hekate as she descends. Her power to facilitate access into and out of Hades also is expressed at *Philops.* 22, where Lucian describes the earth splitting open at Hekate's command to reveal all of Hades and its inhabitants. Finally, the goddess who allowed souls to exit from the Underworld naturally also controlled the entrance of men into the Underworld: Vergil's Sibyl (*A.* VI.258), seeking access to Hades, calls on and sacrifices to Hekate, "mighty in Heaven and Hell" first of all before Persephone, Night and Earth, for it is she who must open the passageway; as the earth splits open, dogs bark and the goddess is felt to be near. Lucan's Erictho, seeking to reanimate a corpse, stands in a cave described as between the upper and lower worlds and exalts Hekate as the goddess who enables her to communicate with the dead (*Bel. Civ.* VI.642 ff.)

Many of the literary expressions of Hekate's involvement with magic, then, emphasize her custodianship over the gates of Hades and thereby her control over the apparitions or souls who ascend to do the magician's bidding. These, in combination with the literary references cited earlier for Hekate's control of wandering spirits, indicate that her ability to aid the magician or witch was based in her control of the passage of souls. The magical papyri also suggest that Hekate's aid to the magician

---

[16]Similarly, she became a goddess who could cause or cure madness and other afflictions, because daemones were imagined to bring the afflictions. See, for example, E. *Hipp.* 142, Arist. *Vesp.* 122, Plut. *De Super.* 166 A and discussion in Nilsson, *GGR* I.3 799.

was based in her domination over wandering souls or daemones released from Hades; she often is invoked with them.[17]

Before the emergence of theurgy, magicians sought the help of such chthonic daemones and disembodied souls; magic was largely a chthonic art. Theurgy, however, placed the power the magician sought in the celestial realm;[18] the daemones or angels who helped the theurgist now were imagined to dwell in the air between the Earth and the Moon. If Hekate was to aid the theurgist, she must control these celestial mediators rather than the chthonic ones, opening not the gate to Hades but the gate to the divine realm. Some of the citations above showed that in popular thought and literature, she became ever more horrific; this was in part due to the increasingly horrific and threatening character of the daemones she led. In theurgy and philosophy, however, as celestial mediators and mediation became ever more important to man's spiritual self-improvement and salvation, Hekate became increasingly beneficent, ever more the savior. By the time of Proclus, it was possible to portray her as the goddess who protected men from sickness, who led the human soul upwards after cleansing it in mysteries and showing it the "divine path," and who brought the worshipper to "safe anchorage in the harbour of devotion."[19]

To sum up: two factors combined to make Hekate the goddess to whom the Chaldean theurgist turned for practical help. First, Hekate long had been depended upon for help in traditional magic. This responsibility began, as was shown, with her connection with daemones, who carried out the magician's wishes, and from her

---

[17]The best example of this is *PGM* IV.2708-84. Lines 2730-4 read: "Hekate, I call you with those who untimely passed away and with those heroes who have died without a wife, and children, hissing wildly, yearning in their hearts," (E.N. O'Neill's translation in Betz's edition). Other spells mention Hekate and ἄωροι together, implying her close connection with them.

[18]Betz, p. xlvii, discusses the growing fascination with the universe as a whole as a potential source of magical power, as opposed to the older reliance on the Underworld alone.

[19]Proclus, *Hymn to Hekate and Janus* (no. VI):

Χαῖρε, θεῶν μῆτερ, πολυώνυμε, καλλιγένεθλε·
χαῖρ', Ἑκάτη προθύραιε, μεγασθενές· ἀλλὰ καὶ αὐτὸς
χαῖρ', Ἴανε προπάτορ, Ζεῦ ἄφθιτε· χαῖρ', ὕπατε Ζεῦ·
τεύχετε δ' αἰγλήεσσαν ἐμοῦ βιότοιο πορείην
βριθομένην ἀγαθοῖσι, κακὰς δ' ἀπελαύνετε νούσους
ἐκ 'ρεθέων, ψυχὴν δὲ περὶ χθονὶ μαργαίνουσαν
ἕλκετ' ἐγερσινόοισι καθηραμένην τελετῇσι.
ναί, λίτομαι, δότε χεῖρα θεοφραδέας τε κελεύθους
δείξατέ μοι χατέοντι· φάος δ' ἐρίτιμον ἀθρήσω,
κυανέης ὅθεν ἐστὶ φυγεῖν κακότητα γενέθλης.
ναί, λίτομαι, δότε χεῖρα καὶ ὑμετέροισιν ἀήταις
ὅρμον ἐς εὐσεβίης με πελάσσετε κεκμηῶτα.
χαῖρε, θεῶν μῆτερ, πολυώνυμε, καλλιγένεθλε·
χαῖρ', Ἑκάτη προθύραιε, μεγασθενές· ἀλλὰ καὶ αὐτὸς
χαῖρ', Ἴανε προπάτορ, Ζεῦ ἄφθιτε· χαῖρ', ὕπατε Ζεῦ·

guardianship of exits and entrances into Hades, but developed to include guardianship over celestial daemones and celestial entrances and exits. Second, she was Soul: for the Chaldeans as for many Platonists, Soul was the medium through which cosmic sympathy worked, and it was on sympathy that the theurgist relied for the success of his magic. Both factors ultimately were due to her basic character as a mediating or transmissive deity. Neither factor can be called predominant with any certainty. Although Hekate's connection with traditional magic and daemones preceded her election to the role of Chaldean Soul, the cosmological importance of Soul in Platonism, and the importance, in turn, of cosmology in Chaldean theurgy together argue that Hekate's role as Soul was an equal contributor to the final result. In the end, the process by which Hekate became the Chaldean theurgist's goddess, like the processes by which many religious concepts or doctrines develop, cannot be described or traced perfectly. The best that can be done is to unravel and study as many of the threads that make up the completed tapestry as possible. Two of the most important threads have been unraveled here, but there were undoubtedly others.[20]

---

[20]The increasing prominence of Isis as both a savior goddess and a magician's goddess during the second century suggests itself as a influence on Hekate's development, for example.

Summary

The Chaldean Oracles emerged during an age when religion and philosophy took increasing notice of one another; the holy man took up anew the tenets of Plato and Pythagoras, the philosopher looked for justification of his cosmologies in traditional religion. The soteriological methods that can be glimpsed in the Oracles and in the comments of their exegetes combined the best of both religion and philosophy, as did Hekate/Soul, the Chaldean deity most directly involved with man's salvation. The preceding chapters elucidated the reasons that Hekate and Soul --a traditional Graeco-Roman goddess and a Platonic entity--became identified with one another. They also examined the specific ways in which the resultant deity aided the theurgist.

The two most important factors that lay behind the identification of Hekate and Soul both sprang ultimately from their roles as intermediary and transmissive entities. The diverse ways in which Hekate's intermediary nature was expressed throughout antiquity were discussed in Part I. Extant versions of the rape of Persephone, for example, suggest that in a lost version she annually escorted Persephone across the boundary between the Underworld and the world of the living; later literature portrayed her as controlling the passage of disembodied souls or living men across that same boundary. Beginning in classical times, she held such names and titles as "Ἐνοδία" and "τριοδῖτις," indicating her guiding presence at liminal points such as the crossroads and the door. In late classical and Hellenistic times, she became linked with the Moon, itself mediator between the mortal and divine spheres, and with the daemones, mediators between gods and men.

The Soul was the cosmic intermediary, transmitter and liminal marker of the Platonic system. Plato had placed Soul on the border between the Sensible and Intelligible Worlds and made it the entity through which life was transmitted from the divine into the mortal sphere. Later Platonism made it the conduit through which other things as well as life, including the Ideas and their magical counterparts the iynges/*symbola*, passed from one realm to the other. Later Platonism also developed its role as a mediator by positioning it between opposites, such as "Time" and "Eternity," that represented the mortal and divine spheres that Soul originally was imagined to connect.

Soul and Hekate were both entities who guided or transmitted material--especially disembodied souls--from one realm to another. But this similarity of function alone would not have been enough to prompt the identification, of course. Chapter V discussed a tendency in the second century to sanction philosophical ideas by identifying them with religious "truths." The Chaldean Oracles were influenced by this movement; the development of the Chaldean iynx from a combination of magician's tool and Platonic daemon is one example of the way in which the Chaldean system melded philosophy and religion. When the originators of the Chaldean system sought a deity with whom they could identify Soul, a transmissive entity crucial to their theurgic practices and to the cohesion of their physical cosmos, it was natural that they should elect Hekate, long a transmissive or guiding deity herself and, as mistress of the Moon, specifically a guide between the terrestrial and celestial worlds.

The second factor contributing to the identification was the important role that both Hekate and Soul played in magic or theurgy. This factor, too, can be traced back in each case to the intermediary or transmissive role that the deity played. Hekate became the patroness of magicians for several reasons that reflect her control of liminal situations.[1] For instance, because Hekate was present whenever souls crossed the boundaries between life and death--at birth and at burial--she naturally took charge of the disembodied souls that lingered between life and death, unable to complete the transition between states of existence. It was just such souls that the magician or witch manipulated to bring about the completion of their spells. Her association with these restless souls was encouraged by her role as the goddess of the crossroads, the place where such souls lingered; she could protect the wayfarer against them, but also release them to do the magician's bidding. Hekate's control over passage of liminal points also included opening and shutting the gates of Hades; she could allow souls to ascend when invoked or permit magicians and seers to descend. In short, without Hekate to help him bridge the gaps between heaven and earth or earth and the underworld, the magician was powerless.

Theurgy concentrated on finding ways to manipulate the natural sympathy that existed between the divine and human worlds. The Cosmic Soul was important in the establishment of sympathy because it stood between the two worlds, dividing yet unifying them. Any sympathetic link forged between the worlds required the participation of Soul; any material or communication that passed in either direction was transmitted by Soul. Among the materials that passed through Soul were the Platonic Ideas, identified in the Chaldean system with the theurgically important iynges/*symbola* and deemed essential to the successful utilization of cosmic sympathy. These iynges/*symbola* were themselves mediating links, allowing the man who correctly used them to control the celestial powers. The mediating, transmissive status of Soul and her regulation of the Ideas, then, made her an entity of great importance to the Chaldean theurgist.

Chaldean Hekate/Soul was a beneficent goddess, willing and able to aid the theurgist. Some of the specific ways in which she did so were examined in Part II.

---

[1]For further details, see Chapter III, "The Mistress of the Moon," Chapter X and Johnston, "Crossroads."

SUMMARY

The mediating iynx-daemones, that travelled between the celestial and terrestrial realms, sprang from and were under the control of Hekate/Soul. The corresponding iynx-top, whose whirling and sounds represented and strengthened the cosmic sympathy upon which the theurgist depended, was dedicated to Hekate. As mistress of these iynges, Hekate/Soul helped the theurgist utilize cosmic sympathy and thus prepare for psychic ascension.

Hekate/Soul appeared to and instructed the theurgist who knew how to invoke her properly. She might tell him about the universe, its entities and their interrelationships. Such basic information was important, for understanding the construction and operation of the cosmos was a prerequisite to putting its forces to work. On the other hand, she might give him information of a more immediately practical type--telling him how to create and animate a telestic statue, for example. Information of both types was essential to the soteriological process. Hekate's physical position between the mortal and divine worlds made her a natural teacher of the theurgist; her role as teacher made her a savior goddess.

Chapters VII and VIII explored the ways in which Hekate/Soul aided the theurgist. Chapter IX, "The Chaldean Daemon-dogs," further illustrated the generally beneficent character of Chaldean Hekate/Soul by showing how the Chaldean system transferred the less desirable traits of the traditional Hekate onto Physis, a goddess imagined to "hang suspended" in a position subordinate to Hekate/Soul herself. Hekate/Soul didn't lead the daemon-dogs that dragged the theurgist's soul towards the temptations of the hylic world; Physis did. In effect, the Chaldean system dichotomized Hekate. Hekate herself retained control of "good" daemons or mediators (iynges/*symbola*) that aided men; this Hekate was identified with Soul.

The influence of the Chaldean Oracles on the religion, philosophy and mysticism of subsequent ages was immense. The Neoplatonists constantly quoted them in support of their own cosmological and soteriological doctrines. The Emperor Julian, who tried to revive paganism during the late Empire, was a student of Chaldean theurgy. Proclus, according to his biographer Marinus, considered the Chaldean Oracles and Plato's *Timaeus* the masterpieces of ancient literature, ahead of Homer, for example (*Procl.* 38). Elucidation of the Oracles and the beliefs that lay behind them, therefore, helps to elucidate the religious history of later paganism as a whole. Hekate was one of the very few traditional Greek deities that the system retained; she was its most accessible deity and the one that most immediately affected men's lives. Study of her roles in Chaldean theurgy significantly illuminates the way in which Chaldean theurgy worked. Moreover, Chaldean Hekate influenced the portraits of Hekate in subsequent magical, mystic or philosophical thought; a better understanding of Chaldean Hekate's nature, then, not only can shed significant light on the Chaldean system, but also on other, contemporaneous or later forms of magic, religion and philosophy.

Previously, scholars of the Oracles have been at a loss to explain Hekate's exaltation adequately, vaguely suggesting that it was due to her earlier role as a witches' goddess or to the extent to which she had been syncretized with other goddesses by the second century A.D. Certainly, both these factors contributed to Hekate's prominence in the Oracles. But only by closely analyzing Chaldean Hekate in the light of the goddess' intermediary and guiding roles throughout antiquity, as this study has shown, can her importance to the theurgist fully be understood and appreciated.

Appendix:
Evidence For Hekate's Equation With Soul

Although modern scholars of the Oracles are unanimous in equating Hekate with the Platonic Cosmic Soul,[1] none has presented thoroughly the evidence that supports making such an equation. This appendix will collect evidence for the equation taken from the Oracles themselves, from the Oracles' commentators and from authors approximately contemporaneous with the Oracles' composition.

The most significant evidence is that which portrays Hekate as the goddess who ensouls the universe and all in it.[2] Ensouling the universe is the role of the Cosmic Soul from her appearance in the *Timaeus* onwards, where she is represented as providing the entire universe with soul or life, two commodities that are understood as identical in Platonic thought.[3] *Timaeus* 36 e ff. states that Soul supplies "the All" with a "divine source of unending life for all time." *Timaeus* 38 e, more specifically, says that "ensouling chains" enabled the planets to become living creatures; the phrase "ensouling chains" refers to the statement at 36 e that Soul was woven throughout and tightly bound to the physical world. This same role of ensouling or enlivening regularly is given to Soul throughout Middle Platonism and in the Chaldean Oracles themselves; in fr. 53, Soul says that she "ensouls (ψυχόω) the All."

Hekate herself is portrayed as responsible for ensouling (ἐμψυχόω) all the parts of the universe in Oracle fr. 51:[4]

---

[1] See Kroll, pp. 27-29, who assumes either that Hekate and Soul are to be identified or, at the least, that Soul is to be understood as contained within Hekate; see also Kroll, p. 46, where he notes that Soul is within Hekate, and Kroll, p. 69, where he adduces Porphyry's equations of Hekate and Soul (to be examined below) as *comparanda* for the nature of Chaldean Hekate. Lewy identifies Soul and Hekate throughout his book; see particularly pp. 85-95 and 353-66. Des Places assumes the equation in his notes to several fragments (e.g., fr. 53) and explicitly identifies the two in his preface *"La Doctrine des 'Oracles',"* p. 13. Wallis, p. 106, identifies Chaldean Hekate with Soul. Dillon, pp. 394-95, expresses the relationship between the two as follows: "from Hecate is derived the World Soul (fr. 51). In a sense, Hecate herself may be viewed as the transcendent World Soul, while the entity which springs 'from her right flank' (*ibid.*) can be taken as Soul in its immanent aspect." Cremer, p. 100, Geudtner, p. 35, and Tardieu, p. 216, assume the equation. The most cautious expression of the equation is found in Dodds' review of Lewy ("New Light") p. 268: "...the Cosmic Soul...is somehow equated with Hecate." Dodds seems not to be doubting the equation itself but rather to be criticizing Lewy's inadequate explanation of it.

[2] I can find only one other deity or entity in philosophical or pseudo-philosophical literature who is given this role of providing soul to the Cosmos or "The All." Porphyry says that earlier philosophers identified the *anima mundi* with Hekate or Jove. For analysis of these equations and explanation of why "Jove" should be taken allegorically, see further pp. 161 ff. below.

[3] See Lewy, p. 356 n. 168, who gives some of the most important supporting citations for the equation of "life" and "soul" from Plato and the Platonists.

[4] See further pp. 62 ff. on this fragment.

> For all around the hollows of the cartilage of [Hekate's] right flank,
> The abundant liquid of the Primal Soul gushes unceasingly,
> Completely ensouling the light, the fire, the aether and the Cosmoi.
>
> Δεξιτερῆς μὲν γὰρ λαγόνος περὶ χήραμα χόνδρων
> πολλὴ ἄδην βλύζει ψυχῆς λιβὰς ἀρχιγενέθλου
> ἄρδην ἐμψυχοῦσα φάος πῦρ αἰθέρα κόσμους.

The fragment says that Hekate produces from within herself the substance that ensouls the light (the noetic sphere), the fire (the empyrean sphere), the aether and the cosmoi--in other words, All. Chaldean Hekate is Soul in its eternal, constant form; the liquid she provides is Soul in its active, emanated form, or as Lewy, p. 88, expresses it, "the potency of the Cosmic Soul."[5] The Oracles regularly portrayed concepts or cosmic substances as both personified entities and unpersonified essences in this way. For example, the Oracles speak of "Intelligence" both as an independent entity and as the essence of thinking (the "noetic essence") itself. Fragment 20[6] says that

> The Intellect does not exist far from the noetic essence and the noetic essence
> does not exist far from the Intellect.
>
> Οὐ γὰρ ἄνευ νόος ἐστι νοητοῦ, καὶ τὸ νοητὸν
> οὐ νοῦ χωρὶς ὑπάρχει.

and fr. 20 *bis* says

> [The Father], having within himself the ability to think, is the noetic essence.
>
> ...νοητόν, ἔχων τὸ νοοῦν ἐν ἑαυτῷ.

In the same way, one might say either that the Sun is light or that light flows from the Sun and express the same idea: the Sun is responsible for providing illumination. Putting the source of Primal Soul's liquid--her power to ensoul--in Hekate is the same as saying that Hekate is Soul; Chaldean Hekate, like Soul in the *Timaeus* and in Oracle fr. 53, ensouls All.[7]

---

[5] Compare the remark of Dillon, above, n. 1.

[6] Fragment 20 = Kr. 11 = Proc. *In T.* III.102.10-11; Dam. II.16.20-21; 57, 26-28. Fragment 20 *bis* = Dam. II.16.18 (not in Kroll).

[7] In one of the oracles from Porphyry's *Philosophy From Oracles* Hekate similarly brags that she can "ensoul even the highest world of all" (*ap.* Eus. *PE* V.7, 191 c = 122 Wolff). Although there is no doubt that Porphyry grew to know the Chaldean Oracles quite well at some point in his life (see the Introduction) the question of which specific oracles from *Philosophy from Oracles* are Chaldean in origin is still unresolved. J. Bidez, "Note sur les mystères néoplatoniciens" *Rev. Belg. de Phil. et. d'Hist.* 7 (1928) 1477 ff.) argued that Porphyry did not know the Oracles at the time he wrote this

Hekate and Soul both are said also to be the source of individual souls. The provision of individual souls first is described as a function of Soul in the *Philebus* (30 a ff.), where Socrates argues that if our bodies are to be understood as derived from the great Body of the cosmos, then logically, our souls could come from nowhere else but the Soul of the cosmos.[8] At about the time of the Oracles' composition, this idea began to re-emerge among Platonists. For example, Apuleius (*De Plat.* 9) describes Soul as the *fons* of individual souls, as well as the source of the universe's generative power.[9] An implication that first- and second-century Stoics also understood the Cosmic Soul to be the source of individual souls is found in Plotinus' apparent arguments against this belief (*Enn.* IV.3.2-7). (In contrast, some scholars of Plotinus also understand *him* to have held this opinion.[10]) Oracle fr. 44[11] alludes to this doctrine as well. Discussing the origin of the human soul, it says:

---

work. Des Places, however, following N. Terzaghi "Sul Commento di Niceforo Gregorio al ΠΕΡΙ ΕΝΥΠΝΙΩΝ di Synesio," *Studi italiani di filologia classica*, XII (1904) p. 191 ff., includes several of them among his *fragmenta dubia;* Lewy, p. 47 ff., argued for the Chaldean origin of more of them than Des Places does, including the one under consideration here. Kroll, p. 69, cited the oracle considered here because of the close analogy it offers to the Chaldean Oracles but did not suggest that it was Chaldean in origin. Dodds, in his review of Lewy's book ("New Light"), finds Lewy's arguments for accepting this specific oracle as Chaldean to be strong but ultimately unconvincing.

Even if a Chaldean origin for this oracle cannot be proven, the oracle nonetheless provides valuable evidence for Hekate's role as ensouler of the All at approximately the time of the Oracles' composition. The Oracles were composed during the second half of the second century, Porphyry wrote during the second half of the third century; his stated aim in the *Philosophy from Oracles* is to review and analyze *earlier* oracles. Moreover, it should be noted in support of using this oracle as evidence for equating Hekate and Soul that Eusebius himself cites it in order to elucidate Porphyry's own beliefs about Soul for his readers. "Perhaps," Eusebius says, immediately after quoting the oracle, "on this account is Soul three-fold and of three parts (τριμερής and τρίμορφος). Don't take these for my ideas, however, rather, these are things you would learn from [Porphyry]."

[8] This is not a task accorded to Soul in the *Timaeus;* there, the Demiurge takes the substance left over from the creation of Soul, mixes it with some other, unspecified material and divides it into individual souls. Thus, Soul is similar to, but not the source of, souls. Sometimes, Middle and Neoplatonic writers, following the *Timaeus*, made the Demiurge the distributor (but not source) of individual souls.

[9] See discussion in Dillon, pp. 315-17.

[10] The main obstacle to determining whether Plotinus understood individual souls to be derived from the Cosmic Soul lies in the question of whether Plotinus agrees with most Middle Platonic doctrine and understands there to be two souls--the individual and the Cosmic--or idiosyncratically understands there to be three souls--the individual, the Cosmic and a "Universal Soul" from which both the Cosmic Soul and individual souls are to be derived. In the latter case, the Cosmic Soul and the individual souls would be "sisters" rather than "parent" and "children," to use the metaphor of Hans Blumenthal, who analyzes this problem in "Soul, World Soul and Individual Soul in Plotinus," in *Le Néoplatonisme*, Proc. of Colloques internationaux du Centre National de la Recherche Scientifique, Royaumont, Sciences humaines (Paris 1971) pp. 55-66. E. Zeller, *Die philosophie der Griechen* (Leipzig 1881) III.ii[4] 538, understood there to be but two souls, the individual souls being derived from the Cosmic Soul; his opinion long has influenced Plotinian scholarship. Blumenthal's important contribution is a close analysis of the pertinent passages and the contradictions they present to the reader. He reaches no conclusions about the specific question that concerns us here-- whether individual souls are to be understood as derived from the Cosmic Soul--but he does argue that, at the very least, the Cosmic Soul is to be understood as the entity that oversees the enforming of individual bodies with individual souls (p. 60). Although this function does differ from that of

156   APPENDIX

> [The Father, having mingled] a spark of Soul with
> two mutually agreeing substances--
> divine intellect and divine will--added to them a third substance,
>   Holy Eros,
> the binder and holy guide of all things.
>
> ...ψυχαῖον σπινθῆρα δυσὶν κράσας ὁμονοίαις,
> νῷ καὶ νεύματι θείῳ, ἐφ' οἷς τρίτον ἁγνὸν Ἔρωτα,
> συνδετικὸν πάντων ἐπιβήτορα σεμνόν, ἔθηκεν.

Soul was the primary ingredient of the mixture out of which the Father created souls.[12]

The evidence for Hekate's role as source of individual souls in Chaldean doctrine comes mainly from the Oracles' commentators, although the statement in fr. 51 that she ensouls "the cosmoi" can be understood to include ensouling the cosmoi's inhabitants--men. Damascius (II.235.8), discussing the individual soul, says that its source is in Hekate. Proclus (In R. II.201.10), discussing the ensouling of individual men, says that "the Oracles speak rightly" when they say that the source of souls is she who ensouls all things; he then quotes Oracle fr. 51, which describes Hekate as ensouling All (quoted above, p. 154). Psellus several times says that the Chaldeans made Hekate the source of individual souls. He says that they "derive souls from Hekate," or "place the source of all souls in her flank," or simply call her "the Source of souls."[13] Porphyry similarly explains that one of the emblems of Hekate's statue represents the fact that a multitude of souls "dwell within her" (ap. Eus. PE III.11, 113 d). The question of Porphyry's use of the Chaldean Oracles as sources has been discussed briefly in Chapter I (pp.4-5) and will be discussed again in some depth below (pp.161 ff.). It is likely that he uses Chaldean doctrine here to explain the statue's attributes; at the very least, his remarks show that Hekate was known as a source of souls at a time not long after the composition of the Oracles.[14]

---

serving as the *source* of souls, it nonetheless places the Plotinian Cosmic Soul in a position of control and even nurture with reference to the individual soul.

[11]= Kr. 26 = Lydus *de Mens*. I, 11 [p. 3, 14-16 W.] = Schol. Paris gr. 1853, f. 312 r⁰.

[12]Psellus, *PG* 122, 1152 c 5 ff., eliminates the divine will and Eros and makes the Soul and the Paternal Intellect the two components of individual souls. See also Kroll, p. 46, who interprets the fragment as meaning that individual souls spring from Soul, and Lewy, pp. 179-81, who suggests that Soul provides the human soul with mortal life and with the potential to obtain immortal life, that Intellect enables it to comprehend the noetic ("think divine things") and that the inclusion of "divine will" expresses the fact that it accords with the Father's decision to send it to earth.

[13]*Scripta Minora*, edited by Des Places in his edition of the Oracles, p. 221 l. 9, following (with Lewy's emedantion) E. Kurtz-F. Drexl, *Michaelis Pselli scripta minora* (Milan 1936) I 446 16 ff.; *PG* 122 1136 b 1 ff.; *Assyrian Exposition*, edited by Des Places in his edition of the Oracles, p. 194, following D. Bassi, *Rivista di filologia e d'istuzione classica*, XXVI (1898) 123.14.

[14]J. Bidez, *Vie de Porphyry* (Gent 1913; rpt. Hildesheim 1969;) p. 15* (hereafter cited as Bidez,

The source of souls for the universe and individual men, then, uniquely is portrayed as residing in both Hekate and Soul. A related role that both are given is that of "Mistress" or "giver" of Life. In the Oracles themselves, Psyche is called "Mistress of Life," "ζωῆς δεσπότις" (fr. 96). Fragment 174 states that "she" provides life to others, rather than to herself; the fifth-century Hermias, source for the fragment (*In Phaedr.* 110 5 C.), says that "she" refers to Soul. Hekate is said to have a "life-giving" ("ζῳογόνος") womb in fr. 32.2, and is said to send forth a "life-giving whir" ("ζωογόνον ῥοίζημα").[15]

The commentators also provide extensive evidence for equating both Psyche and Hekate with the Chaldean ζωογόνος θεά, and, resultantly, with each other. For example, Proclus (*In T.* II.260.20 ff.) discusses Psyche's "life-giving forces;" ("γονίμους δυνάμεις"). He interprets them with reference to her temples, hands and womb, citing Oracle fr. 52, which describes Hekate's statue and mentions her by name. Psellus often refers to Hekate as being ζωογόνος or as having control over the ζωογόνοι processes in the universe, e.g., *Hypotyposis* pg. 74.19 and 74.34 (Kroll). Des Places, in his notes to fr. 32, cites further exegetical passages in which Hekate or Soul are described as ζωογόνος. By applying these adjectives to both Soul and Hekate--and no one else--the commentators indicate their identity in Chaldean doctrine.

Sometimes the commentators reflected the identity of Psyche and Hekate with each other and with Zoë or the ζωογόνος θεά by making them separate members of a triad. Both the triadization of entities or concepts and the hypostatization of entities' traits ran rampant in Neoplatonism.[16] These trends especially affected interpretation of the Oracles. Kroll, p. 13, suggested that this was because the Oracles genuinely spoke of several triads, at least one of which--Father, Paternal Intellect and Paternal Power--included hypostatized traits of its prime member. The existence of this triad encouraged exegetes to seek out triads elsewhere in Chaldean doctrine and, where none were to be found, to create them.[17]

Proclus and Psellus (who relied heavily on Proclus) industriously sought to harmonize several theological systems, notably the Orphic, the Platonic and the Chaldean.[18] Triadization and hypostatization were two of their favorite tools. They

---

Vie) makes this fragment part of Porphyry's *Concerning Statues* (Περὶ Ἀγαλμάτων; "ἄγαλμα" is a term used frequently to signify telestic statues used in theurgic practice).

[15] Kr. 29 = Damascius II.154.18; Des Places does not include it among his fragments. See also Chapter VII pp. 108.

[16] See Chapter I, pp. 15-16, for a brief discussion of triadization.

[17] Lewy, Theiler and Des Places all discuss the results of this tendency throughout their works; other scholars of the Oracles and Neoplatonism, such as Wallis and Dillon, discuss the ways in which it affected other Neoplatonic philosophers.

[18] A brief discussion of how the Chaldean, Platonic and Orphic systems were "adjusted" by Proclus and a helpful accompanying chart can be found in Lewy, Excursus VII, pp. 483-4.

sometimes split a single deity or concept into several parts in order to match deities or concepts in another system or to make some cosmological point. For example, the Oracles genuinely mention the Father, His Intellect and His Power. Proclus and Psellus, however, subdivided these entities, declaring that each of them, in turn, had its own "Father, Intellect and Power." Proclus and Psellus also took Hekate a step further and subdivided her. They made her the leading member of a triad whose members were Hekate, the Primal Soul and the Primal Virtue. The triad as a whole was called by Psellus the ζωογόνοι ἀρχαί--the life-giving Primals. Thus, those qualities with which Hekate is identified, or which she bestows, including Soul, become independent, subordinate entities.

Finally, the Oracle fragments identically describe Hekate and Soul as possessing wombs.[19] Fragment 96 says:

> Soul, being a brilliant fire by the power of the Father,
> Remains immortal and is the Mistress of Life
> And holds the plenitude of the full womb of the cosmos.
>
> Ὅττι ψυχή, πῦρ δυνάμει πατρὸς οὖσα φαεινόν,
> ἀθάνατός τε μένει καὶ ζωῆς δεσπότις ἐστὶν
> καὶ ἴσχει [κόσμου] πολλῶν πληρώματα κόλπων.

and fragments 32.2 and 35.3 describe the:

> life-giving womb of Hekate
>
> τὸν ζῳογόνον...Ἑκάτης...κόλπον

and the

> ...lightning-receiving womb of the splendid brilliance of Father-born Hekate
>
> ....πρηστηροδόχοι κόλποι παμφεγγέος αὐγῆς πατρογενοῦς Ἑκάτης

Fragment 51 and 52.1 tell us that[20]:

> For all around the hollows of the cartilage of [Hekate's] right flank,
> The abundant liquid of the Primal Soul gushes unceasingly,
> Completely ensouling the light, the fire, the aether and the Cosmoi

---

[19] Rhea is also described as having a womb (fr. 56). With the exception of Lewy, however (who thinks "ῥείη" is here an adjective), scholars of the Oracles agree that the Rhea of fr. 56 represents Hekate (see Chapter IV p. 66 n. 42).

[20] For analysis of these fragments, see Chapter IV, pp. 62 ff. The entity to whom the flank belongs in fr. 51 has to be supplied from the context in which the fragment is quoted. Proclus cites or refers to the fragment four times, each time making the subject "the Source of souls" ("πηγὴ ψυχῶν") or Hekate. Moreover, the subject can be inferred from fr. 52, which continues this Oracle by describing the left flank of Hekate; there, the name "Hekate" is contained within the fragment.

Δεξιτερῆς μὲν γὰρ λαγόνος περὶ χήραμα χόνδρων
πολλὴ ἄδην βλύζει ψυχῆς λιβὰς ἀρχιγενέθλου
ἄρδην ἐμψυχοῦσα φάος πῦρ αἰθέρα κόσμους

and that

In the left flank of Hekate resides the source of Virtue

Λαιῆς ἐν λαγόσιν Ἑκάτης ἀρετῆς πέλε πηγή

As was suggested in Chapter IV, the specific organ within Hekate's flanks, in which Soul and Virtue were imagined to be contained, probably was her womb. The commentators also mention wombs of Hekate and Soul several times.

The enlivening function of Hekate's womb has been discussed in detail in Chapter IV. Here I note only that the womb appears to be related to Hekate's and Soul's roles as "mistresses of life:" Soul's possession of a womb is mentioned in connection with her description as immortal and a mistress of life, and Hekate's womb is called "life-giving." Hekate's womb also is said to "receive lightning." (fr. 35.3). "Lightning," as several chapters have noted, symbolizes the Ideas/ iynges/ *symbola* sent forth by the Father and transmitted by Hekate. Similarly, Soul's womb is said by Proclus to be the place from which iynges/*symbola* descend towards Earth (see Chapter VII, pp. 108-109.). Thus, Soul and Hekate are described in very similar language as possessing wombs that perform identical functions; clearly, the womb actually belongs to one goddess, variously called Soul or Hekate.

In conclusion: the extant Oracle fragments, when clarified by some of their commentators' statements, indicate that Soul and Hekate are the same deity, described as having identical attributes and roles shared by no other deity or entity. Further statements from the commentators, which are not tied to the exposition of any specific Oracle fragment but rather seek to elucidate the Chaldean system as a whole, support this view of Hekate and Soul as identical.

One indication that commentators understood the Chaldean Cosmic Soul and Chaldean Hekate to be identical is the fact that they apply the unusual adjective "ἀμφιπρόσωπος" and related adjectives to both Hekate and Soul.[21] At *In T.* II. 129.25-130.23, Proclus calls Hekate "ἀμφιπρόσωπος" and "ἀμφιφαής;" the statement is part of Proclus' discussion of Soul's position between gods and men. Damascius calls Hekate "ἀμφιφαής" at I.315.20 and II.152.23. At *In T.* II.246.19 and II.293.23, Proclus calls Soul "ἀμφιπρόσωπος" and "ἀμφίστομος." In all these cases, the attribution of the adjectives to Hekate and/or Soul arises during

---

[21]Des Places lists "ἀμφιπρόσωπος" as Chaldean fr. 189. See also Chapter IV pp. 59-61; Lewy, pp. 93-4; Kroll, p. 30.

discussion of the mediating, liminal role between the Sensible and Intelligible Worlds that each is said to play.

Another indication arises during Iamblichus' discussion of how the epiphanies of various types of entities--gods, angels, heroes, souls, etcetera--differ from one another (*De Myst.* II.7; 84,6). Iamblichus describes the epiphany of the "Soul of the Whole" i.e., the Cosmic Soul, as being a "formless fire (ἀνείδεον πῦρ) visible throughout the cosmos." Cremer, who has argued convincingly that Iamblichus relied on the Oracles for many of his statements about epiphanies,[22] has shown that this fragment in particular is based on the Chaldean description of an epiphany in Oracle frs. 146, 147 and 148 (discussed in Chapter VIII, "The Epiphany of Hekate"), which also describes a formless fire visible throughout the "depths of the cosmos."

Cremer and others have argued that the three Chaldean fragments are part of a single Oracle describing the epiphany of Hekate, who is to be identified with the "formless fire."[23] A misunderstanding of Oracle fr. 147 by Michael Italicus (Letter XVII.182.28) and his source, Psellus, confirms this. Psellus transmits the first line of the fragment not as "If you say this to me many times, you will see all things growing dark," but rather as "If you say this to me many times, you will see all things 'in the form of a lion'," "πάντα λέοντα." He then procedes to explain this as a reference to the adjective "λεοντοῦχος." As Chapter VIII, pp. 112-114 argued, Psellus' reading is obviously a mistake. But significantly, when Michael Italicus, who depended largely on Psellus for his information about the Oracles, later discusses the nature of Chaldean *Hekate,* he says that the Oracles called her "λεοντοῦχος." "Λεοντοῦχος" is an uncommon word; surely Italicus' source must have been Psellus' transmission of Oracle fr. 147. Italicus' remarks, therefore, indicate that his sources--Psellus and perhaps later exegetes of the Oracles who depended on Psellus--understood fr. 147 to describe Hekate's epiphany. This epiphany, recorded in fr. 146, 147 and 148, closely matches Iamblichus' description of the "Soul of the Whole's" epiphany. Iamblichus' "Soul of the Whole," then, is identical to the Chaldean Hekate.

The descriptions of Hekate and Soul in Oracle fragments and the remarks of Oracle commentators indicate that Hekate was equated with Soul in Chaldean doctrine. Two final observations close the case. First, there is, in fact, a direct statement identifying Hekate and Soul in Porphyry. Although the source is later than the Oracles it can be traced with almost complete certainty back to Chaldean doctrine.

---

[22] See especially Cremer, pp. 45-6.

[23] That the three fragments are part of a single Oracle describing Hekate's epiphany first was suggested by Lewy, pp. 243-4. Des Places concurs with this decision in his edition of the Oracles.

Augustine (*Serm.* 241.6-7)[24] quotes at length a passage from Porphyry's *De Regressu Animae* [25] in which the concept of the Cosmic Soul is examined (Augustine translates the passage from Porphyry into Latin). Porphyry discusses previous philosophical theories that the world is an immense animal in possession of its own soul. According to these previous philosophers, Porphyry says, this *anima mundi* can be called "Jove" or "Hekate."

Lewy, following E. Zeller, *Die Philosophie der Griechen* III ii[4] 680, traces the identification of Jove with the Cosmic Soul back to Plotinus, Porphyry's teacher. As was noted above (p. 155 and n. 10). Plotinus' concept of the Cosmic Soul generally differed from that of the other Platonists.[26] Lewy traces the second of Porphyry's identifications--Hekate and Soul--back to the Chaldeans. It cannot be proven definitively that Porphyry was thinking of the Oracles (or other Chaldean works) when he made the identification, but two observations lend overwhelming support to Lewy's suggestion.

First, Porphyry is known to have written several works about Chaldean doctrine (see the Introduction); Hadot and O'Meara have argued convincingly that Porphyry's works, in fact, were the essential agents in transmitting Chaldean doctrines to later Neoplatonists.[27] More to the case in point, Augustine elsewhere tells us that Porphyry cites the Chaldean Oracles frequently throughout *De Regressu Animae*, the work from which the citation considered above is taken.[28] Ancient sources and modern scholars, then, join in support of Lewy's suggestion.

Second, the Chaldean system was the only philosophical system (so far as we currently know) that exalted Hekate to any great degree. It certainly is the only one known to have posited a close relationship of any type between Hekate and the

---

[24] Kroll and Lewy erroneously cite the passage in Augustine as *Serm.* 242.7.

[25] That this passage genuinely is from Porphyry is agreed upon by scholars of his work, including J.J. O'Meara, *Porphyry's Philosophy from Oracles in Augustine* (Paris 1959) pp. 92-3 and J. Bidez, *Vie*, p. 38* n. 4 (O'Meara, however, suggests that it comes from *Philosophy from Oracles*, which, he argues, made up a single work with *De Regressu Animae*). Lewy, p. 455 n. 26, and Kroll, p. 69, in citing it as proof of Chaldean Hekate's equation with Soul, assume that it is Porphyrian.

[26] Plotinus' identification of Jove with Soul reflects not an actual belief of Plotinus that the two are to be identified, but rather an attempt by Plotinus to show how the Homeric and Hesiodic myths hint at reality. Discussing the succession myth, Plotinus identifies Cronos with Mind (Νοῦς) and, because he understands Soul to be derived from Mind, equates Jove with Soul (Ouranos is implicitly the first, transcendent principle). For discussion of Plotinus' use of this and other Homeric/Hesiodic myths, see Robert Lamberton, *Homer the Theologian; Neoplatonic Allegorical Reading and the Growth of the Epic Tradition*, Transformation of the Classical Heritage, no. IX (Berkeley 1986), pp. 104-5.

[27] P. Hadot, *Porphyry et Victorinus*, 2 vols. (Paris 1968) and J.J. O'Meara, *Porphyry's Philosophy from Oracles in Eusebius's Praeparatio Evangelica and Augustine's Dialogues of Cassiciacum* (Paris 1969).

[28] Aug. *De Civ. Dei* X.9-32. See further J. Bidez, *Vie*, pp. 27*-44*, and Lewy, p. 7 and nn. 16-17; p. 449.

Cosmic Soul, whether that relationship be understood as one of equation (as is argued here) or of some other type.[29]

In short, Lewy's suggestion that Porphyry was thinking of the Chaldean system when he said that previous philosophers called Soul "Hekate" is convincing. But even if Porphyry were thinking of some other, previous philosophical system, rather than of the Chaldean system, it must be admitted that Porphyry's comment reflects the establishment of an equation between Hekate and Soul at some time previous to his essay. That it was established well before his essay is implied by the statement he makes just before setting forth the views of the previous philosophers he discusses: *"Sed nolo hinc diutius disputare"* (as quoted in translation by Augustine).

The first observation was that Porphyry, writing in the century after the Oracles' composition and avowedly a dedicated student of Chaldean doctrine, understood Hekate to be identical with Soul. The second observation is that no other theory can be found that adequately explains Hekate's roles in the Oracles and their commentators. To vaguely say, for instance, that the Chaldean system exalted Hekate because it was a system created by theurgists and she was a witches' goddess does not explain why she is portrayed in fr. 51 as sending forth the potency of Soul, why she is the "mistress of life" possessing a full womb, or why her cosmological position is described as "between the two Fathers" in fr. 50. Accepting her equation with Soul, on the other hand, does explain these things, and others that have been discussed in this book. Such an identification between Soul and Hekate in second-century Platonic mysticism should not be surprising. Chapter V discussed the gene-

---

[29]There is one possible exception to my statement, although the evidence is so slight as to prevent definitive conclusions. R. Merkelbach, *Mithras* (Hain 1984), pp. 234-5, suggests that Hekate represented the Cosmic Soul in the Mithraism of late antiquity. He bases this suggestion on 1) the fact that statues of Hekate have been found in three Mithraic sanctuaries, 2) the apparent reliance of the Mithraic cosmological system on that of the *Timaeus* and 3) most importantly, remarks in a passage of Firmicus Maternus that discusses Mithraic beliefs (*De er. prof. rel.* 5). The passage from Firmicus supposedly interprets a three-headed statue of Hekate as representing three different goddesses who in turn represent the three parts of the soul. "Minerva" represents that part called *ira*, "Diana" represents *mens* and "Venus" represents *libido*. Merkelbach's conclusion that Hekate therefore represented the Cosmic Soul in the Mithraic system, seems weak for several reasons. First, there is an absence of any other evidence connecting Hekate with Soul in the Mithraic system. Second, the passage that Merkelbach adduces comes from a fourth-century work that railed against pagan religions of all types; the three-headed statue Firmicus describes may have been Mithraic but the exegesis he brought to bear on it may not have been. Indeed, he may have borrowed the connection between Hekate and Soul from the Chaldean system, which by his day was widely known. (moreover, the passage of Firmicus is marred badly by a lacuna; the name "Hekate" is never attached to the statue described. Editors have suggested it was a statue of Hekate because it was a triplicate statue.) Third, as Merkelbach admits, Firmicus' exegesis pertains only to the individual soul; that Hekate might be the Mithraic *Cosmic* Soul is Merkelbach's own suggestion. In short, although Merkelbach's suggestion is very attractive to one seeking *comparanda* with which to elucidate Chaldean Hekate/Soul, his arguments for it are unconvincing. See also Robert Turcan, *Mithras Platonicus: Recherches sur l'hellénisation philosophique de Mithras* (Leiden 1975) pp. 90-104. Turcan suggests that the triplicate goddess of the Mithraic system, described by Firmicus Maternus, should be identified with the Persian goddess Anâhitâ, rather than with Hekate.

ral trend at the time the Oracles were composed to equate philosophical concepts with deities, and to validate philosophical truths with religious tradition. The Chaldean divinity variously called Hekate or Soul fits this trend admirably.

Bibliography

PRIMARY SOURCES

This list includes only lesser known works. Volume, page and line numbers cited in the text refer to the editions listed below, unless otherwise noted. Citations within this book of better known authors, such as Aeschylus and Vergil, use the standard means of reference.

Apuleius. *De Dogmata Platonis*. P. Thomas, ed. and trans. (French). In *De Philosophia*. Paris: 1908.

Calcidius. *In Platonis Timaeum*. J. Waszink, ed. London and Leiden: 1962.

Corpus hermeticum. A.D. Nock and A.J. Festugière, ed., comm., and trans. (French). Paris: Vols. I-II 1945; Vols. III-IV 1954.

Damascius. *Dubitationes et Solutiones de Primis Principiis, in Platonis Parmenidem*. C.-A. Ruelle, ed. 1889; rpt. Paris: 1966. Vols. I and II.

----------. *In Phaedonem*. *Versio* 1 and *versio* 2. In *The Greek Commentaries on Plato's Phaedo*. L.G. Westerink, ed. Amsterdam: 1977. Vol. 2.

----------. *Vita Isidori reliquiae*. C. Zintzen, ed., comm. and trans. (German). Hildesheim: 1967.

Eusebius. *Praeparatio Evangelica*. E.H. Gifford, ed., comm. and trans. 4 vols. Oxford: 1903.

Hermias. *In Phaedrum*. P. Couvreur, ed. Paris: 1901.

Iamblichus. *Les Mystères d'Egypte*. E. Des Places, ed., comm. and trans. (French). Paris: 1966.

----------. *Vita Plotinus*. A. Nauck, ed. Leipzig: 1884.

(pseudo-Iamblichus) *Theologumena Arithmeticae*. Vittorio de Falco, ed. Leipzig: 1922.

Italicus, Michael. *Letter* XVII. E. Des Places, ed. and trans. In *Oracles Chaldaïques avec un Choix de Commentaires Anciens*. Paris: 1971.

Lydus, Joannes. *De Mensibus*. R. Wünsch, ed. Leipzig: 1898.

Marinus. *Vita Procli*. J. F. Boissonade, ed. Paris: 1862.

Numenius. *Fragmenta*. E. Des Places. Paris: 1973.

Oracles Chaldaïques avec un Choix de Commentaires Anciens. E. Des Places, ed., comm., and trans. (French). Paris: 1971.

Orpheus. *Hymni*. W. Quandt, ed. Berlin: 1955.

----------. *Orphica*. Eugene Abel, ed. 1885; rpt. Hildesheim: 1971.

----------. *Orphicorum Fragmenta*. Otto Kern, ed. Berlin: 1922.

Papyri Graecae Magicae; Die griechischen Zauberpapyri. K. Preisendanz and (2nd ed.) A. Henrichs, ed. and trans. (German). 2 vols. 1928-31; rpt. Stuttgart: 1973.

Plotinus. *Enneads*. A.H. Armstrong, ed. and trans. Cambridge, MA: 1966-87. Vols. I-VII.

Porphyry. *De Abstentia*. In *Opuscula*. A. Nauck, ed. 1886; rpt. Leipzig: 1963.

----------. *De Philosophia ex oraculis haurienda librorum reliquae*. G. Wolff, ed. and comm. Berlin: 1856.

----------. *Lettera ad Anebo*. A. Sodano, ed. and trans. Naples: 1958.

----------. Opuscula (incl. *Concerning Statues, Return of the Soul*). In *Vie de Porphyry*. J. Bidez, ed. and comm. 1913; rpt. Hildesheim: 1964.

----------. *Sententia ad intelligibilia ducentes*. B. Mommert, ed. Leipzig: 1907.

Poseidonius. *Die Fragmente*. W. Theiler, ed. and comm. 2 vols. Berlin and New York: 1983.

Proclus. *Elements of Theology*. E.R. Dodds, ed., comm. and trans. Oxford: 1963.

----------. *Extraits du Commentaire sur la Philosophie Chaldaïque*. E. Des Places, ed., comm. and trans. In *Oracles Chaldaïques*. Paris: 1971.

----------. *Hymni*. Eugene Abel, ed. In *Orphica*. 1885; rpt. Hildesheim: 1971.

----------. *In Parmenidem*. V. Cousin, ed. Paris: 1864.

----------. *In Platonis Cratylum commentaria*. G. Pasquali, ed. Leipzig: 1908.

----------. *In Rem Publicam*. W. Kroll, ed. 2 vols. Leipzig: 1899-1901.

----------. *In Timaeum*. E. Diehl, ed. 3 vols. Leipzig: 1903-1906.

----------. *Theologia Platonica*. AE. Portus, ed. Hamburg: 1618.

Psellus, Michael. Opuscula discussing the Chaldean Oracles are found in *Oracles Chaldaïques avec un Choix de Commentaires Anciens*. E. Des Places, ed., trans. and comm. Paris: 1971. For full citations see pp. 153-56 of Des Places.

----------. *De operatione daemonum*. J. F. Boissonade, ed. Nürnberg: 1838.

----------. *Scripta Minora*. E. Kurtz and F. Drexl, eds. Milan: 1936.

Simplicius. *In Aristotelis Physicorum Libros Posteriores Commentaria*. H. Diels, ed. *C.M.A.G.*, IX-X. Berlin: 1882-95.

Synesius. *Hymni*. N. Terzaghi, ed. Rome: 1939.

----------. Opuscula (incl. *De Insomniis*). In *Synesii Cyrenensis Opuscula*. N. Terzaghi, ed. Rome: 1944.

Victorinus, Marius. *De trinitate contra Arium*. P. Henry, ed. and trans.; P. Hadot, comm. Paris: 1960.

SECONDARY WORKS

Allier, R. *Magie et Religion*. Paris: 1935.

Armstrong, A.H. "Was Plotinus a Magician?" *Phronesis*, 1 (1955), 73 ff.

Audollent, A. *Defixionum Tabellae*. Paris: 1904.

Aune, D.E. "Magic in Early Christianity." *ANRW*, II.23:2 (1980), 1507-57.

Barb, A.A. "Diva Matrix." *Journal of the Warburg and Courtauld Institute*, 16 (1953), 193-238.

----------. "The Survival of the Magic Arts." In *The Conflict Between Paganism and Christianity in the Fourth Century*. Ed. Arnaldo Momigliano. Oxford: 1963, pp. 100-125.

Betz, Hans Dieter, ed. *The Greek Magical Papyri in Translation*. Chicago: 1986. Vol. I.

----------. "Fragments from a Greek Catabasis Ritual." *HR*, 19 (1980), 287-95.

Bianchi, U. "Observations on Valentinianism." In *The School of Valentinus*. Vol. I of *The Rediscovery of Gnosticism.*. Ed. Bentley Layton. Leiden: 1980, 103-117.

Bicknell, P.J. "The Dark Side of the Moon." In *Maistor. Classical, Byzantine and Renaissance Studies for Robert Browning,*. Ed. Ann Moffatt. Canberra, Australia: 1984, pp. 667-75.

Bidez, J. "Note sur les mystères néoplatoniciens." *Rev. Belge de Phil. et d'Hist.*,7 (1928), 1477 ff.

---------- and F. Cumont. *Les Mages Hellenises*. Paris: 1938. Vol. I.

Blumenthal, H. "Soul, World Soul and Individual Soul in Plotinus." In *Le Néoplatonisme: Colloques internationaux du Centre National de la Recherche Scientifique, Royaumont, Sciences humaines*. Ed. P. Hadot. Paris: 1971, pp. 55-66.

Boedeker, Deborah. "Hecate: A Transfunctional Goddess in the *Theogony?*" *TAPA*, 113 (1983), 79 ff.

Bremmer, Jan. *The Early Greek Concept of the Soul*. Princeton: 1983.

Breton, S. "L'homme et l'âme humain." *Diotima*, 8 (1980), 21-24.

----------. "Teléologie et ontogénie. Variations sur les Oracles Chaldaïques." *RecSR*, LXVI (1978), 5-26.

Burkert, Walter. *Griechische Religion der archaischen und klassischen Epoche*. Stuttgart: 1977. (English trans. by John Raffan, Cambridge: 1985; all references herein refer to the German edition, however).

----------. *Homo Necans*. Trans. Peter Bing. Berlin: 1972; English ed., Berkeley: 1983.

----------. *Lore and Science in Ancient Pythagoreanism*. Trans. Edwin L. Minar, Jr. Nürnberg: 1962; English ed., Cambridge: 1972.

----------. *Structure and History in Greek Mythology and Ritual*. Berkeley: 1979.

Clay, Jenny Strauss. "The Hecate of the *Theogony*" *GRBS*, 1984 pp. 27-38.

Cook, A.B. *Zeus. A Study in Ancient Religion*. 2 vols. 1914; rpt. New York: 1964.

Cremer, F.W. *Die Chaldäischen Orakel und Iamblich De Mysteriis*. Beitr. z. Klass. Philol. 26. Meisenheim am Glan: 1969.

Culianu, I.P. *Psychoanodia I. EPRO* 99. Leyden: 1983.

Cumont, Franz. *Afterlife in Roman Paganism*. 1922; rpt. New York: 1959.

----------. *Recherches sur le symbolism funéraire des Romains*. Paris: 1942.

----------. *Lux Perpetua*. Paris: 1949.

----------. *The Mysteries of Mithra*. Trans. T.J. McCormack. 1902; English edition, New York: 1956.

Des Places, E. "Les Oracles Chaldaïques" *ANRW*, II 17.4 (1984), 2299-2335.

----------. "Notes sur quelques '"Oracles Chaldaïques'." In *Melanges Edouard Delebecque*. Aix-en-Provence Cedex: 1983, pp. 321-9.

Detienne, M. *The Gardens of Adonis: Spices in Greek Mythology*. Trans. Janet

Lloyd. Sussex: 1977.

Deubner, L. *Magie und Religion*. Freiburg: 1922.

Diehls, Charles and Georges Cousin. "Inscriptions de Lagina." *BCH*, 11 (1887), 5-39.

Diels, H. *Antike Technik*. Leipzig and Berlin: 1914.

Dieterich, A. *Eine Mithrasliturgie*. 1903; rpt. Leipzig: 1923.

Dillon, John. "The Descent of the Soul in Middle Platonic and Gnostic Theory." In *The School of Valentinus*. Ed. Bentley Layton. Vol. I of *The Rediscovery of Gnosticism*. Leiden: 1980, pp. 357-364.

----------. *The Middle Platonists: 80 B.C. to A.D. 220*. Ithaca: 1977.

Dodds, E.R. "New Light on the Chaldean Oracles" *HThR*, 54 (1961) 263-73

----------. "Theurgy and its Relationship to Neoplatonism." *JRS*, 37 (1955), 55 ff. Rpt. as "Theurgy," Appendix II of *The Greeks And The Irrational*. Berkeley: 1951, pp.283 ff.

----------. *Pagan and Christian in an Age of Anxiety*. 1965; rpt. New York: 1970.

----------. *The Ancient Concept of Progress and Other Essays on Greek Literature and Belief*. 1973; rpt. Oxford: 1985.

Douglas, Mary. *Purity and Danger: An Analysis of the Concepts of Pollution and Taboo*. London: 1966.

Droysen. "Enodia." *RE* V.II, Halbband X, 2634-36.

Eitrem, S. "Die σύστασις und der Lichtzauber in der Magie," *Symb. Oslo.*, VIII (1929), 49 ff.

----------. "La Théurgie chez les Néoplatoniciens et dans les Papyrus Magiques" *Symb. Oslo.*, XXII (1942), 49-79.

----------. *Hermes und die Toten*. Christiania VidenskabsSelskabs I Forhandlinger for 1909 no. 5. Christiania [Oslo], Norway: 1909.

Faraone, C. "The Protection of Place: Talismans and Theurgy in Ancient Greece." In *Magika Hiera: Ancient Greek Magic and Religion*. Ed. C. Faraone and D. Obbink. Oxford: forthcoming 1990.

Farnell, L.R. *Cults of the Greek States*. 5 vols. Oxford: 1896-1909.

Festugière, A.-J. *Études de philosophie grecque*. Paris: 1971.

----------. *Proclus, Commentaire sur la "Republique."* 3 vols. Paris: 1955.

----------. *Proclus, Commentaire sur le "Timée."* 5 vols. Paris: 1966-68.

----------. "Un Vers Méconnu des Oracles Chaldaïques dans Simplicius." *Symb. Oslo.*, 26 (1948), 75-77.

Finamore, John F. *Iamblichus and the Theory of the Vehicle of the Soul.* American Philological Association American Classical Studies no. 14. Chico, CA: 1985.

Fowden, Garth. *The Egyptian Hermes: A Historical Approach to the Late Pagan Mind.* Cambridge: 1986.

----------. "Pagan Versions of the Rain Miracle of A.D. 172." *Historia*, 36/1 (1987), 83-95.

Friedländer, P. "Jacobys Hesiodi Carmina." *GGA* 193 no. 7 (1931). Rpt. in *Hesiod*. E. Heitsch, ed. Darmstadt: 1966.

Fuchs,W. "Unerkannte Hekate-Heiligtümer. *Boreas,* 2 (1979).

Garland, Robert. *The Greek Way of Death.* Ithaca: 1985.

Geertz, H. and K. Thomas. "An Anthropology of Religion and Magic." *Jnl. of Interdisc. Hist.*, VI.1 (1975), 71-109.

Geudtner, O. *Die Seelenlehre der Chaldäischen Orakel.* Beitr. z. Klass. Philol. 35. Meisenheim am Glan: 1971.

Goergemanns, H. *Untersuchungen zu Plutarchs Dialog de Facie in orbe lunae.* Bibliothek der klassichen Altertumswissenschaft, neue Folge 2 Reihe Band 33. Heidelberg: 1970.

Golden, M. "Did the Ancients Care When their Children Died?" *G&R,* 35 (1988), 152-63.

Goulet, Richard "L'Oracle D'Apollon dans la *Vie De Plotin.*" In *Porphyre: La Vie de Plotin.* Ed. L. Brisson et al. Vol. I. Paris: 1982, pp. 371-412.

Goulet-Cazé, M.O. "L'Arrière-Plan Scholaire de la *Vie de Plotin*" In *Porphyre: La Vie de Plotin.* Ed. L. Brisson et al. Vol. I. Paris: 1982, pp. 231-281.

Gow, A.S.F. "῎Ιυγξ, ῾Ρομβός, Rhombos, Turbo." *JHS,* 54 (1934), 1-13.

Graf, Fritz. *Eleusis und die orphische Dichtung Athens in vorhellenistischer Zeit. RGVV* XXIII. Berlin: 1974.

----------. *Nordionische Kulte.* Rome: 1985.

----------. "Prayer in Magic and Religious Ritual." In *Magika Hiera: Ancient Greek Magic and Religion.* Ed. C. Faraone and D. Obbink. Oxford: forthcoming 1990.

Haarløv, Britt. *The Half-Open Door. A Common Symbolic Motif within Roman Sepulchral Sculpture.* Odense: 1977.

Hadot, P. "Physique et Poésie dans le *Timée* de Platon." *Rev. Theol. Philos.*, 115 (1983), 133-33.

----------. *Porphyre et Victorinus*. 2 vols. Paris: 1968.

----------. "Citations de Porphyre chez Augustine (response to J.J. O'Meara's *Porphyry's Philosophy from Oracles in Augustine)." REAug.*, VI (1960), 205-244.

Halliwell, Stephen. "Where Three Roads Meet: a neglected detail in the *Oedipus Tyrannus.*" *JHS* , 106 (1986), 187-190.

Hatzfeld, J. "Inscriptions de Lagina en Carie." *BCH,* 44 (1920), 70-100.

Heckenbach. "Hekate." *RE* VII.II, Halband XIV, 2769-82.

Hopfner, Th. "Die Kindermedien in den griechisch-ägyptischen Zauberpapyri." In *Recueil N.P. Kondakov.* Prague: 1926, pp. 65-74.

----------. *Griechisch-Aegyptischer Offenbarungszauber.* Studien zur Paläographie und Papyruskunde XXI and XXIII. 2 vols. Leipzig: 1921 and 1924; vol. 1 and part 1 of vol. 2 rpt. Amsterdam: 1974, 1983. (citations herein refer to section numbers, which are consistent between the original printing and reprinting).

----------. "Nekromantie." *RE* XVI.2 Halbband XXXII, 2218-2233.

----------. "Theurgie." *RE* VI.1, Halbband XI, 258-70.

----------. "Τρίοδος." *RE* VII.1, Halbband XIII, 161-66.

Hubert, H. and M. Mauss. "Esquisse d'une théorie général de la Magie." *Année Sociol.,* 7 (1902), 1-140.

Hull, J.M. *Hellenistic Magic and the Synoptic Tradition.* London: 1974.

Johnston, S.I. "Crossroads." *ZPE* (forthcoming 1990).

Jordan, David. "A Survey of Greek Defixiones not Included in the Special Corpora." *GRBS,* 26 (1985) 151-197.

----------. "Defixiones from a Well Near the Southwest Corner of the Athenian Agora." *Hesperia,* 54 no. 3 (1985), 205-55.

----------. "'Εκατικά." *Glotta,* LVIII (1980), 62-5.

----------. "Two Inscribed Lead Tablets from a Well in the Athenian Kerameikos." *AthMitt,* 95 (1980), 225-39.

----------. "CIL VIII 19525 (B) .2 QPVVLVA = q(uem)p(eperit) vulva." *Philologus,* 120 (1976), 127-32.

Kahn, L. "Hermès, la frontière et l'identité ambigue"." *Ktema*, 4 (1979), 201-211.

Köhler, W. "Die Schlüssel des Petrus." *ArchRW.*, VIII (1924), 214-243.

----------. "Kleiduchos." *RE* XI.I, Halbband XXI, 593-600.

Kraus, Th. *Hekate*. Heidelberg: 1960.

Kroll, W. *De Oraculis Chaldaicis*. Breslauer Philol. Abhand. VII.1. 1894; rpt. Breslau: 1962.

Lamberton, Robert. *Homer the Theologian: Neoplatonist Allegorical Reading and the Growth of the Epic Tradition*. The Transformation of the Classical Heritage series no. IX. Berkeley: 1986.

Laumonier, Alfred. *Les cultes indigènes en Carie*. Paris: 1958.

Lewy, Hans. *Chaldean Oracles and Theurgy*. 1956; rpt. Paris: 1978.

Lloyd, G.E.R. *Magic, Reason and Experience*. Cambridge: 1979.

Lobeck, C. A. *Aglaophamus*. 1829; rpt. Hildesheim: 1964.

Luck, Georg. "Theurgy and Forms of Worship in Neoplatonism." In *Religion, Science and Magic: In Concert and in Conflict*. Eds. Jacob Neusner, Ernest S.Frerichs and Paul V.M. Flesher. New York and Oxford: 1989, pp.185-225.

----------. *Arcana Mundi*. Baltimore: 1985.

----------. *Hexen und Zauberei in der Römischen Dichtung*. Zürich: 1962.

MacMullen, Ramsey. *Paganism in the Roman Empire*. New Haven: 1981.

Majercik, R.T. "Chaldean Oracles: Text, Translation, Commentary." Diss. University of California at Santa Barbara 1982.

Marquardt, Patricia A. "A Portrait of Hecate." *AJP*, 102 no. 3 (1981), 244-60.

Mazon, P. *Hesiode*. Paris: 1928.

Merkelbach, R. *Mithras*. Hain: 1984.

Merlan, Phillip. *From Platonism to Neoplatonism*. The Hague: 1960.

----------. "Plotinus and Magic." *Isis*, 44 (1959), 341-8.

----------. "Religion and Philosophy from Plato's *Phaedo* to the Chaldean Oracles." *Journ. Hist. Philos.*, I.2 (1963) 163-76.

Meyer, M.W. *The "Mithras Liturgy"* Missoula, MT.: 1976.

Miller, Patricia Cox. "In Praise of Nonsense." *In Mediterranean Spirituality.* Ed. A.H. Armstrong. Vol. 15 of *World Spirituality: An Encyclopedic History of the Religious Quest* New York: 1986, pp. 481-505.

Morenz, Siegfried. "Anubis mit dem Schlüssel." In *Religion und Geschichte des Alten Aegypten.* Vienna and Cologne: 1975, pp. 510-20.

Mikalson, Jon D. *The Sacred and Civil Calendar of the Athenian Year.* Princeton: 1975.

Nelson, Grace. "A Greek Votive Iynx-wheel in Boston" *Am. Journ. Arch.,* XLIV (1940), 443 ff.

Nilsson, Martin. *Geschichte der griechischen Religion.* 2 vols. Vol. I, Munich: 1940, 3rd ed. 1967; vol. II, Munich: 1950, 2nd ed. 1961 (citations herein refer to the more recent editions).

----------. *Griechische Feste.* Berlin: 1906.

Nock, A.D. "Tertullian and the Ahori" *VigChr.,* 4 (1950), 129-41; rpt. in *Essays on Religion in the Ancient World.* Ed. Zeph Stewart. Cambridge: 1972, pp. 712-19.

----------. "Oracles théologiques." *REA,* 30 (1928), 86 ff; rpt. in *Essays on Religion in the Ancient World.* Ed. Zeph Stewart. Cambridge: 1972, pp. 160 ff.

O'Meara, J.J. *Porphyry's Philosophy From Oracles in Augustine.* Paris: 1954.

----------. *Porphyry's Philosophy From Oracles in Eusebius's Praeparatio Evangelica and Augustine's Dialogues of Cassiacum.* Recherches augustiennes vol. VI, suppl. à la *Revue des etudes augustiniennes.* Paris: 1969.

Parke, H.W. *Festivals of the Athenians.* Ithaca: 1977.

Parker, Robert. *Miasma: Pollution and Purification in early Greek Religion.* Oxford: 1983.

Petersen, E. *Die dreigestaltige Hekate.* 2 vols. *AEM,* 4 (1880) and *AEM,* 5 (1881).

Pfister, F. "Die Hekate-Episode in Hesiods *Theogonie.*" *Philologus,* 84 (1928), 1-9.

----------. "Epiphanie." *RE* suppl. IV, 277-323.

Phillips, Charles Robert. "The Sociology of Religious Knowledge in the Roman Empire to A.D. 284." *ANRW,* II.16.3 (1986), 2677-2773.

Preisendanz, K. "Fluchtafel (Defixio)." *RAC,* 8 (1969), 1-24.

Reinach, S. ""Αωροι βιαιοθάνατοι." *ArchRW,* 9 (1906), 312-20.

Richardson, N.J., ed. and comm. *The Homeric Hymn to Demeter.* Oxford: 1974.

Rike, R.L. *Apex Omnium: Religion in the Res Gestae of Ammianus.* Berkeley: 1987.

Rist, John M. "Mysticism and Transcendence in Later Neoplatonism." *Hermes,* 92 (1964), 213-225.

Ritner, Robert. "A Uterine Amulet in the Oriental Institute Collection." *Jnl. Near East. Studies,* 43 (1984), 209-221.

Rohde, Erwin. *Psyche: The Cult of Souls and Belief in Immortality among the Greeks.* Trans. W.B. Hillis. 1894; rpt. 1898; English ed., London: 1925.

Rosan, L. *The Philosophy of Proclus.* New York: 1949.

Roscher, W.H. "Hekate." *Lex.* II.1, 1885-1910.

Rose, H.J. *Religion in Greece and Rome.* New York: 1959.

Rubin, H.Z. "Weather Miracles under Marcus Aurelius." *Athenaeum* NS., 57 (1979), 357-58.

Saffrey, H.D. "Les néoplatoniciens et les Oracles Chaldaïques." *REAug.,* 28 (1981), 209-225.

----------. "Nouveau Oracles Chaldaïques dans les Scholies du *Paris. Gr.* 1853." *Rev. de Philol.,* 43 (1969), 59-72.

Sagnard, F. *Clément d'Alexandrie. Extraits de Théodote.* Sources chretiennes 23. Paris: 1948.

Schlam, Carl. *Cupid and Psyche: Apuleius and the Monuments.* University Park, PA: 1976.

Segal, Charles. "Simaetha and the Iynx." *QUCC,* 15 (1973), 32-43.

Shaw, Gregory. "Theurgy: Rituals of Unification in the Neoplatonism of Iamblichus." *Traditio,* XLI (1985), 1-28.

Sheppard, Anne. "Proclus' Attitude to Theurgy." *CQ,* 32 (1982), 212-24

Smith, A. *Porphyry's Place in the Neoplatonic Tradition.* The Hague: 1974.

Sokolowski, F. *Lois Sacrées de l'Asie Mineur.* Paris: 1955.

Stroumsa, Gedaliahu G. "Chaldean Oracles: (review of the second edition of Hans Lewy's *Chaldean Oracles and Theurgy*). *Numen,* XXVII fasc. 1 (1981), 167-171.

Tardieu, M. "Les Oracles Chaldaïques." In *The School of Valentinus.* Vol. I of *The Rediscovery of Gnosticism.* Ed. Bentley Layton. Leiden: 1980, pp. 194-237.

Tavenner, E. "Iynx and Rhombos." *TAPA,* LXIV (1933), 109-27.

Terzaghi, Nicholas. "Sul Commento di Niceforo Gregorio al ΠΕΡΙ ΕΝΥΠΝΙΩΝ di Synesio." *Studi italiani di filologia classica*, XII (1904), 181-217.

Theiler, W. *Die chaldäischen Orakel und die Hymnen des Synesios*. Schriften der Königsberger Gelehrten Gesellschaft XVIII.1. Halle: 1942; rpt. in *Forschungen zum Neuplatonismus* (Berlin 1966), pp. 252 ff.

Tupet, Anne-Marie. *La magie dans la poésie Latine des origines jusqu'a la fin du règne d'Auguste*. Paris: 1976.

Turcan, Robert. *Mithras Platonicus: Recherches sur l'hellenisation philosophique de Mithras*. Leiden: 1975.

Versnel, H.S. "Religious Mentality in Ancient Prayer." In *Faith, Hope and Worship*. Ed. H.S. Versnel. Vol. II of *Aspects of Religious Mentality in the Ancient World*. Leiden: 1981, pp.1-64.

Wallis, R.T. *Neoplatonism*. New York: 1972.

Waszink, J.H. "Biothanati." *RAC*, 2 (1954).

West, M.L., ed., proleg. and comm. *Hesiod. Theogony*. Oxford: 1966.

---------. *The Orphic Poems*. Oxford: 1983.

Wilson. N.G. *Scholars of Byzantium*. Baltimore: 1983.

Winkelmann, Michael. "Magic: A Theoretical Reassessment." *Curr. Anthr.*, XXIII no. 1 (1982), 37-66.

Zaganiaris, N.J. "Sacrifices de chiens dans l'antiquite classique." *Platon*, XXVII (1975), 322-329.

Zeller, E. *Die Philosophie der Griechen*. 1923; rpt. Darmstadt 1963. Vol. III 2[4.]

English and Greek Indices of Topics Discussed

English

N.B.: Readers should check for the names of ancient authorities (e.g., "Porphyry," "Damascius") in the "Index of Passages Discussed" as well as in this index.

Adrasteia	96-97 and n. 20.
Aion	106-107 and nn. 44, 46; 116, n. 14.
Albinus	2, n. 5.
Alcamenes	24.
Alphabet, letters of as *symbola*	97-98.
Anāhitā	162, n. 29.
Angels	121-126; 136.
Anubis	30, n. 5.
Apollo	3; 22, n. 3; 73; 112.
Apollonius of Tyana	3; 72; 119.
Apuleius	3, n. 9; 155.
Archangels	121-122.
Aristotle	4; 17.
"Armour," theurgical skills as	127-130.
Artemis	24, n. 10; 27 and n. 24; 31 and n. 8; 141 and n. 26
Astrology	86; 112.
Atlas	53, n. 15.
Augustine	5; 79; 161-162 and n. 24.
Bendis	24, n. 10.
"Boundary" ("Ορος) (Gnostic deity)	71.
Brimo	24, n. 10.
Calcidius	20.
Caria (worship of Hekate there)	21-22.
Chaeremon	72-73.
Christos (Gnostic deity)	71.
Coercion (of gods by mortals)	85; 131-132 and nn. 60, 61.
"Connectives" or "Maintainers"	64.
Cosmic Soul, Evil or Bad (see also, "Physis")	13; 19; 136 and n. 12.
Crossroads	Chp. II *passim;* 73-74; 150.

Curse Tablets	145 and nn. 10, 11.
Dacians, Julian's participation in battle with	3.
Daemon(es)	16; Chp. III, "The Mistress of the Moon," *passim;* 71; 92; 107 and Chp. VII, *passim;* 121-126; Chp. IX, *passim;* 144-148; 149-151.
Damascius	7.
Demeter	22.
Demiurge (Second Intellect)	52-58; 60; 108; 109.
Diotima	71; 92.
Dogs	81; 87; Chp. IX, *passim;* 151.
Enodia (Ἐνοδία)	23-24; 27; 149.
Ensouling (as duty of Soul)	Chp. IV, "Hekate as Ensouler," *passim;* 127; 153-157.
Epiphany	82; 87-88; Chp. VIII, *passim;* 137.
Er	39; 43-44.
Eros, erotes	1, n. 1; 71; 107, n. 47; 156.
Eudorus	18.
Fate(s)	43-44 and n. 38; 87, n. 22; 89; 97, n. 22; 137 and n. 13.
"Ferrymen"	91; 102-103.
Ficino, Michael	8.
Fire, fieriness: see "Lightning"	
Four	45-47.
Hades, keys to; deities controlling access to	41 and nn. 25, 27, 28, 30; 73 146-148; 150.
Helios	1, n. 1; 22; 116.
Hephaestus	54, n. 19.
Hermes	23, n. 9; 26, n. 19; 28, n. 27; 145.
Heroes	119; 124, n. 34.
Hexad	18.
Horses	111; 121-124.
Iamblichus	5-7; 16; 18; 78-89; 113-114; 117; 120; 124; 160-161.
Ideas or Forms	17; 19; 30; Chp. IV, *passim;* 50-58; 70; 93; 103-104; 107; 109-110; 122; 159.

INDICES OF TOPICS DISCUSSED

Initiations	81-82; 134.
Intermediary principles (cf. "Princ. of Continuity")	15; 72.
Isis	30; 72; 148.
Italicus, Michael	8; 112, n. 3; 113, n. 6; 160.
Iynx, iynges	82; 84; 87; Chp. VII, *passim;* 132; 135; 143; 149-151; 159.
Iynx, the nymph	95, n. 17.
Janus	25, n. 17; 59; 147 and n. 19.
Jove	153, n. 2; 161 and n. 26.
Julian(i) (authors of the Oracles)	2; 3, n. 6; 71; 80.
Julian, Emperor	30; 151.
Kronos	50, n. 5.
Lagina (Stratonice)	41-42.
Lightning; lightning and thunderbolts; fire	49-58; 103; 108; 111; 119; 159.
Lions	111-114; 160.
Magi	96-97.
Marcus Aurelius	3.
"Mathematicals," mathematical proportions	14; 17-18.
"Measuring"	55-58; 70.
Mediumistic Prophecy	88.
"Mistress of Life" (Soul as...) (see also Greek cognates of ζωή)	64-68; 157-159.
Mithras, mithraism	116; 162 and n. 29.
"Mithras Liturgy"	116 and n. 14.
Moderatus	18.
Molpoi, cult regulations of	21, n. 3.
Moon	Chp. III, *passim;* 57, n. 27; 71; 73; 89, n. 29; 137, n. 14; 138, n. 18; 141; 149-150.
Music, musical proportions (see also next entry)	14; 17; 46.
Music of the Spheres	101-103; 109; 143.
Nicomachus of Gerasa	18.
Number(s)	17; 19; 44-47; 50-58.
Numenius	2, n. 5.
nymphs	1, n. 1.
Orpheus; "orphic" beliefs	4; 9; 39 and n. 23; 40; 42; 45; 63, n. 38; 67, n. 42; 72; 157.
"Orphic" Rape of Persephone (frs. 42, 49)	23, n. 6.

Osiris	30; 72.
Paternal (First) Intellect (Νοῦς)	50; 51, n. 7; 52-58; 64, n. 39; 65 and n. 40; 106 and n. 44.
Paternal (First) Power (Δύναμις)	51, n. 7; 56, n. 25; 65 and n. 40; 66-67 and nn. 43, 44.
Paternal Will	55, n. 22.
Persephone	22-23; 24, n. 10; 25; 26; 27; 36 and n. 21; 146; 149.
Persuasion (πειθώ)	98-100.
Peter, Saint	44.
Pheraia, goddess of Pherai	24, n. 10; 27 and n. 24.
Philo	72-73 and n. 3.
Philolaus	44-47.
Physis	10; 45; Chp. IX, *passim;* 151.
Plotinus	2, n. 5; 5-6; 16; 77; 137 and n. 13; 155 and n. 10; 161 and n. 26.
Plutarch	19; Chp. III, "Mistress of the Moon, *passim;* 72.
Porphyry	2, n. 5; 4-6; 63; 79; 88; 131; 141-142; 154-155, n. 7; 160-162.
Poseidonius	18.
"Principle of Continuity" or "Mediation"	15; 59; 71; 147.
Proclus	7; 79-80; 147; 151.
Prophecy	86-88 and n. 222.
Psellus, Michael	7-8.
Quadi, Julian's participation in battle with	3.
Rain miracles	3; 90, n. 2; 95; 97.
"Restless Souls" (cf. ἄωροι, βιαιοθάνατοι)	34; 36; 136; 150.
Rhea	1, n. 1; 66-69; 158.
Salt (sea water)	81 and n. 14.
Second Intellect: see "Demiurge"	
Selene	31, n. 6.
Silence	81; 129 and n. 51.
Sirens	98-102; 109.
Sophia (Gnostic deity)	69, n. 50; 71.
Sounds, as *symbola* (cf. "Music of the Spheres)	97-103; 128; 143.
"Spindle of Necessity"	101; 108.

INDICES OF TOPICS DISCUSSED

Symbola, synthemata	82 and n. 16; 83; 85-89 and n. 28; 98; 103-110; 122; 127-131; 134-135; 141-142; 143; 149-151; 159.
Sympathy (συμπάθεια)	77; 79; 88 and n. 26; 97-98; 101-102; 107; 131; 143-144; 148; 150-151.
Synesius	9.
Telestika (τελεστικά)	3 and n. 7; 87-88 and n. 23; 131-132 and nn. 55-58; 151.
Ten; the Decad	44-47.
Tetractys	45-47; 101, n. 32.
Thresholds	Chp. II, *passim;* 47, n. 46; 73.
Triads, trinitization	9; 16; 18; 54-57; 64, n. 39; 128-129 and n. 51; 157-158.
Trivia	24.
Turbo	94-95 and n. 15; 102.
Valentinus, Valentinian Gnosticism	11; 71.
"Virtue"	62; 159.
"Whirling" or "Whirring" motion and sounds (cf. " ἐνθρῴσκω," "ῥοιζέω")	66-68; 93; 101, n. 31; 104; 106; 108-110; 126.
Womb(s) (κόλπος)	49-52; 56-57; 60; Chp. IV, "Hekate as Ensouler," *passim;* 107-109; 158-159.
Wryneck (iynx-bird)	93-94 and n. 12; cf. 102, n. 34.
Zeus (cf. "Jove")	1, n. 1.
Zoë	10; 67.

Greek

ἄγαλμα	109; 137 and n. 14.
ἀλκή	59, n. 30; 128-130 and n. 50
ἀμφιπρόσωπος	Chp. IV, "Hekate as Dividing Bond," *passim;* 159-160.
ἀμφιφαής	Chp. IV, "Hekate as Dividing Bond," *passim;* 159-160.

ἀμφίστομος	Chp. IV, "Hekate as Dividing Bond," *passim;* 159-160.
ἀναγωγή	89.
ἅπαξ ἐπέκεινα	50, n. 5; 57, n. 27; 61.
αὐτοζῷον, τό	64, n. 39.
ἀφομοιωτικός ("assimilative")	92.
ἄωροι, βιαιοθάνατοι	35; 119; 122-123 and n. 30 136 and n. 9; 144-47 and nn. 9-15, 17.
γοητεία	77 and *passim* Chp. VI and Chp. X.
γυλλός	21, n. 3.
δεῖπνα (Hekate suppers)	26-27.
δέμα (band)	55-58.
διακόσμησις (regulation of the Cosmos)	52; 92.
διαπόρθμιος: see "Ferrymen"	
δὶς ἐπέκεινα	50, n. 5; 57, n. 27; 61.
δύναμις (cf. "Paternal Power)	59, n. 30; 64; 67.
ἑκατηβελέτις	18.
ἐλάτειρα ("chariotress")	134; 140.
ἐνθρῴσκω (cf. "Whirling" or "Whirring" motion and sounds, ῥοιζέω)	103; 49-50.
ἐργάτις (workwoman)	64-67.
ἐργοτεχνίτις	54, n. 19.
ζωῆς δεσπότις: see "Mistress of Life"	
ζωηφόρος	64; 67-69; 108.
ζωογονική	68.
ζῳογόνος, ζωογόνος	64; 67-69; 157-159.
κηληδόνες	98, n. 25 and 99, n. 26.
κλειδοῦχος (key-holder)	Chp. III, "Hekate Κλειδοῦχος" *passim;* cf. "Hades, keys to."
κλειδοφόρος; κλειδὸς πομπή or ἀγωγή	41-42.
κοσμαγοί	61.
λαγών	62-63 and n. 38; 159.
λεοντοῦχος	112-113 and n. 6; 160.
λιμενοσκόπος, λιμενῖτις	27, n. 24.
μαγειῶν πατέρες	91-92 and n. 6.
νουμηνία (New Moon)	26; 31, n. 7; 73.
πειθώ: see "Persuasion"	
πηγαῖοι πατέρες	61.
Προθυραία	27; 40, n. 24; 147, n. 19.

INDICES OF TOPICS DISCUSSED

Προπύλα	24.
ῥοιζέω, ἐκροιζέω (cf. "Whirling" or "Whirring" motion and sounds)	58, n. 28; 101, n. 31; 108;
῾ροίζημα	108.
ῥόμβος (bull-roarer)	94-95 and n. 15; 102.
στροφάλιγξ	96, n. 19; 101, n.31; 105-106.
στρόφαλος	90 and n. 1; 91 and n. 3; 105.
σύστασις	88.
τριοδῖτις	24; 27; 36, n. 21; 38; 149.
ὑμήν (membrane)	53 and n. 16; 57-58 and n. 29 70.
φαντάσματα	34-35; 135-136.

Index of Ancient Passages Discussed

Included herein are passages that are discussed in some depth, or passages that offer critical substantiation of an argument. Some passages that are mentioned only briefly, as *comparanda* in footnotes for example, are not included. Oracle fragments are listed in the index that follows this one, under the numerical designations given them by Des Places.

Aeneas of Gaza	
Theophrastus, p. 51	5, n. 16.
Aeschylus	
Pers. 989	91, n. 4.
Pr. 173-74	100.
TrGF 388 Radt	21; 24.
Anastasius	
PG 89, 525 a	3, n. 9.
Antoninus Liberalis	
Meta. IX	95, n. 17.
Apollodorus	
FrGH 244 F 109	26, n. 20.
Apollonius Rhodius	
II.697	116.
III.758-60	96, n. 19.
III.1211 ff.	140.
III.1218	116.
Schol. on Apollonius Rhodius I.1139	95, n. 16.
Apuleius	
ap. Aug. *De Civ. Dei* VIII.18	34, n. 14.
de Plat. 9	155.
Meta. XI.2	146.
Aristophanes	
Schol. on *Plut.* 594	26, n. 20.
Ran. 465 ff.	41, n. 25.
Vesp. 804	24.
Aristotle	
Ath. Pol. 56.2	26.
Met. 986 a 8	46, n. 42.
Probl. 910 b 31	46, n. 42.
Arnobius	
Adv. nat. 3.29	27.
Augustine	
De Civ. Dei X.9-10	124 and n. 36.
X.11	98.
Basilius of Cappadocia	
Serm. Contub., PG 30, 816.11	44.
Calcidius	
In Plat. Tim. 53	20.
129-36	34, n. 13.
Callimachus	
Dian. 259	27, n. 24.

INDEX OF ANCIENT PASSAGES DISCUSSED

fr. 466	23, n. 6.
fr. 685	95, n. 17.
Calvenus Taurus	
ap. John Philoponus *De. Aet. Mund.* p. 145, 13 ff. (Rabe)	30.
Catullus	
61.159-160	25, n. 16.
Cedrenus, George	
Hist. comp. I p. 287.7 ff. Bekk. = Orph. fr. 316	45, n. 40.
Chariclides	
fr. 1	27.
Cornutus	
ND 34	24, n. 11.
Corpus Hermeticum	
Treatise X.11	53, n. 16.
Damascius	
In Phaed. [*vers*. 1 Westerink] 496.1 ff	74.
[*vers*. 2 Westerink] 108.1 ff	74, n. 7.
Pr. I.286.9	92.
I.291.11-13	55, n. 21.
I.315.20	59-61.
II.29.15	106, n. 44.
II.43.27	61.
II.89-90	61.
II.95.15	90.
II.131.27 ff.	53, n. 15.
II.152.23	59-60.
II.154.18-19	68; 108.
II.156.15	108.
II.157.15	138, n. 19.
II.201.3-6	103.
II.235.8-15	68; 138, n. 19; 156.
Is. fr. 200, p. 173.15 Zintzen	102, n. 34.
Empedocles	
ap. Plut. *De Is*. 361 c	32, n. 9; 34, n. 14.
Diels I p. 267 no. 115	
Etym. Magn. 706.29	95, n. 16.
Eudorus	
ap. Plut. *De Proc. An.* 1013 b	18.
Euripides	
Ba. 1084 ff.	116.
Hel. 569-70	24 and n. 10; 34, n. 15; 35, n. 19.
1361	95, n. 16.
Ion 1048 ff.	34, n. 15 and 16; 36, n. 19.
Eusebius	
PE V.13, 201 c-d	131, n. 56.
V.14, 202 d	131, n. 56.
V.15, 203 d	131, n. 56.
Firmicus Maternus	
De er. prof. rel. 5	162, n. 29.
Greek Anthology *(AP)*	

184 INDEX OF ANCIENT PASSAGES DISCUSSED

5.205	91, n. 4; 95, n. 16.
6.165	95, n. 16.
7.694	25, n. 18.
7.391	41, n. 25.
"Herodotos"	
V. Homer. 410-20	144, n. 7.
Hesiod	
Theog. 411-52	22; 144, n. 7.
WD 122-28	34, n. 13; 36.
Schol. *Theog.* 411	44, n. 38.
Hesychius	
Προπύλα	24.
Hippocrates	
Morb. Sacr. 6.362	34, n. 15 and 16; 35, n. 19.
Homer	
Il. XIII.18	116.
Homeric Hymn to Artemis 6-7	116.
Homeric Hymn to Demeter	22-23; 27.
Horace	
Sat. I.8.33	140.
Iamblichus	
ap. Stob. *Anth.* I.364 ff. Wachs	18.
De Myst. I.5-6; 16,6-20,19	34, n. 14.
II.4; 75,11	113-14; 117.
II.4; 77,10-19	119-120 and n. 21; 125 and n. 39.
II.7; 84,6	120; 160 ff.
III.6; 112,10 ff	120, n. 21.
III.26; 161,10-16	79, n. 6.
III.31; 176,3 ff	125, n. 37.
V.15; 220,6-9	78.
V.16; 221,1-4	78.
V.23; 233,10	131, n. 56.
VP 85	46, n. 44.
pseudo-Iamblichus	
Theol. Ar. 28.13 (de F.)	45.
59. (de F.) = Orph. fr. 315	46, n. 42.
81.14 (de F.)	45.
IG 14.1746	41, n. 25.
Italicus, Michael	
Letter XVII, 181.26 ff.	104, n. 41; 112 ff. and nn. 3, 6; 160 ff.
Julian	
Caes. 307 c	30.
Lucan	
VI.642 ff.	146.
Lucian	
De Domo 13	98.
De Luctu 4	41, n. 25.
Cata. 4	41, n. 25.
Philps. 12	131.
15	146.
22	116; 146.

INDEX OF ANCIENT PASSAGES DISCUSSED 185

V. Auct. 4	46, nn. 41 and 44.
Lycophron 1175 ff.	140.
Schol. on Lycophron 1180	27 and n. 24.
Lydus, Joannes	
De Mens. I.15 = p. 9, 4 Wünsch = Orph. fr. 315	44-46.
Marinus	
Procl. 13	4, n. 13.
26	4, n. 13; 7, n. 28; 131.
28	80; 95, n. 16; 97; 104, n. 41.
38	4, n. 13; 15; 151.
Moderatus	
ap. Porph. *VP* 48	46, n. 42.
Nicomachus	
Theol. Ar. p. 49, 11 (De Falco)	18.
"Orpheus"	
Argo. 986	41.
fragments (Kern)	
42	23, n. 6.
49	23, n. 6.
315	44; 46, n. 41 and 42.
316	39 and n. 23; 45, n. 40.
Hymns (Quandt)	
I.7 (Hekate)	40, n. 24; 41, n. 29; 42, n. 36.
II.5 (Prothuraia)	40, n. 24.
XVIII.4 (Plouton)	40, n. 24.
XXV.1 (Proteus)	40, n. 24.
LIV.4 (Eros)	40, n. 24.
LXXIII.6 (Daimon)	40, n. 24.
Ovid	
Am. I.8.7	95, n. 16.
Fasti I.125-28	41, n. 26.
Meta. VII.234	146.
Papyri Graecae Magicae	
I.65	117.
I.74	117-18.
IV.475-829 (the "Mithras Liturgy")	116.
IV.1434	27.
IV.1903	118.
IV.2292	41.
IV.2296	95, n. 16.
IV.2335	41.
IV.2563	27.
IV.2708-84	27, n. 25; 136, n. 9; 147, n. 17.
IV.2724-28	27.
IV.2795	44, n. 38.
IV.2858	44, n. 38.
IV.2871-76	88, n. 28.
IV.2940-41	117.
VII.614	118.
XIII.734-1077	116.

186 INDEX OF ANCIENT PASSAGES DISCUSSED

	LXX.10	41.
Pausanius		
	II.30.2	24.
Philolaus		
	fr. 11 Diels I.313,5	46, n. 42.
Philostratus		
	VA 1.5	119, n. 17.
	1.25	96 ff.; 101, n. 31.
	4.10	140, n. 25.
	6.11	98-100.
Photius		
	"ἴυγξ"	95, n. 17.
Pindar		
	P. IV.212-215	91, n. 4; 95, n. 16.
	IV.219	100 and n. 28.
	XI.38	25, n. 18.
	N. IV.35	91, n. 4.
	Pa. XI.8-9	98-99, nn. 25 and 26.
Plato		
	Epin. 984 e 4	92.
	Lg. 799 c	25, n. 18.
	828 d	39.
	896 e-898 d	13; 19; 136, n. 12.
	Phd. 107 d ff.	35.
	107 d-108 c	74.
	Phdr. 245 c	62, n. 34; 67, n. 46.
	Phlb. 30 a ff	13; 19; 155.
	R. 614 b	39-41.
	616 c ff.	108-109.
	617 b	101-102.
	617 c	44.
	Smp. 190 b	29, n. 2.
	202 e	32, n. 9; 92.
	Ti. 30 b ff.	13; 68.
	34 b-37 c	13-14; 136, n. 12.
	35 a-b	14; 16.
	36 b	14; 109.
	36 d-37 c	14.
	36 e	16; 153.
	38 e	153.
	41 d ff.	14-15; 19.
	69 c ff.	14-15.
Plotinus		
	Enn. I.9	5, n. 20.
	IV.3.2-7	155.
Plutarch		
	De E 394 c	34, n. 14.
	De Fac. 928 c	30.
	937 f	24, n. 11; 36, n. 21.
	942 e ff.	36, n. 21.
	943 a ff.	36-37.
	943 e	33, n. 10.
	944 c-f.	36; 37.

INDEX OF ANCIENT PASSAGES DISCUSSED 187

945 c	33, n. 10; 37-38.
945 d 3	44, n. 37.
De Fato 568 e ff.	44, n. 38.
De Gen. Socr. 591 b	43-44.
De Is. 360 e	34, n. 14.
361 c	32, n. 9.
368 e-f	30 and n. 5.
369 e-370	19, n. 13-15.
De Proc. An. 1026 e-1027 a	19, n. 13.
Dio 2	34.
Numa 19.11	59-60.
Obs. Orac. 416 c-f	31-33; 37.
Quaest. Conv. 745 c 1	44, n. 37.

Polyaenus
    VIII.43   24, n. 10.

Porphyry (cf. also *frag. dub.* 219-225)
ap. Aug. *De Civ. Dei* X.9-11	34, n. 12; 131, n. 56.
ap. Aug. *Serm.* 241.6-7	138, n. 20; 154-55 and n.7; 160-62.
De Regr. An. 27*.21-28*.15 (Bidez)	79, n. 8.
ap. Eus. *PE* III.11, 113 c-d	38 and n. 22; 63, n. 37; 156.
III.16, 126 c	34, n. 12.
IV.23, 174 a	34, n. 12.
IV.23, 175 c-d	141 ff.
V.7, 191 c	63; 154, n. 7.
V.24, 202 c, d	34, n. 12.

Posidonius
    ap. Plut. *De Proc. An.* 1023 b-d =   18.
    fr. 391 a Theiler

Proclus
Hymn to Hekate and Janus	38; 147, n. 19.
In Alc. 4, 2-3 Westerink	81, n. 14.
68, 13 Westerink	105.
In Cr. 33.14-17	91-92; 103; 105.
35.2	82, n. 16.
58.19-22	50, n. 5.
67.19	104, n. 41.
74.26	92-93 and n. 11; 104, n. 41.
In. Pr. 821.7	138, n. 16.
1199.31-38	91-92; 103.
In R. II.93.28-29	138, n. 19.
II.113-122	39-40; 43-44.
II.133.15-17	137, n. 14.
II.150.21	138, n. 19.
II.168-171	46, n. 41.
II.201.10	156.
II.212.20 ff.	109.
II.224.28. ff.	53, n. 15.
II.337.18	134, n. 1.
In T. I.11.19	138, n. 19.
I.142.23	54, n. 19.
I.408.14-15	54.
II.57.9	92, n. 9.

188 INDEX OF ANCIENT PASSAGES DISCUSSED

II.61.19-24	54.
II.89.25	54, n. 19.
II.129.25-130.23	59-61.
II.246.19	59-60.
II.255.24 ff.	109.
II.260.20 ff.	157.
II.293.23	59-60.
III.248.5 ff.	63, n. 38.
III.256.32-257.2	62, n. 34.
III.271.2 ff.	138, n. 19.
Scholion to Hesiod, *WD* 155	134, n. 1.

Propertius
2.28.35	95, n. 16.
3.6.26	95, n. 16.

Psellus
Epistle 87 (Sathas)	131, n. 56.
Hyp. Keph. 73, 7 K	92, n. 9; 104, n. 41.
74, 10 K	68.
74, 12 K	61.
74, 11 K	138, n. 19.
74, 19 K	68; 157.
74, 34 K	157.
74, 41 K	61.
75, 3 K	68.
75, 20 K	139, n. 23.
PG 122, 1125 d	5, n. 20.
1133 a ff.	90 ff.; 104, n. 41.
1136 b	61.
1137 a 1-10	139, n. 23.
1141 d	52; 67.
1152 a	61.
1152 c 5	65, n. 41; 156, n. 12.
Script. Min. I.446.25 K-D	98, n. 25.
I.446.28 K-D	3, n. 7.

Seneca
Oed. 568 ff.	146.

Simplicius
Phys. 613.7	120, n. 21.

Sophocles
Rhiz. fr. 492	22, n. 5; 23; 24, n. 10.
fr. 535	24, n. 12.

Sophron
ap. Plut. *Super.* 170 B (= fr. 2 Demiańczuk)	144, nn. 7 and 8.

Strabo
XIV.660, 663	42.

Suidas
"ἴυγξ"	91, n. 4; 95, n. 16.
"Ἰουλιανός" (433 Adler)	2, n. 4.
"Ἰουλιανός" (434 Adler)	2, n. 4; 3, n. 6.

Synesius
De insomn. 132 c	97 and n. 23.
Hymn 1 (3) 96-97	135, n. 4.
5 (2) 52-53	139, n. 23.

Syrianus
>*In Arist. Metaphys.* 106, 14 ff.=
>>Orph. fr. 315   46, n. 42.

Tacitus
>*Ann.* III.62   42.

Theocritus
>*Id.* II   24, n. 12; 27, n. 25; 35, n. S 19; 91, n. 4.

Schol. on Theocr. *Id.* II   95, n. 17.

Theognis
>*Eleg.* I.911   25, n. 18.

Theopompos
>*ap.* Porph. *de Abst.* 2.16   26, n. 20.

Thucydides
>5.54-55   25, n. 17.
>5.116   25, n. 17.

Trag. Incert. fr. 375   34, n. 15; 35, n. 19.

Vergil
>*Aeneid* IV.609   140.
>   VI.256-8   116; 140; 146.

Xenocrates
>*ap.* Plut. *De. Fac.* 943 f = fr. 56 Heinze   29.
>*ap.* Plut. *Obs. Orac.* 416 c-d = fr. 23 Heinze   29; 32.
>*ap.* Plut. *Plat. Quaest.* IX, 1007 f =   30.
>>fr. 18 Heinze

Xenophon
>*Mem.* III.2.18   91, n. 4.

Index of Oracle Fragments Discussed

Oracle fr. 1	59, n. 30; 84-85; 129, n. 5.
2	59, n. 30; 83; 105, n. 42; 128-30 and nn. 50, 52; 133.
5	65, n. 40; 66, n. 44.
6	53 ff. and n. 15, 16.
7	54, n. 17.
14	99.
20	154.
20 *bis*	50, n. 6; 154.
23	55-56 and n. 24.
24	55, n. 21.
25	65, n. 41.
26	55, n. 22.
27	55, n. 22.
28	55-57 and n. 23.
30	56, n. 25.
31	55; 57.
32	1, n. 2; 64; 67; 157-58.
33	54, n. 19.
34	50-52; 59, n. 30; 103.
35	1, n. 2; 51-52; 158.
37	51, n. 11; 57, n. 28; 104; 108; 122.
38	1, n. 3; 52; 127.
44	1, n. 2; 155.
45	1, n. 2.
49	59, n. 30; 106.
50	1, n. 2; 57, n. 27; 162.
51	59; 62 ff. and n. 38; 131; 153-54; 156; 158-59; 162.
52	1, n. 2; 59; 62; 63, n. 38; 131; 157; 158-59.
53	1, n. 3; 63; 127; 153.
54	138.
56	1, n. 2; 66-68 and n. 42; 108, n. 49.
67	54.
68	54.

INDEX OF ORACLE FRAGMENTS DISCUSSED

70	137.
72	1, n. 3; 127-30 and n. 52; 133.
75	91, n. 5.
76	91, n. 5; 92 ff; 101; 103; 108, n. 48.
77	91, n. 5; 92 ff.; 103.
78	91 ff. and n. 4.
81	50, n. 5; 99.
82	50, n. 5; 59, n. 30.
87	93, n. 11; 101; 105.
88	139-40.
90	134 ff.; 103, n. 35; 105, n. 42.
91	134 ff.
94	65, n. 41.
96	51, n. 11; 52; 63-64; 67; 157-58.
101	137; 138.
102	137; 138.
107	86; 112.
108	105.
109	105, n. 42.
110	83-84; 105, n. 42.
112	82; 85.
115	65, n. 41.
116	82; 84.
117	59, n. 30; 129, n. 51.
118	59, n. 30; 129, n. 51.
119	59, n. 30.
127	85.
128	129, n. 51.
130	87, n. 22.
131	81.
132	81; 129, n. 51.
133	81 and n. 14.
134	139, n. 21.
135	81; 134 ff.
136	65, n. 40.
142	126, n. 43.

146	1, n. 3; 86; Chp. VII, *passim* ; 160-61.
147	1, n. 3; 86; Chp. VII, *passim*; 160-61.
148	1, n. 3; 86; Chp. VII, *passim*; 160-61.
149	82, n. 16; 88-89.
150	88-89.
153	87, n. 22.
156	134 ff.
157	135 ff.
163	82; 84; 139, n. 21.
172	83; 84; 139, n. 21.
174	67; 157.
180	139, n. 21.
186 *bis*	131, n. 58.
189	59-61; 159-60.
206	90, n. 1.
210	82, n. 16.

fragmenta dubia

213	139, n. 21.
215	1, n. 2.
216	1, n. 2.
217	87, n. 21; 139, n. 21.
218	1, n. 2.
219	1, n. 3; 99.
220	86, n. 20; 132, n. 60.
221	1, n. 2 and 3; 86, n. 20; 126, n. 42; 131, n. 59; 132-33.
222	1, n. 3; 86.
223	1, n. 3; 86, n. 20; 91; 100; 126, n. 42; 131, n. 59; 132; 104, n. 41; 105, n. 42.
224	1, n. 3; 86; 88, n. 27; 130-31 and n. 52; 133.

www.ingramcontent.com/pod-product-compliance
Ingram Content Group UK Ltd.
Pitfield, Milton Keynes, MK11 3LW, UK
UKHW011832190326
469160UK00012B/999